DARWIN IN AMERICA

Paul L. White
12/8/76

Charles Darwin, 1809–1882. (Courtesy of The Bettman Archive, Inc.)

DARWIN IN AMERICA

The Intellectual Response
1865-1912

CYNTHIA EAGLE RUSSETT

YALE UNIVERSITY

W. H. Freeman and Company
San Francisco

Library of Congress Cataloging in Publication Data

Russett, Cynthia Eagle.
  Darwin in America.

  Includes bibliographical references and index.
  1. Darwin, Charles Robert, 1809–1882. On the
Origin of Species. 2. Natural selection.
3. Biology—United States—History. I. Title.
QH365.08R87   301.24′3   75-40476
ISBN 0-7167-0564-8
ISBN 0-7167-0563-X pbk.

Printed in the United States of America

9 8 7 6 5 4 3 2 1

CONTENTS

DISCARD

PREFACE

 OREN EISELEY refers in an essay to "the great synthesizer who alters the outlook of a generation, who suddenly produces a kaleidoscopic change in our vision of the world. . . . Such a man is a kind of lens or gathering point through which past thought gathers, is reorganized, and radiates outward again into new forms." Charles Darwin was preeminently such a man. His own contribution to science was enormous in itself, but it also served, in Eiseley's words, as "a kind of lens or gathering point" that focused ideas across the widest possible range of thought and sent them forth transformed.

The times were ripe for that transformation. By 1859 English natural science had already proven its pragmatic value in a series of technological developments that advanced industry, raised the yield of agriculture, and improved the national health. Throughout the second half of the nineteenth century, the prestige of the natural sciences and of their spokesmen, men like Thomas Henry Huxley, professor of biology at the Royal School of Mines, and Herbert Spencer, philosopher of cosmic evolution, reached its zenith. For this reason the message of Darwin's epochal book, *On the Origin of Species,* could not be ignored by the nonscientific community, nor could its ideas be confined to the animal kingdom.

This book is an attempt to describe what happened to some important areas of American culture after their permeation by Darwinian ideas. The response to Darwinism on the part of theologians, philosophers, novelists, and social theorists was bewilderingly diverse; it would take a book much larger than this one to chronicle all its manifestations. I have not tried to do so. Rather, I have tried to suggest some of the patterns that emerged from the intellectual ferment, and to indicate, by means of intellectual portraits of some prominent or representative thinkers, how people tried to work through the new and disturbing perspectives of Darwinism to some kind of reconciliation of old and new ideas. This book, then, is in the nature of an essay, with no pretense to inclusiveness. Nor has it any pretense to research in manuscript or obscure sources. My approach was designedly to focus on the published record as the arena in which controversial issues were thrashed out.

The figures that I have selected for discussion were by and large part of an American intellectual elite, men whose professional concern was with ideas. Many of them were university professors. If the purpose of intellectual history is solely to describe a "climate of opinion" in the broadest sense—that is, the ideas that are held by a majority of the common people of a period—then this essay is not intellectual history. I prefer to believe, however, that there is an important relationship between the beliefs of intellectuals and those of their society more generally and, moreover, that even if there were no discernible relationship, the ideas of serious thinkers are worthy of study. In the case of Darwinism, though I have for the most part restricted myself to the "high intellectuals," we have abundant evidence in newspapers, letters, and memoirs that familiarity with Darwinian ideas was by no means restricted to a cultured few. The rise of fundamentalist religion marks one response of the common people to the complex of modern ideas of which Darwinism was one important strand.

Throughout the book, and explicitly in Chapter 4, I have made clear my own conviction that Darwinism, as a set of ideas, was an intellectual phenomenon first and foremost, whatever social consequences its popularization may secondarily have caused. Some businessmen may have found that the categories of Darwinian thought provided them with a useful scientific rationale for ruthless business practices. Some apologists for the "white man's burden" may have hoped to strengthen their case for Anglo-Saxon superiority by adopting Darwinian maxims. In the main, however, the challenge of Darwinism was not directed to practice but to thought—how to accommodate old ideas, values, and faiths to the vision of a world of incessant strife at every moment evolving new forms and discarding others in perpetual flux.

In seeking to provide for undergraduates an intelligible account of the impact of Darwinism on American intellectual life, I particularly wanted to try to sort out the lasting effects from those that were transient. John Dewey, reflecting on Darwin's philosophical influence, remarked that "intellectual progress usually occurs through sheer abandonment of questions. . . . We do not solve them: we get over them." The changes in outlook wrought by Darwinism were in many cases permanent, but some of the knottiest religious and philosophical puzzles were not truly resolved. They were "gotten over" at the time, but they rise anew to shake the complacency of succeeding generations. We ask ourselves today, as those who pondered Darwinism did, what are the limits of scientific evidence? Is science the only road to real knowledge? Can religion and science live harmoniously together? Are science and scientists trustworthy guides to ethical values? Is there an ideal equilibrium to be struck within a culture between the power and influence of the scientific community and that of the humanities? We answer variously, having by no means reached an intellectual consensus, but our answers will gain perspective if we view them against the backdrop of earlier controversies.

For reading this manuscript in whole or in part I am debted to Edmund Morgan, Sydney Ahlstrom, and John Blum. William Goetzmann's detailed criticisms were unvaryingly helpful. Miriam Miller's first-rate editorial skills smoothed many rough edges. Those others "without whom" I will attempt to thank not in word but in action.

Cynthia Eagle Russett

September 1975

DARWIN IN AMERICA

THE EALL OF MAN.

Man was by Heaven made to govern all,
But how unfit, demonstrates in his fall.
Created pure, and with a strength endu'd
Of grace divine, sufficient to have stood,
But alienate from God he soon became
The child of wrath, pride, misery and shame.

The Fall of Man. Pennsylvania Dutch fraktur, early 1800s. (Courtesy of The New York Historical Society.)

ONE

ORIGINS

N THE WINTER OF 1859 AMERICA unwittingly hastened toward two convulsions—one physical, the other intellectual. Both were to reshape the national spirit. Both were to propel the country decisively forward to its confrontation with the twentieth century. Few Americans in 1859 could foresee either of these great crises. But John Brown had already marched on Harper's Ferry. And in Cambridge, Massachusetts, a Harvard botanist named Asa Gray pored over a book with a formidable name, *The Origin of Species by Means of Natural Selection, Or the Preservation of Favoured Races in the Struggle for Life.*

Gray's initial reaction was measured and judicious, quite lacking the drama of an intellectual explosion. That was to come later. But already the lines were clear, and early in 1860, in a review of Darwin's book written for the *American Journal of Science and Arts* (often called *Silliman's Journal* after its founder), Gray prophesied a controversy "not likely to be settled in an offhand way," a "spirited conflict" of ideas which, like the struggle Darwin had revealed among plants and animals in nature, would winnow out the weak and preserve the strong.[1]

In this rather sober fashion the Darwinian revolution broke upon the American intellectual horizon. It came to a nation ill prepared to receive it in the short run—distracted as it was by sectional conflict and the alarums of approaching war—but immensely receptive in the long. The dominant mind of nineteenth-century America, romantic, transcendental, individualist, was even then in the process of undergoing that slow dissolution that would make it vulnerable to later caricature as a bloodless, prudish, elaborately hypocritical "Genteel Tradition." At its height, nevertheless, American romanticism had been an impressive construct, welding religion, philosophy, and social theory into a unified set of beliefs about the nature of the universe.

Perhaps the central feature of this faith was its sturdy assurance of the fundamental moral order of the cosmos and of man's immediate access thereto. It was given to mankind, so Americans widely believed, to enjoy an intimate relationship with ultimate reality, whether through reason, as traditional Calvinism and its offshoot, Unitarianism, taught, or through the intuitive faculty celebrated by transcendentalism. Rightly perceived, the universe showed itself to be orderly and beneficent. Evil existed, no doubt, but evil incident to greater good. The pattern of history was upward. Men and nations were progressing toward new heights of civilization and morality, and they were doing so free of the tragic incubus of depravity and predestination that had burdened their Calvinist ancestors. Unitarianism, evangelical Protestantism, transcendentalism, even the tempered Calvinist orthodoxy of theologians like Horace Bushnell—all united to throw off the divine determinism of their Genevan inheritance and to preach what secular experience daily proved—the liberty of the democratic individual.

In the schools, this certitude of the basic rightness of things was undergirded by the teachings of the philosophy of common sense. Originating in Scotland as a response to the skepticism of Hume, common sense philosophy crossed the Atlantic in the mid-eighteenth century with John Witherspoon when he answered a call to the presidency of the College of New Jersey (later Princeton). Common sense quickly became the dominant academic philosophy in America, a position it easily maintained until the Civil War and the dual challenges of German idealism and British Darwinism. Against Hume's reduction of knowledge to a mere stream of sense impressions with no necessary connection to the external world, the Scottish philosophers stoutly opposed the "common apprehensions of mankind," which vouched for the reality of our knowledge of the world. Hume had based his argument on the Lockean distinction between the ideas in our minds, which alone we know, and the real world of sense objects outside. Nonsense, declared the Scotsmen and their American disciples: we do not know ideas, we know things, and we know them reliably. The common sense of mankind (otherwise known as "intuitive reason") had attested to this fact; further metaphysical quibble was idle. Common sense philosophy, at once empirical and intuitive, was thus admirably fitted to counter transcendental speculation, on the one hand, and to quell antireligious skepticism, on the other.

Empirical knowledge, in this scheme of things, was valued less perhaps for its own sake than for the evidence it offered of the wonderful cosmic pattern. Relations between science and religion were cordial, since it was taken for granted that the findings of natural scientists would reinforce the revelations of Scripture. Commonplace in the curriculum of liberal arts colleges in the nineteenth century was a course entitled "Evidences of Christianity," which enlisted natural science in demonstrations of the divine wisdom. Transcendentalists similarly looked to nature to provide them with a symbolic incarnation of divinity. In his celebrated essay, *Nature*, Ralph Waldo Emerson wrote that "the noblest ministry of nature is to stand as the apparition of God. It is the organ through which the universal spirit speaks to the individual, and strives to lead back the individual to it." Nature, symbol and conduit of divinity, nourished, as no human intercourse could, the soul of the transcendent individual.

To this cluster of ideas animating the mid-century American mind Darwinism posed a massive challenge. It confounded with a stern biological determinism the nineteenth century's hardwon affirmation of moral freedom. It destroyed the traditional reliance of orthodox religion on the works of nature as evidence of the hand of God. It destroyed, just as surely, the transcendentalist's conduit of divinity. For the benevolent, spirit-impregnated nature of the transcendental vision it substituted an iron maiden presiding over endless panoramas of anguish and extinction. The serene cosmic pattern was replaced by the blind movement of mindless forces eternally sifting and shaping all living things, men as well as the lowliest mollusk, toward ends unperceived and perhaps nonexistent. Assaulting the optimistic democratic faith in the worth of the individual, Darwinism disclosed a slaughter of the innocents sanctioned, as it seemed, by a nature concerned with the preservation not of the individual but of the type. Taken in large draughts, the Darwinian gospel could be intellectually exciting and liberating, but it could also be overwhelming.

The Origin of Darwinism

No episode more forcefully illustrates the tendency for movements of thought to escape their original boundaries than does the diffusion of Darwinism. As originally presented, Darwin's theory pertained solely to natural science. Darwin had set out to explore the vexing question of variation: why animals and plants frequently diverge from their predecessors to develop characteristics not present in earlier generations. A close study of the process of variation might shed light on "that mystery of mysteries," the origin of species.

The problem of variation had first come to Darwin's attention while he was circumnavigating the globe in the *Beagle* in the years 1831–1836. He was at this time a believer in the doctrine of special creation, the orthodox alternative to theories of transmutation and change. According to this view, each species had been created independently of every other species, and had never varied in any important way down through the ages. Monkeys had always been exactly like the monkeys of the nineteenth century, and chimpanzees had always been chimpanzees, and the two species had no physical, genetic link whatsoever to one another. Each had come into being through a separate act of creation. Darwin found it difficult to square special creation with the dramatically obvious fact that in the Galapagos Islands plants and animals on one island were always similar to, yet slightly different from, those on another island, and yet all resembled the flora and fauna on the South American mainland nearby. Darwin resolved to give the matter more thought.

The theory of separate creation was the dominant view among English scientists at the time that Darwin began to reflect on the problem. It was not, however, the only possible view. Evolution, or "the development hypothesis" as it was commonly called, had surfaced from time to time in philosophic and scientific speculation since the days of ancient Greece. By the middle of the nineteenth century evolutionary notions had acquired a modicum of respectability: in various ways Hegel and Comte, Goethe, Lamarck, and Darwin's own grandfather, Erasmus Darwin, among others, were preoccupied with developmental ideas. The refined heroine of Disraeli's novel *Tancred* (1847) presents a parodied but probably not atypical understanding of the development hypothesis:

> You know, all is development. The principle is perpetually going on. First, there was nothing, then there was something; then—I forget the next—I think there were shells, then fishes; then we came—let me see—did we come next? Never mind that; we came at last. And at the next change there will be something very superior to us—something with wings. Ah! that's it: we were fishes, and I believe we shall be crows.[2]

For scientists the problem was not that there was no alternative to special creation, which many of them found less than satisfactory, but that there was no *scientifically convincing* alternative. Lamarck had made a brave attempt to invest evolution with plausibility, but his resort to a mystical animal will to live, in order to explain how evolution occurred, forfeited credibility. Thomas Henry Huxley, the renowned naturalist and friend of Darwin, wrote that his own reaction to this impasse of the scientific imagination was to declare "a plague on both your houses" and to maintain a resolute skepticism about both theories. This was the situation when Darwin made his seminal voyage around the world.

By 1838 Darwin had become, after much reflection, a convert to the idea that species change over time and had decided to devote himself to the problem of how and why species vary. He knew what breeders had of course long known, that animals under domestication varied, and could be made to vary, one from another, in striking ways. Variability within species was an incontrovertible fact. Equally important, these variations could be inherited by the offspring. Darwin reasoned that the same sort of process must go on in nature—that variations must perpetually arise and be passed on (or fail to be passed on) to the offspring. Assuming, then, that organisms varied and evolved over time, the question was how they did so. It was only after a chance reading of the political economist Thomas Malthus's *Essay on the Principle of Population* that Darwin found the clue that he needed to the mechanism of evolution. Malthus argued that since human population increases geometrically while the plants and animals that furnish mankind's food supply increase only arithmetically, pressure and struggle to keep alive are permanent conditions of human existence. Population, which would otherwise be unrestrained, is held in check by dint of scarce resources, and a certain degree of human misery is at all times inevitable.

The idea of a struggle for existence struck Darwin forcibly as a notion that could profitably be extended to the entire organic world. It was evident that plants and animals, if unchecked by any restraints on reproduction, would very quickly overrun the earth. Darwin calculated that one pair of elephants, which are the slowest breeding animal species, would produce 19,000,000 descendants after a period of 750 years. Overreproduction in relation to available resources would inevitably cause a struggle for existence. But Darwin theorized, quite in contrast to Malthus, that such a struggle would result in weeding out the feeble and preserving the strong; that Natural Selection (Darwin habitually capitalized the term) operated to preserve individuals with favorable variations and to destroy those with injurious ones. Over the course of time, then, individuals with variations that somehow aided them in the competition for life would survive to reproduce themselves and thus to multiply the favorable variations. Modifications of character and structure would gradually lead to divergence of type and to the formation of new variations and species.

An example will serve to illustrate the process. The flounder originally lacked spots, but at some point in time a few baby flounders were born with spots which camouflaged them when they swam over pebbles or sand and thus lessened the chance of their becoming dinner for a hungry predator. A greater number of spotted than nonspotted flounders would therefore live to become parents of a new generation—some without spots, but many spotted. Extended over vast stretches of time, this process of selection would lead to permanent modification of the flounder into a species all members of which possessed spots. And as selected individuals might form a distinct variety, so, with a greater effort of imagination, one might suppose varieties being elevated into separate species.

Darwin's theory was thus a great deal narrower and more specific than much previous evolutionary speculation. Its specificity, together with its avoidance of metaphysics, was precisely what made it so astoundingly successful in carrying the day for evolution. Evolution *without* natural selection might be an interesting philosophical hypothesis; evolution *with* selection became a convincing scientific explanation. It is necessary to distinguish Darwin's particular theory of natural selection from the general notion of evolution in order to be aware that the "impact of Darwin" can mean either or both of two things: (1) the impact of the general idea of evolution, or (2) the impact of Darwin's specific explanation of evolution. The latter was a good deal harder to swallow than the former.

Just because it was so impeccably scientific, the theory of natural selection legitimized certain tendencies already present in the social and philosophical thought of Darwin's time. A fellow Englishman, Herbert Spencer, for example, had already published an essay entitled "The Development Hypothesis" in 1852, and by 1860 was circulating a prospectus for a "synthetic philosophy"—a kind of survey of all knowledge—based squarely on evolutionary principles. Where such tendencies did not already exist, Darwin's theory created them. One of the most brilliant works of social theory of the later nineteenth century, Walter Bagehot's *Physics and Politics*, is subtitled *Thoughts on the Application of the Principles of 'Natural Selection' and 'Inheritance' to Political Society.*

And so it went in fields as widely separated as aesthetics and economics: Darwin's theory, a biological principle, became transmuted into Darwinism, a set of principles of presumably universal application. The *Origin of Species* thus triggered a tremendously varied inquiry into every aspect of the human condition; learned as well as popular articles explored Darwinism and ethics, Darwinism and politics, Darwinism and religion. If much that was written under the impetus of evolutionary concepts proved to be ephemeral, nevertheless the net effect was truly revolutionary.

To the progenitor of the original doctrine, such widespread application of his discoveries was bewildering. Darwin confessed that he had not realized that his views on biological species were germane to questions of society. What Darwin did foresee, however, was the certainty of controversy over the *Origin* on scientific and religious grounds. In 1844 he had confided to his friend and close consultant Joseph Hooker, "I am almost convinced . . . that species are not (it is like confessing a murder) immutable."[3] Thomas Henry Huxley, Darwin's self-appointed "bulldog," warned Darwin of the probable effects of publication: "I trust," he wrote, "you will not allow yourself to be in any way disgusted or annoyed by the considerable abuse and misrepresentation which, unless I greatly mistake, is in store for you." Later on he added, "I am sharpening up my claws and beak in readiness."[4]

The Scientific Reception of Darwinism in America

The response to Darwinian ideas in America was neither as immediate nor as clear-cut as it was in England, partly because the famous confrontation between Huxley and Bishop Samuel Wilberforce at Oxford in June of 1860 early crystalized the formation of Darwinian and anti-Darwinian parties in England, partly because of the intervention of civil war in America. The process of reception began auspiciously enough with the publication of Gray's exceedingly penetrating review of the *Origin*. Correctly foreseeing a struggle, Gray concerned himself less with the truth or falsity of Darwin's ideas than with ensuring them fair play in the intellectul marketplace. Evolution by natural selection, he affirmed, "must be regarded as a legitimate attempt to extend the domain of natural or physical science."[5] At the same time, Gray was greatly impressed by the cogency of Darwin's argument and his marshaling of a truly staggering quantity of evidence. The most striking feature of Gray's review seen in retrospect is, however, its discussion of the religious issues raised by Darwinism. Clearly perceiving that the central philosophical problem in the theory of natural selection was that of chance versus design, or mechanism versus teleology, Gray tried from the outset to make a case for the compatibility of natural selection with the two latter alternatives. Since these issues will come up in greater detail at a later point, it need only be said here that Gray had, at the very beginning of the great debate, divined the essential philosophical challenge of Darwinism with remarkable clarity.

Though Gray was no bulldog, his scientific reputation and his openness to the theory of natural selection put him at the head of the Darwinian party in America. The leader of the anti-Darwinians

Louis Agassiz, 1807–1873. (Courtesy of William Tenney.)

was a figure of even greater contemporary renown, the zoologist Louis Agassiz. Gray's colleague at Harvard, Agassiz was undoubtedly the best-known scientist in America. Yet, so unremittingly idealistic a thinker was he that he could in all earnestness describe a species as "a thought of the Creator." Agassiz' master, Cuvier, had been the leading antievolutionist of the early nineteenth century, doing battle with both Lamarck and Geoffroy Saint-Hilaire. It was a foregone conclusion that Agassiz would react violently to Darwin's book. Gray reported gleefully to Hooker that Agassiz "growls over it, like a well-cudgeled dog—is very much annoyed by it—to our great delight—and I do not wonder at it."[6]

Gray had been familiar with Darwin's basic ideas for over two years before the publication of the *Origin*. Darwin's research fed Gray's long smoldering discontent with Agassiz' idealist method (Gray considered himself a strict empiricist) and with his dogmatic insistence on separate creation. In a celebrated series of debates in the spring of 1860, the two Harvard colleagues finally crossed swords before a gathering of literary, social, and scientific luminaries such as only Boston could assemble. The results were inconclusive, however. Perhaps this was because the issues remained purely scientific, rather than becoming philosophical or theological. Had the religious question arisen, Gray's theism would have been found to be, as a matter of fact, a good deal more traditional than Agassiz'.

Agassiz issued from the clash still fixed in his antagonism, and so he remained until his death in 1873. For Gray, the debates signified a public commitment to Darwinian ideas and to the compatibility of natural selection with theism. Initially, the immense prestige of Agassiz weighed heavily against the acceptance of Darwin by American scientists. But idealism proved no match for Darwinism, and Agassiz died, as would Herbert Spencer many years later, in the knowledge that his lifelong beliefs had become intellectual relics of an earlier age. By the early 1870s American scientists had begun to make substantial contributions of their own to evolutionary theory. By 1900 natural scientists in this country (Agassiz' son among them) had virtually ceased to challenge the Darwinian verities.

Any implication of a sweeping acceptance of Darwinism by American scientists needs qualification, however. It would be more accurate to say that American scientists accepted their own interpretation of Darwinism, which was not in fact pure Darwinism. They did not, that is to say, attribute evolutionary changes in organic structures solely to the influence of natural selection. Though they took natural selection to be one factor in evolution, they stressed as equally important and, for human evolution, paramount, the Lamarckian theory of the inheritance of acquired characteristics. They did this for several reasons: Darwin himself had given increasing ground to Lamarckian speculation in later editions of the *Origin*, and paleontological evidence being uncovered at that time lent some credence to Lamarck's insistence on direction, rather than randomness, in the evolutionary process. More important, almost certainly, was the greater congruence of Lamarckianism with religion, since direction could be translated into theological terms as providence. Lamarckianism obviated the sharpest form of warfare between science and religion.

Probably the strongest reason why neo-Lamarckianism was so prevalent among American scientists that it became known as "the American school" was none of the above. It was that Lamarckianism offered, as Darwinism did not, firm scientific support for the efficacy of education in improving humanity. As Joseph Le Conte, prominent geologist, evolutionist, and reconciler of science and religion, feelingly wrote:

> All our schemes of education, intellectual and moral, though certainly intended mainly for the improvement of the individual are glorified by the hope that the race also is thereby gradually elevated. . . . All our hopes of race-improvement, therefore, are strictly conditioned on the efficacy of these factors—i.e., on the fact that useful changes, determined by education in each generation, are to some extent inherited and accumulated in the race.[7]

Arguments like this, rather than strictly scientific reasons, explain the pertinacity with which Lester Frank Ward and other scientist-reformers clung to neo-Lamarckianism long after scientific evidence began pointing decisively in the other direction. In the end, Darwinian natural selection carried the day; but in retrospect it appears that neo-Lamarckianism may well have performed a valuable service for its rival by muting the initial harshness of the Darwinian challenge to established truths and thus facilitating its general acceptance.

Opposition from the Nonscientific Community

In areas of thought other than science the victory of Darwinism was scarcely less complete, if harder won. An editor of the *Galaxy* noted with amusement the "universal drenching" of literature and journalism with ideas taken from Darwin.[8] Wherever Darwinian categories penetrated, they produced at the very least a shaking up and airing out of received materials and methods. Actually, a distinction should be made between the content and the method of Darwinism. The particular principles of Darwinian theory—chiefly the struggle for existence, natural selection, and survival of the fittest—were adopted outright by many disciplines outside the natural sciences. But equally, and in the long run more importantly, the *Origin* revolutionized methods. Darwinism promoted the study of origins, histories, developments. Not that the *Origin* itself was a historical document in its methodology, or that Darwin had a highly developed historical sense; on the contrary, Darwin appended a historical sketch of pre-Darwinian evolutionary speculation only in the third edition of his book, and then only at the urging of friends. But the whole thrust of his argument directed attention to beginnings and to the processes by which things come to be what they are. For this reason, the genetic method became perhaps the characteristic hallmark of Darwinian scholarship in the humanities and social sciences.

In the academic disciplines Darwinism kindled controversy. "Pre-Darwinian" became in more than one instance an epithet. So long as these disputes remained within the confines of the university they did not agitate the national mind. Certain areas, however—notably philosophy, ethics, and religion—always belong at least in part to the common culture. In the years before Darwin these fields had become especially vulnerable by virtue of being tied to questionable scientific assumptions. Here Darwinism appeared to threaten not an airing out, but an emptying out; not a tinkering and readjustment merely, but a whole new construction. Try as Darwin himself might to avoid metaphysics, the Darwinian theory of evolution undeniably contradicted Genesis. What was worse, it contradicted the argument for the existence of God based on cosmic design, a favorite strategem of natural theologians since the seventeenth century. This argument sought to prove God's existence by pointing to complicated natural phenomena like the eye and claiming that only a supernatural intelligence could have contrived them. Closely related to the chance/design antithesis was another metaphysical riddle that had long agitated nineteenth-century philosophers, the question of mechanism versus free will. With the idea of natural selection, Darwinism thus went straight to the heart of a highly sensitive area of concern.

At first many of those who opposed Darwin's theory believed that it could be controverted on purely scientific grounds, but this proved a false hope. More influential (outside fundamentalist circles) were those who felt that a truce could be arranged between Darwinism and religion, provided that a special place be reserved for man in the creative scheme. Darwin, so it was argued, had only meant to include plants and the lower animals in his evolutionary scale. Or, if man's body had evolved, there was yet something special about his mind. In the *Origin* Darwin himself had carefully skirted the issue of man, expressing only the cautious opinion that "much light will be thrown on the origin of man and his history."[9]

Hopes for a reconciliation on some such basis unfortunately received a powerful setback from the master himself with the publication of his *Descent of Man* in 1871. Man, Darwin declared, was the descendant of "a hairy quadruped, of arboreal habits, furnished

MR. BERGH TO THE RESCUE

The Defrauded Gorilla: "The Man wants to claim my Pedigree. He says he is one of my Descendants."

Mr. Bergh: "Now, Mr. Darwin, how could you insult him so?"

Darwin and Bergh (founder of the Society for the Prevention of Cruelty to Animals). Drawing by Thomas Nast, 1871. (Courtesy of The Bettman Archive, Inc.)

with a tail and pointed ears." His mental and moral equipment differed in degree only, and not in kind, from that of the animals.[10]

Even for some of Darwin's associates the fixing of man's place in evolution rankled. Sir Charles Lyell, whose *Principles of Geology* entitles him to rank as the John the Baptist of Darwinism, balked at "going the whole orang." Could not Darwin make room for divine direction, a smattering of "prophetic germ?" Darwin could not. While the English, already prepared by Huxley and others, took the news with remarkable aplomb, Americans were greatly distressed. After 1871, positions hardened and emotions deepened all around.

In the long run, the message of the *Origin* on evolution prevailed. But many philosophers and theologians continued to distinguish between the Darwin of the *Origin* and the Darwin of the *Descent*. It was dreadful enough, but perhaps acceptable, to swallow man's apish ancestry on condition that his soul be divinely infused.

To deny the soul, to consider that our minds were as apelike in origin as our bodies, was clearly inadmissible. As passions cooled, however, it could be seen that the question of man's origin was not necessarily crucial to determining his place in nature—what man *had been* (or what he had evolved from) could clarify but could not settle the question of what man *now was*. Thus the philosophical dispute over the existence of mind (or spirit or soul) did not in the end come to rest with Darwin.

Herbert Spencer and Cosmic Evolution

In the area of social thought, American intellectuals had to reckon not only with Darwin but with Herbert Spencer as well. At the very time that they were endeavoring to make sense of natural selection, Spencer, civil engineer by training, philosopher and moralist by instinct, was preparing to offer to the world a system of thought which would relegate Darwin to a chapter, which would do for the cosmos what Darwin had done for terrestrial life. Years before Darwin published the *Origin*, Spencer had been reflecting on the possibility of organizing a general philosophical system around the principle of evolution. In his autobiography, Spencer tells us that he had been an evolutionist in a vague sort of way for almost as long as he could remember, but that it was the German embryologist Von Baer who gave him a clue as to what precisely evolution meant. Von Baer's description of the development of the ovum from structural homogeneity to heterogeneity laid the groundwork for Spencer's own famous definition of evolution as "an integration of matter and concomitant dissipation of motion, during which the matter passes from an indefinite incoherent homogeneity to a definite coherent heterogeneity; and during which the retained motion undergoes a parallel transformation."[11]

To this definition, couched in the terms of physics and not of biology, Darwin's researches could add little but confirmation; still, as confirming his own speculations, Spencer welcomed them. It always rankled just a bit that he, who had coined the term "survival of the fittest" in an article on human population, had not thought to extend the principle to the plant and animal world as Darwin had done. He tended to be touchy about the degree of his indebtedness to Darwin, as indeed he was about the degree of his indebtedness to the French social theorist August Comte, from whom he bor-

Herbert Spencer, 1820–1903. (Courtesy of The Bettman Archive, Inc.)

rowed the term "sociology." In both cases his sensitivity was need-less. If ever ideas sprang full-blown from the brow of any man, that man was Spencer. In fact, his greatest resemblance to Comte may have been in his single-minded absorption in his own thoughts.

Spencer's accomplishment was to weld together two previously distinct worlds of discourse—that of philosophy and that of sci-ence.[12] Heir to the social and political individualism of a noncon-formist family, he set forth his principles of innate struggle, survival of the fittest, and a laissez-faire so strict as to amount to virtual anarchism, within the framework of nineteenth-century science. In an age when the tremendous accomplishments of science had given scientists a stellar role in shaping intellectual life, this marriage of science and philosophy gave his work its powerful appeal. What was more, Spencer applied his principles—persistence of force, evolution, and eventual equilibrium—to *everything*, from the inor-ganic world to mind itself. William James rather acidly remarked that "Mr. Spencer's task, the unification of all knowledge into an articulate system, was more ambitious than anything attempted since St. Thomas or Descartes. Most thinkers have confined them-selves either to generalities or to details, but Spencer addressed himself to everything."[13] Nevertheless, to many, Spencer's system appeared to open up new and wholly enthralling vistas. Jack Lon-don, the novelist, records his awe on first reading *First Principles:* "Here was the man Spencer, organizing all knowledge for him, reducing everything to unity, elaborating ultimate realities, and pre-senting to his startled gaze a universe so concrete of realization that it was like the model of a ship such as sailors make and put into glass bottles. . . . All the hidden things were laying their secrets bare. He [Martin Eden, London's fictional alter ego] was drunken with comprehension."[14]

Herbert Spencer's impact upon American thought was profound. Serious philosophers, among them James, Dewey, and Royce, had to clear their paths of Spencer before proceeding on their own way. He was one of the founders of the new study of society called sociology, and theorists as widely divergent as Lester Frank Ward and William Graham Sumner turned to him for guidance. At the level of popular culture his presence was similarly inescapable. He served as the common man's Darwin, proffering the intellectual certainties of Darwinism on a cosmic scale, without Darwin's scien-

A DARWINIAN

Scientific Monkey: "Cut it off short, Tim; I can't afford to await developments before I can take my proper position in Society."

Drawing by Frederick Stuart Church, from *Harper's Bazaar,* 16 September 1876. (Courtesy of Culver Pictures, Inc.)

tific rigor. Indeed, thanks to vigorous promotional efforts by his American disciples Edward Youmans and John Fiske, his popularity soon outstripped Darwin's. And this was only fitting, for was not Spencer's the grander and more comprehensive perspective? Darwin, after all, had "made no attempt to elucidate the general law of evolution." The point was worth stressing: " 'Evolutionism' and 'Spencerism' are synonymous terms," wrote Fiske, " 'evolutionism' and 'Darwinism' are not . . . "[15]

Darwin appealed above all to the harder, clearer intellects—the Grays, Deweys, Jameses. But Spencer appealed to the multitudes —he was, in William James's telling phrase, "the philosopher whom those who have no other philosopher can appreciate."[16] Few today appreciate Herbert Spencer; perhaps we have other philosophers. But in the Gilded Age, Spencer's brand of evolution, no less than Darwin's, appeared to be the wave of the future.

Darwinism and Culture

From the vantage point of a century later, it is clear that the rise and spread of Darwinian ideas throughout the nonscientific cultural community constitutes one episode in the constantly shifting relationship between science and culture. Prior to Galileo and Newton, science had been a pursuit now more and now less respected, but of value largely in making possible technological advance. The great discoveries of Newton, however, came to mean much more than that. They were transmuted into a cosmic world view that set the pattern for every area of intellectual endeavor. Mechanism reigned in philosophy and politics, economics and ethics. Newtonian physics was the first great instance of science as a paradigm, i.e., when not only the method but the very substance of science spills over into the humanities. On a cosmic scale, Newton's achievement promoted a conception of the universe as a great machine operating in accordance with certain specified laws. At a lower level, it suggested that men and societies could similarly be interpreted as acting under fixed laws. More than one version of "social physics" attempted to chart the paths of attraction and repulsion along which the atomistic units of society were presumed to move.

It was against the mechanistic view of life and mind stemming from Newtonianism that nineteenth-century romantic philosophers, above all Hegel and his successors in Germany, raised the standard of revolt. They emphatically rejected the machine metaphor to which Newtonian mechanics had given rise. Ironically, however, the romantic revolt against science ended by enshrining another scientific metaphor, the organic, which was to become one of the most recurrent themes of nineteenth-century biology. In effect, romantic philosophy appealed to a more congenial scientific concept, that of the organism, against a less congenial one, the machine. The proliferation of organic models in philosophy and social thought in the period just preceding Darwin probably contributed much to the readiness with which Darwinian concepts were taken up by ethical and social theorists. At any rate, the ruling model remained scientific, though the dominance passed from physics to biology.

Darwinism reigned over Victorian culture as supremely as Newtonian mechanics had over the previous century. Indeed, its hegemony was probably greater, both because the terms in which it was couched were so commonplace as to be easily absorbed, and because it dealt with a world of plants and animals much more recognizable as our own than was the cogwheel world of Newtonian physics. From monkey to man, unflattering as that coupling might be, demanded a shorter mental leap than from machine to man.

One distinctive feature of the Darwinian era, in contradistinction to the Newtonian, was the fact that some of the most heretical inferences from Darwin's theory were the work of Darwin himself. It could always be argued, for example, that Newtonian science had not itself converted man into a machine; Newton after all remained devoutly orthodox about the nature of God and man. But the description of man's animal ancestry and its ethical consequences came not from an interpreter but from Darwin. That which appeared to be most unorthodox had also to be acknowledged as the essence of Darwinian theory. So it came about that many of those most critical of unbridled Darwinism in social thought, such as the pragmatists, differed from their opponents not over the validity of applying Darwinian norms to man, but rather over the *proper* application of those norms.

The Darwinian Era Gives
Way to Modern Uncertainty

The exploration and appropriation of Darwinism went on over several decades. But the history of intellectual life suggests that the foundations of any governing world view may be sapped before the superstructure has ever been completed. Even as the meaning of evolution was being amplified and extended, certain undercurrents in the field of physics threatened to sweep away the whole carefully constructed scientific cosmology. The work of Planck, Einstein, Bohr, Heisenberg, and others left deep clefts in the dike of scientific certitude. Victorian science had never doubted that beneath flux lay order, an order which men could, little by little, apprehend. The new physics called this assumption into question. It replaced ultimate certainty with ultimate uncertainty, insisting that precision could be no more than a statistical average. What is more, the new science forfeited its claim to laying hold of reality: the concepts of science, it was now suggested, were conveniences rather than absolute truths. Even order, that cherished ultimate of Victorian science, might originate not in nature, but in the minds of men.

The complexity of the physical universe as it was revealed by physicists in the early decades of the twentieth century greatly altered the intellectual configuration of the previous generation. It became more difficult to believe as confidently as Victorian science had believed in a universe of absolute scientific laws discoverable by man. Clearly, if such laws existed, men were further from having delineated them than the giants of the Darwinian age had ever dreamed. To this doubt about the eternal verity of scientific facts was added in midcentury a doubt about scientific values: could science prescribe beneficent values for others when its own work led in the end directly to Hiroshima? The layman's faith was shaken.

In our own time, science has become more and more conspicuous in terms of magnitude, of achievement, of public recognition. Yet at the same time it has become circumscribed; it has rejected, by and large, the intellectual imperium of the Darwinian era. The scientific findings of the Darwinians have long since been accepted as a permanent enrichment of our knowledge of the world. Not so their social and philosophical inquiries. We still seek revelations among the animals, but we no longer assume that such discoveries are necessarily normative for men. At the flood tide of scientific confidence, Carl Snyder wrote a summary of the growth of science in which he anticipated the day when historians of his era would write, "It was at about the beginning of the twentieth century that man attained at last a true picture of the world . . . "[17] After Einstein and Heisenberg such a pronouncement is no longer thinkable.

The relative autonomy of the humanities and social sciences in relation to the natural sciences is surely one of the more striking features of intellectual life in our own time. Those who decry the rise of a scientific culture and the decline of the humanities at present ought perhaps to reread Tennyson's *In Memoriam* to see how thoroughly saturated with science Victorian culture really was. If history and belles lettres cannot today command the financial support accruing to microbiology, neither do they feel they must await the latest report of the scientists before getting on with their own work. Such a separation of intellectual spheres is by no means necessarily good. For one thing, it has made possible the rift between the two cultures pointed out by C. P. Snow. Still, there may well be some creative gain in an atmosphere which permits the individual to explore other modes of experience, other values, perhaps even other kinds of truth than the purely scientific. With culture as with politics, perhaps, there is merit in a world made safe for diversity.

A situation such as we seem to find ourselves in does, of course, entail the willingness to live more or less permanently in a state of uncertainty. If science cannot offer us metaphysical certainty, then certainty is nowhere to be found (except, perhaps, for believers, in religion). But uncertainty seems in any case to be the lot of modern man. Few are the institutions of modern life which instill a sense of permanence; transience appears everywhere ascendant. One might speculate that only in the stability of Victorian society could the Darwinian verities have been taken for transcendent truths. Similarly, in today's world scientific uncertainties and social instabilities reinforce each other.

In an epoch so different from the one we are about to examine, and in some ways so much more terrifying, it takes an effort of will to recapture the genuine fear and shock on the part of some, and the elation and triumph on the part of others, which greeted the Darwinian revolution. By contrast with nuclear fission, earlier scientific revelations seem to pale in significance. Yet, that effort must be made if we are to take the Darwinian episode as seriously as it deserves. There is an inclination in the modern mood to dismiss past intellectual controversies as tempests in teapots, and to stress continuities of thought over discontinuities. But that tendency is a privilege of hindsight. We can now see, as Darwin's contemporaries could not, not only that the path to Darwinism was well laid out before Darwin, but that in many areas of thought Darwinism either failed in the long run to work a lasting revolution or else merely dramatized and legitimized tendencies already present. Even so have the Renaissance and the French Revolution been rationalized out of existence by some historians. Certainly, however, Darwin's generation believed it was experiencing a revolution, and it might be well for us to grant each age the final word on its own revolutions. Whether or not its effects were permanent, the crisis of thought which the *Origin of Species* initiated was truly a revolution in the history of thought.

NOTES

1. Asa Gray, "The Origin of Species by Means of Natural Selection," reprinted in Asa Gray, ed., *Darwiniana* (New York, 1876), p. 10.
2. Benjamin Disraeli, *Tancred,* 1: 225–226, quoted in Gertrude Himmelfarb, *Darwin and the Darwinian Revolution* (Garden City, N.Y.: Doubleday Anchor Press, 1962), p. 216.
3. Francis Darwin, ed., *Life and Letters of Charles Darwin* (New York, 1887), 2: 23, quoted in Himmelfarb, *Darwin,* p. 198.
4. Leonard Huxley, ed., *Life and Letters of Thomas Henry Huxley*, 2 vols. (New York, 1902), 1: 189.
5. Gray, *Darwiniana*, p. 14.
6. Letter of Jan. 5, 1860, in Jane Loring Gray, ed., *The Letters of Asa Gray*, 2: 455, quoted in A. Hunter Dupree, *Asa Gray* (Cambridge, Mass.: Harvard University Press, 1959), p. 269.
7. These two paragraphs are based on George W. Stocking, Jr., "Lamarckianism in American Social Science, 1890–1915," in *Race, Culture and Evolution: Essays in the History of Anthropology* (New York: Free Press, 1968). The quotation is on p. 8.
8. "Darwinism in Literature," *Galaxy*, 15 (1873): 695, quoted in Richard Hofstadter, *Social Darwinism in American Thought* (Boston: Beacon Press, 1955), p. 24.
9. Charles Darwin, *On the Origin of Species by Means of Natural Selection, Or the Preservation of Favoured Races in the Struggle for Life* (New York: Washington Square Press, 1963), p. 469.
10. Charles Darwin, *The Descent of Man; and Selection in Relation to Sex*, 2 vols. (New York, 1871), 2: 372.
11. Herbert Spencer, *First Principles* (New York, 1891), p. 396.
12. "Herbert Spencer," in John Dewey, *Characters and Events*, 2 vols. (New York: Henry Holt & Co., 1929), 1: 58.
13. "Herbert Spencer's Autobiography," in William James, *Memories and Studies* (New York: Longmans, Green & Co., 1911), p. 110.
14. Jack London, *Martin Eden* (New York: The Macmillan Co., 1908), p. 108.
15. John Fiske, *Edward Livingston Youmans, Interpreter of Science for the People* (New York, 1894), pp. 54, 29fn.
16. James, "Spencer's Autobiography," p. 124.
17. Carl Snyder, *The World Machine* (New York and London: Longmans, Green & Co., 1907), p. 7.

Rocky Mountains, "Lander's" Peak. Painting by Albert Bierstadt, 1863. (Courtesy of the Fogg Art Museum, Harvard University. Bequest of Mrs. William Hayes Fogg.)

TWO

NATURE'S GOD

O F THE TROUBLES BESETTING religion in post-Civil War America, the coming of Darwinism does not seem, in retrospect, the gravest; yet it created the greatest stir and quickened the most intense emotions. It was the misfortune of organized religion at this particular juncture in its history to be undergoing a triple intellectual assault—from Biblical criticism, from the comparative study of religions, and from Darwinian biology. At the same time, the churches confronted an unprecedented social challenge, "the problem of the unchurched masses" as it came to be known, created by massive industrialization and urbanization. Nineteenth-century Protestantism, typically small-town, middle-class, and individualistic in outlook, came up against a range of problems involving city dwellers and members of the working class, problems with which it had no previous experience and for which it had no aptitude.

Partly because the churches made very little attempt to keep pace with large-scale economic and social changes, partly because they were losing the spiritual impetus that had been provided in times past by the great revivals, Protestantism did not face these challenges from a position of strength. "Never before," as one historian has written, "had the church been materially more powerful or spiritually less effective."[1] Paralleling the alienation of the working classes was the alienation of many intellectuals no longer willing to tolerate the hell-fire and brimstone Calvinism of orthodoxy. Those who, like Robert Ingersoll, "The Great Agnostic," directly attacked the churches for their failings remained a distinct minority. Far more to be feared was the possibility that the churches would come to be ignored as intellectually and ethically irrelevant. The problem for the churches, then, was twofold: they had to come to grips with a new society without losing sight of the essentially spiritual nature of the churches' mission; they also had to work out, in the light of new scientific and historical evidence, a theology both intellectually satisfying and prophetically vigorous. Paradoxically, the coming of Darwinism, in forcing a direct confrontation with theological issues, may actually have contributed in the long run to strengthening the American churches. But at the time the possibility of such a benign outcome occurred to few.

The initial reaction of American Protestant churchmen to Darwin's theory was overwhelmingly hostile. To chronicle the myriad attempts of ministers and concerned laymen to conjure away the Darwinian specter with ridicule or pseudo-science would serve no purpose but to entertain. The intellectual level of their arguments may be suggested by the query of the Reverend De Witt Talmadge, a well-known Brooklyn preacher, whether the generals who died in the Civil War had not been as good as those who lived through it—whereby he thought to disprove the theory of the survival of the fittest.

On a much higher intellectual plane was the resounding dissent of Charles Hodge, professor at Princeton Theological Seminary, author of the massive *Systematic Theology*, and probably the foremost theologian of his day. Hodge's *What Is Darwinism*, appearing in 1874, proceeded from the dictum that "science, so called, when it comes in conflict with truth, is what man is when he comes in conflict with God." Hodge went on to argue that the distinguishing feature of Darwinism was neither the notion of evolution nor that of natural selection but the rejection of "teleology, or the doctrine of final causes." That was sufficient to damn Darwinism in Hodge's view, since "the denial of design in nature is virtually the denial of God." Thus Hodge arrived at a succinct answer to the question of his title: "What is Darwinism? It is Atheism." A clearer instance of "science in conflict with truth" could not, in his view, be found.[2]

In point of fact, Hodge was even more adamant than these quotations reveal, for he opposed not only the Darwinian version of evolution but the general concept of evolution itself. He confessed an inability to reconcile evolution with Scripture, arguing that evolution and creation were mutually exclusive alternatives. There was no room in his cosmology for "half-way-evolutionism" which "professes to have a creator somewhere behind it," as the equally embittered J. W. Dawson of McGill phrased it in an obvious thrust at the conciliatory theology of his less militant colleagues.[3] Clearly, Hodge was on dangerous ground, leaving theologians no room for graceful withdrawal should evolution win general scientific approval, as appeared increasingly likely even in 1874. That Hodge was not alone in his sentiments, however, is shown by the approval with which his book was greeted by a number of Protestant journals as well as by the *Catholic World*. The *World* reviewer even singled out for praise the "quiet moderation" of Hodge's tone.

More prudent thinkers realized that Hodge's summary rejection of evolutionary theory did no service to the cause of religion. The botanist Asa Gray, himself something of a lay theologian and a shrewder mind than Hodge, remarked on the danger of wholesale condemnation of Darwinism: "All former experience shows that it is neither safe nor wise to pronounce a whole system 'thoroughly atheistic' which it is conceded may be held theistically, and which is likely to be largely held, if not to prevail on scientific grounds."[4] And James McCosh, celebrated president of Princeton and exponent of Scottish common sense philosophy, warned against "the undiscriminating denunciation of evolution from so many pulpits, periodicals, and seminaries." Such denunciation, he feared, might very well "drive some of our thoughtful young men to infidelity, for they could see for themselves that development was everywhere in nature." McCosh attested to the gratitude of his own students because "in showing them evolution in the works of God, I showed them that this was not inconsistent with religion, and thus enabled them to follow science and yet retain their faith in the Bible."[5]

The Reconciliation
of Science and Religion

Pockets of resistance remained, but the main body of religious thought in this country gradually embraced some scheme of reconciliation with science in the years after 1870. This reconciliation commonly took the form of discriminating, as Hodge had refused to do, between evolution and Darwinism; that is, between some notion of developmental change (often quite vague) and the particular hypothesis of natural selection. In its most popular guise, this view restricted natural selection to the animal world, while claiming a special exemption for man. Alfred Russel Wallace, codiscoverer with Darwin of natural selection, took this approach, as did James McCosh, in his dismissal of "evolution by physical causes" as the source of intelligence and morality. So, too, did the University of California geologist Joseph Le Conte. One of the most influential reconcilers, Le Conte, in his widely read *Evolution, Its Nature, Its Evidence, and Its Relation to Religious Thought*, enumerated six evolutionary mechanisms in all, including both Lamarck's use and disuse of organs and Darwin's natural selection. On the theory that evolution proceeded by levels, each with a distinctive operative factor, Le Conte argued that the appearance of man had introduced a new factor, the rational, which superseded natural selection.[6] All three writers, Wallace, McCosh, and Le Conte, were thereby enabled to ignore the darker side of natural selection, the side that exhibited "nature red in tooth and claw," by claiming that whatever it might mean for brute creation, natural selection had only a subsidiary role in the evolution of humanity. By preserving for the final stage of evolution a rational, hence purposeful, element, they could also evade Hodge's charge that Darwinism destroyed teleology. Reconciliation of Darwinian science with orthodox religion meant for the majority of reconcilers that the received religious truths retained all their former validity.

For one Calvinist theologian, George Frederick Wright, the Darwinian dispensation actually enhanced the standing of the old-time religion. Wright, a Congregationalist, was pastor of a church in Andover, Massachusetts, a man whose proficiency as a geologist—he was a recognized authority on glaciation—led him to explore with some concern the relationship between science and religion. It was he who prompted Asa Gray to collect the series of essays that appeared in 1876 as *Darwiniana*. Wright recognized in Gray a fellow proponent of the middle way between "the infidel class of Darwinian expositors" on the one side and "such opponents as Hodge and Dawson . . . [who] have made matters still worse" on the other.[7] Wright was later to accept an appointment at Oberlin

College as Professor of New Testament Language and Literature and then as Professor of the Harmony of Science and Revelation, the latter a chair endowed expressly for him.

In an article entitled "Some Analogies Between Calvinism and Darwinism," Wright made clear his dissent from evolutionary optimism by pointing out that Darwinism had not promised a happy ending. Natural selection could work for degradation as well as for progress. Organisms well-fitted to one environment might perish in another. Extinction was a paleontological fact. Such evidence, in Wright's opinion, did little to bolster the case for a cosmically unfolding perfection but was fully consonant with the Calvinistic doctrine of the fall of man from original grace. And, moreover, was it not central to Calvinism to discount the importance of individual happiness in the face of God's grandeur and His divine plan for the universe? Where but in the Darwinian cosmos, with its imperfect adaptations and its coercion of all creatures to "the reign of general laws and the requirements of their fellow travellers" could a more apt analogy be found? Wright concluded, "If Calvinism is a foe to sentimentalism in theology, so is Darwinism in natural history."[8]

Wright, and with him the majority of American churchmen, satisfied themselves that the challenge of Darwinism could be met and weathered without any serious remodeling of the orthodox theological edifice. There were a few theologians, however, who joyously undertook to modernize that structure in the light of the new science. For the most part, these men occupied the left wing of the American theological spectrum, the wing that sheltered Congregationalism, its offspring Unitarianism, and, at the farthest extreme, the rationalistic speculations of free religion. Freed of binding ties to orthodox creeds and confessions, such men as Lyman Abbott, Minot J. Savage, James T. Bixby, Francis Ellingwood Abbot, and Octavius B. Frothingham tried their hands at the construction of a genuinely evolutionary theology.

Evolutionary Theology

As a group, the evolutionary theologians were inspired rather more by Herbert Spencer than by Charles Darwin. Darwinism, as George Frederick Wright had correctly observed, lent itself to cosmic pessimism as readily as to optimism, but Spencer outlined a universe ever ascendant toward a more perfect equilibrium. It was easy, given the enormous prestige Spencer enjoyed in America, to relegate Darwin and natural selection to a tightly defined niche in a grander whole. "Darwinism is not evolution," affirmed Lyman Abbott, successor to Henry Ward Beecher at Brooklyn's Plymouth Church, and an immensely influential liberal theologian. "The doctrine that struggle for existence and the survival of the fittest is an epitome of life . . . is a hard and cruel view of life, and it is not the view of the great evolutionists."[9] But if Darwinism was not compatible with Christianity, evolution emphatically was. In *The Theology of an Evolutionist,* Abbott reshaped the old faith in the new light.

Probably the most important doctrine of the new theology was that of God's immanence in the world as a creative force. The old theology had supposed a God apart from the world and ruling over it in the manner of a king governing his empire. Evolutionary theology, on the contrary, confessed "that God is the one Resident Force, that He is in His world; that His method of work in His world is the method of growth; and that the history of the world . . . is the history of a growth in accordance with the great law interpreted and uttered in that one word evolution."[10]

This taming of the old Calvinist ferocity, this narrowing of the distance between God and man, was a marked feature of the new theology. So man ceased to be the depraved creature who had fallen with Adam and became a being in the process of developing from an animal to a spiritual condition. Sin was "a falling back into the animal condition," a momentary lapse on the upward path. Christ became fully human, a man uniquely filled with the divine nature, whose divinity differed, however, not in kind but only in degree from the divinity of other righteous men and women. God redeemed men, but He did not redeem them to a former high estate from which they had tragically fallen. Rather, He redeemed them to a glorious future, whose consummation "will not be until the whole human race becomes what Christ was, until the incarnation so spreads out from the one man of Nazareth that it fills the whole human race, and all humanity becomes an incarnation of the divine, the infinite, and all-loving Spirit."[11]

A text so flexible as both to encourage and to deflate optimism, to confirm and to deny the providential hand of God, all according to the eye of the beholder, was clearly open to endless varieties of interpretation. But at the very least, two central issues required resolution if science and religion were to coexist. The first and more superficial of these was the disparity between the Darwinian and the scriptural accounts of creation. This issue did not begin with Darwin; it arose in the 1830s and 1840s when geology was becoming very nearly a national mania in England. Geological findings, principally fossil evidence of the coexistence of man with creatures long extinct, began to undermine the traditional dating of prehistory based on the Old Testament. By adding up the life spans of all the patriarchs listed in the Mosaic genealogy, Archbishop Ussher in the seventeenth century had arrived at 8:00 p.m., Saturday, October 22, 4004 B.C. as the moment of creation. But this calculation had become shaky well before the *Origin*. By 1836 even one of the Bridgewater Treatises, written expressly to show "the Power, Wisdom, and Goodness of God, as manifested in the Creation," had had to concede a vast and indefinite period of pre-Adamite time between the creation of the world and the beginning of the Mosaic series.

Coming on the heels of this chronological readjustment, the *Origin* struck at Genesis in a more fundamental way by rendering dubious its entire description of creation. The progressive development of living things from simpler forms, as revealed by evolution, was held to be a flat contradiction of the scriptural story of creation. Apprehension on this account was doubly and trebly reinforced by the appearance of the *Descent of Man*, wherein Darwin expressly disclosed the presence of an ape in man's ancestral closet. The Scriptures had made reference only to mud in the fashioning of Adam, and many Bible readers were hard put to accommodate both mud and monkeys.

In point of fact, reconciling "geology and Genesis," as the phrase of the day went, proved to be a relatively simple matter once the need had been clearly perceived. This was not the first time that science had challenged the accuracy of the Bible—had not Galileo been imprisoned at the behest of the church for daring to deny that the sun could stand still in the sky? The churches began to realize that in binding themselves to a literal interpretation of the Bible they were needlessly handicapping themselves. They did not lack distinguished precedents—St. Augustine, among others, had expounded a metaphorical reading of Genesis some thirteen centuries earlier. (Literal interpretation of the Bible never had affixed itself to

Catholic tradition, a fact which gave Catholics a certain advantage over some of the more orthodox Protestant sects when Darwinism struck home.)

James McCosh showed how an accommodation could be reached:

> The Bible opens, "In the beginning God created the heavens and the earth." The account that follows is not to be regarded as a scientific one, in the nomenclature of biology and geology— sciences which did not exist till within the last century or two. . . . It may be looked on as an ocular description, such as might have been given by an intelligent observer as he witnessed the unfolding scenes.

There were really two records of the beginning of the world, the theological and the scientific, though as a matter of fact the two "have a very wonderful correspondence."[12]

Other theologians, a whit more daring, declined the gambit of the "intelligent observer" as incongruous and denied that the cosmology of Moses and that of modern science corresponded so nicely. An article in the *Bibliotheca Sacra* urged the establishment, "not as anything new, but only as requiring a more rigorous verification . . . than it has hitherto received," of a basic ground rule for biblical interpretation: "The Holy Scriptures were given to reveal moral and spiritual truth, and it was no part of their object to teach the truths of science, upon which consequently, they are no authority."[13] By such relatively gentle adjustments the Genesis of Moses and the genesis of Darwin were made to coexist. It was left to the winds of the higher criticism, even then blowing from across the ocean, to buffet the traditional view of the Bible more severely.

Chance vs. Design:
The Demise of Paleyan Theology

As President McCosh effortlessly harmonized evolution and Scripture, so he made short work of chance and design, the second and far more serious issue posed by Darwinism. Not only did evolution "not undermine or in any way interfere with the argument from design," it actually buttressed that argument. Evolution presupposed coordinated development among several independent parts within a given structure, as, for example, among the "coats and humors, rods and cones, retina and nerves" of the eye. In this concurrence McCosh clearly saw a designing mind which had foreordained the result. Natural selection conflict with Divine Providence? Hardly. "Supernatural design produces natural selection."[14]

More acute minds than McCosh's were not able to settle the question so easily. Darwin himself had worried the problem to an uneasy stalemate. At one time he would be overwhelmed by the inconceivability of man's having evolved through pure chance. At another time he could state flatly, "There seems to be no more design in the variability of organic beings, and in the action of natural selection, than in the course which the wind blows."[15] More and more, as he grew older, the second mood prevailed, but he continued to waver. The issue was metaphysical, and Darwin confessed that he had little taste or aptitude for metaphysics. Nor did he consider the mind a very trustworthy instrument when applied to speculative problems like this. Had it not developed from the mind of lower animals? In his last year of life Darwin listened to the Duke of Argyll argue from the adaptive contrivances of nature to the existence of a cosmic mind. Darwin's reply, characteristically gentle if a trifle weary, was his last recorded utterance on the subject of chance and design: "Well," he said, "that often comes over me with great force, but at other times it seems to go away."[16]

Thomas Henry Huxley did not waver. Convinced that science and religion could not mutually endure, he rejoiced in the Darwinian eclipse of design. What Darwin had done, Huxley pointed out, was to separate the notion of adaptation from that of design, so that the first could be held to even as the latter was discarded. Natural selection offered a convincing alternative to Divine Providence. It alleged that the nice fit between organism and environment, far from being preordained at the outset, was actually the final outcome of a brutally competitive process in which the less efficient went to the wall. "Far from imagining that cats exist *in order* to catch mice well, Darwinism supposes that cats exist *because* they catch mice well—mousing being not the end, but the condition of their existence."[17] Accordingly, Huxley was persuaded on first reading the *Origin* that teleology had "received its deathblow at Mr. Darwin's hands."[18] He did not doubt, any more than had the Princeton theologian Charles Hodge, that the death of teleology was the death of God.

Between the militant extremes marked off by Huxley and Hodge lay the *via media* of the reconcilers, among whom Asa Gray occupied a prominent position. Gray's immediate reaction to a first reading of the *Origin*, unlike Huxley's, was that "the argument for design, as presented by the natural theologians, is just as good now, if we accept Darwin's theory, as it was before that theory was promoted . . . ." Indeed, Gray suggested that Darwin might provide a modern addendum to Paley: Paley's watch, given time, might produce better watches, and even, with a change of environment, a chronometer or a town clock. If, as Darwin had persuasively argued, physical causes rather than separate acts of divine creation could be adduced to explain the origin of species, what was to prevent thinkers from simply referring these causes to Divine Providence? Variation might be likened to a stream whose channel, while no doubt carved out by the stream itself, had in fact been predetermined along "certain beneficial lines."[19]

Gray was perhaps only half serious about the chronometer. But he was entirely serious about his central point—the denial that Darwinism could be parlayed into a new chapter in the philosophical dispute between chance and design. Again and again he iterated that Darwin had not changed the nature of that dispute: "We could not affirm that the arguments for design in Nature are conclusive to all minds. But we may insist, upon grounds already intimated, that, whatever they were good for before Darwin's book appeared, they are good for now."[20] Natural selection was not an alternative to design, as Huxley had claimed it to be; it was a mechanism, a mode of operation, or, as Gray's student Wright put it, an instance of "secondary causation."

Gray was, of course, a very distinguished scientist as well as a convinced Christian. But he was not a professional philosopher, and on the question of Darwin's relevance to the argument from design he seems to have been quite wrong. For Darwin did subvert the empirical foundation of the argument from design.[21] Paley's watch may have required a watchmaker, but Darwin's eye required only a favorable conjuncture of variation and selective force, together with a sufficiency of time. Strictly speaking, it is true, Darwinian theory could not *disprove* design—it could not show that design in nature did not exist, only that its existence was an unnecessary hypothesis. By making explicable in naturalistic terms what had hitherto been inexplicable except in religious terms, the theory of natural selection made it possible to dispense with God in organic nature, just as La Place had found it unnecessary to invoke Him in explaining the cosmic mechanism. One could still affirm God; one could still, indeed, affirm design. But belief in the existence of design in the world, based on a prior belief in God, is far different from belief in God because design exists. After Darwinism, design was no longer an argument but merely a pious affirmation. "I believe in design because I believe in God; not in a God because I see design," wrote Cardinal Newman.[22]

Still, when Gray asserted that the argument for design was as good after Darwin as it had been before, he was very nearly right, though in a sense he did not intend. For design had been moribund before the *Origin* was ever written. If Darwin slew Paley, surely it was a corpse rather than a living, breathing body of thought that was delivered up to destruction. Before Paley ever wrote, the fatal blow had been dealt to Paley's mode of reasoning by the philosopher David Hume. Hume had pointed out, in effect, that, even granting the design analogy to be valid, a God revealed in the cleverly adapted mechanisms of nature would still be nothing more than a God of mechanism, and a finite God at that. Mechanical contrivance in nature could tell no more about God than that He was a cosmic mechanic.

But Hume did more: he went on to demolish the design analogy itself. To that end he offered at least two main arguments. The first begins with the observation that all inferences from design to deity assume that something akin to human reason must be responsible for the order we see in nature. But have we any right to assume that thought is the only causal principle in the universe? Is nature so limited in her resources as to possess no other spring of action? We see the operations of intelligence on our own planet, "this narrow corner,"—can we then legislate for the universe?[23]

Hume's second argument challenged the validity of inferring facts about a situation of which we have no experience. For the universe, he argued, is by definition inclusive of all that is (except God, if there be a God). Hence it is a thing unique and without parallel. But when we infer the existence of a designing mind from evidences of design in nature, we are using a mode of reasoning that applies only in cases of *repeated* experience. "When two *species* of objects have always been observed to be conjoined together, I can *infer*, by custom, the existence of one wherever I *see* the existence of the other: And this I call an argument from experience. But how this argument can have place, where the objects, as in the present case [i.e., the universe and God], are single, individual, without parallel, or specific resemblance, may be difficult to explain. . . . To ascertain this reasoning, it were requisite, that we had experience of the origin of worlds."[24]

Undoubtedly, it was too much to expect many of the controversialists in the dispute over Darwin and design to be conversant with Hume. Certainly, Gray and his fellow scientists can be forgiven their apparent ignorance of Hume's views.[25] But the fact is that the argument from design had been exposed as defective long before Darwin. That it took empirical argument to give the *coup de grace* where logic had failed perhaps gives witness to the inveterate empiricism of the Anglo-Saxon mind, but it does not diminish the prior achievement of Hume.

Post-Darwinian Teleology

There did remain for post-Darwinian theologians the possibility of invoking a "higher teleology"—a "teleology of the world-process as a whole." Such a shift would replace the design argument, or "argument from special contrivances," with "the teleological argument from order in Nature." Arguing for such a substitution, the Anglican F. R. Tennant wrote in 1909, "The higher teleology, the notion of a general design, which, as Professor Huxley admitted, evolution cannot touch, is in no opposition to the lower teleology of special designs, which when based upon Paley's grounds, was disposed of by the teaching of Darwin." Tennant even professed to see in Darwinism a new support for this "higher teleology":

> [Darwinism] may have shown that there is no better argument for teleology to be derived from the organic than from the inorganic world; this indeed it has done, if natural selection be an adequate description of the process of organic evolution. But, by disclosing more of order in the realm of animate Nature, it has served perhaps to intensify the demand for ultimate design behind the proximate causes which so marvellously combine to render the world the harmonious 'cosmos' which we find it on the whole to be.[26]

What Darwin had taken with one hand, he had given back even more abundantly with the other.

An American who took somewhat the same view was the famed minister of New Haven's Center Church and exponent of the "New Theology," Newman Smyth. Smyth took for his own, Lowell's lines in his poem "The Cathedral":

Science was Faith once; Faith were Science now,
Would she but lay her bow and arrows by
And arm her with the weapons of the time.
Nothing that keeps thought out is safe from thought.
For there's no virgin-fort but self-respect,
And Truth defensive hath lost hold on God.

Determined to open religion up to the "ice-cold water of critical reflection," Smyth betook himself to the biology laboratories at Yale to discover what science could tell him about "nature's progressive self-revelation."[27] A slim volume entitled *Constructive Natural Theology* offered to other seekers like himself the fruits of that quest.

Smyth's approach was singularly candid. While not disposed to disparage the older natural theology—the Bridgewater Treatises, Paley, and Butler's *Analogy*—Smyth granted that that approach was "an antiquated and no longer tenable fortification." A new theology of nature awaited construction, one conforming to the mechanical principles of evolution and incorporating the recent discoveries in physics. "Natural theology may not now go forth with Paley to find that remarkable watch in crossing a heath; but it may inquire what the least particle of earth has to tell of its atoms or the energies of electrons, while the flowers in full bloom on the heath may ask us to behold some diviner secret in their flourishing . . . ."[28]

It was perhaps a measure of the time that had elapsed between his own book and that of the early reconcilers that Smyth's temper was so serene, so certain, so assured. Paley may, as Smyth assures us, have been "ruled out of court by Darwinian science," but his dismissal was only an incident in the reconstruction of a viable natural theology. Smyth did not even find it necessary to reassure his audience of the ultimate compatibility of science and religion. Science attended to the cosmos as it was, in the interim between its infinitely remote beginnings and its final end; religion looked to that beginning and that end.

Go back, then . . . —as far back toward the origin of things as the most adventurous science may go; then look to the end—as far toward the end as the vision of the transfigured man, the ascended

Christ, may suffer the most worshipful faith to gaze into the heavenlies. The way of the aeons between let science measure as it may—the materials, the powers, the mechanics of it from age to age; but the beginnings and the end, the origin lost from sight far away, and the glory at the end vanishing into the ineffable—of these what science can tell?[29]

The harmony of science and religion had found its seer.

Obviously, the notion of a higher order beyond the reach of natural selection was as open to Hume's critique as was the Paleyan form of natural theology, but it did circumvent the immediate stumbling block of Darwinism and thereby found great favor with theologians generally, and especially with those acute enough to suspect the eclipse of special contrivance. John Dewey ridiculed this idea of a cosmic design behind the mechanical processes of nature as "design on the installment plan," and it is doubtless true that with biological adaptation no longer acceptable as evidence of God's plan, there remained little, if any, tangible proof of ultimate providence. By the same token, however, if the argument from general design could not be empirically proven, neither could it be disproven, and it was therefore a refuge safe from the shock of a future Darwin.

Religion After Darwin:
The Theology of Experience

Having made some adjustment to the revelation of natural selection, many theologians were able to dismiss the threat of Darwinism to religion. A reading of some leading theological journals in this country suggests that Darwinism may not have deranged the faith of the pious too greatly. True, it was initially seen by many writers as inimical to the faith, and it inspired an enormous amount of explication and clarification after the first, usually unfavorable, reaction. But the bulk of this work was directed to showing why Darwinism did not after all disturb the bedrock of faith. One writer in the *Bibliotheca Sacra* even complained that the whole episode had been inflated beyond reason. "There has been more said about the disturbing influence of Darwin's book in theology and the unsettling of religious belief than facts will warrant," he asserted. "*Some* dry bones may have rattled, but they were neither as numerous nor as representative as is sometimes asserted. My bones never rattled. I passed through the time of whatever perturbation there was in thought because of Darwin's work without agitation myself and I did not find myself lonesome. I found company in plenty in both church and schools."[30]

But it would be wrong to underrate the lasting effect of Darwinism on religious thought. It engendered all those theologies directly based on evolutionary concepts, whose liberalizing influence in the way of softening the older Puritan doctrine extended beyond the relatively small circle of professed religious liberals. These theologies so identified evolution with moral and spiritual progress, with "God's way of doing things," that evolution in the natural world and redemption in the spiritual world could be viewed as analogous processes, with God resident at the center of both.

More important in the long run, probably, was Darwinism's role in turning religion away from metaphysics and toward its roots in experience. Darwinism weakened the dominant apologetic of physical proofs for the existence of God and encouraged recourse to other sources of belief—the experience of God in the individual conscience or in the historic moral sense of mankind. Pure Darwinism, untainted by the optimistic emendations of a Spencer or a Fiske, dashed cold water on the convictions of the godly. Darwin, in the *Origin*, had carefully left the door open to the existence of a creator, but a creator who merely imparted developmental energies to a few germs at the beginning of the world and thenceforth let things run on through the working of secondary agencies.

Nor did Darwin's characteristic stress on the violent, strife-ridden aspects of existence tend toward the disclosure in nature of an all-good and benevolent deity. Lyman Abbott took great pains to show that Darwinism was not synonymous with evolution, that the "Struggle for Others" (as Henry Drummond termed it) existed side by side with the "Struggle for Self." He had to admit that, taken by itself, the Darwinian process did not exactly trumpet the presence of God. In proportion as God faded from sight, natural theology—whose whole object was to trace God in nature—declined.

As theologians began to turn away from a metaphysical approach to God, they turned toward its principal alternative, a theology of experience. Experience as a touchstone of faith was not new; it had been an important element in Western Christianity from the beginning. Those who felt God's presence within them as a living reality had always tended to look askance at the rationalizing, coldly logical enterprise of the natural theologians. Pascal's emphasis on the hidden God stands as perhaps the most vehement denial of the possibility of finding God in nature. "I wonder at the boldness with which men speak of God in addresses to the irreligious," Pascal had written. "Their first undertaking is to prove the Deity by the works of nature." But men who do not believe in God can search nature in vain for any sign of deity: "To say to these that they have only to look at the least thing in the world, and they will see God unveiled, and to give them, as the whole proof of this great and important subject, the course of the moon or of the planets, and to pretend to have completed the proof by such a discourse—this is only to furnish them occasion to think that the proofs of our religion are very feeble . . . ."[31]

In Darwin's day Pascal's dissent was taken up and reaffirmed by John Henry Newman, prominent Anglican clergyman who led a band of followers into the Catholic church. Newman looked in vain for evidence of God in the world. "If I looked into a mirror, and did not see my face, I should have the sort of feeling which actually comes upon me, when I look into this living busy world, and see no reflexion of its Creator." What did Newman see? " . . . tokens so faint and broken of a superintending design, the blind evolution of what turns out to be great powers or truths, the progress of things, as if from unreasoning elements, not towards final causes, the greatness and littleness of man, his far-reaching aims, his short duration, the curtain hung over his futurity, the disappointments of life, the defeat of good, the success of evil, physical pain, mental anguish, the prevalence and intensity of sin, the pervading idolatries, the corruptions, the dreary hopeless irreligion . . . ."[32] In short, the very same panorama as that constructed by the more pessimistic evolutionary naturalists. To try to fashion a proof for God's existence from evidence that was at best ambiguous and at worst contradictory seemed to Newman "jejune." And supposing that its program could be attained, natural theology did not in any case "tell us one word about Christianity proper," but only preached the existence of God and three of his attributes—power, wisdom, and goodness.[33]

Newman's distaste for Paleyan physicotheology, and his conviction that other modes of demonstrating God's reality were needed, led him to concentrate on the argument from conscience to God and immunized him against undue anxiety about the effect of Darwinism on religion. In 1863 Newman confided to his journal the improbability "that monkeys should be so like men with no *historical* connection between them," and in a letter to St. George Mivart, Catholic biologist and foe of natural selection (though not of evolution), he wrote, "You must not suppose I have personally any great dislike or dread of his [Darwin's] theory."[34] Still, though his own reflections on natural religion did not stem from Darwinism, Newman gave cogent expression to a type of reasoning that could be eminently useful to those who saw in the Darwinian controversy confirmation of the danger of basing religion too narrowly on physical proofs.

One well-known American thinker who followed up Newman's lead was George P. Fisher, professor of church history at Yale. In a book entitled *Faith and Rationalism*, Fisher took the position that "the grand peculiarity of religious faith is the part which the heart plays in it." The old arguments from natural theology had not lost their force for Fisher; he remained as convinced of the validity of design after Darwin as did Asa Gray. Indeed, he inclined to the view that scientists who refused to believe in God did so not from lack of evidence but from lack of goodness. In arguing his case, then, Fisher aimed not to belittle the evidence of natural religion, but to reach those who were untouched by that evidence. He pointed out that "many, in these days especially, who come in contact, in their daily studies, with what strike us as marks of design, are not convinced of theism." The evidence did not compel assent as, say, the axioms of logic do. Christ had commanded His hearers to believe in Him, Fisher observed, but "Who ever *commanded* another to believe that two and two are four, or to accept the doctrine of free-trade [!], or the nebular hypothesis?"[35]

Fisher did not regret the incapacity of the evidence to coerce belief. Indeed, his entire argument was a demonstration of the limits of rationalism in matters of religion. Placing himself in the line of religious thinkers that included Augustine, Luther, Pascal, Schleiermacher, and, most recently, Newman, he set himself to vindicate the role of experience, as over against logic, in the assent of faith. "Men do not reason themselves into the exercise of love," he argued, "any more than they reason themselves into the perception of the beauty of a landscape, or into the enjoyment of a painting of Titian." Not reason but experience, the profound sense of man's dependence and guilt,—this is what summons the soul to believe, and, believing, to understand. The intellect has a role, a central role, in examining the doctrines of Christianity and attesting to their reasonableness. Fisher by no means intended to denigrate the uses of intellectual persuasion. (Later he was to write a compact *Manual of Natural Theology* based on the conviction that the proofs for God's existence, being eminently logical, would "elicit, enlighten, and fortify the spontaneous belief which is native to the human spirit.") All that he wished to assert was the priority of feeling over intellect in religious conviction. "We *believe* because we *love*," Fisher wrote, quoting Newman. "How plain a truth!"[36]

Fisher's position is interesting, and may be significant, precisely because he was a staunch theological conservative. Unlike Newman Smyth or Theodore T. Munger or the other restless heirs of the New England theology, Fisher did not feel the need to recast the old orthodoxies into more appealing forms. He did not turn to the category of experience, as some liberal theologians did, in order to reject traditional doctrines. For that very reason his assent to an experiential theology suggests the broad appeal such a theology could have for conservative as well as liberal Christian apologists.

Nor did Fisher turn to experience in order to ward off the threatening implications of Darwinian science. He had made his peace with Darwinism on what he took to be its own terms and required no Kantian demarcation of the line between science and faith. At the same time, the line of thought that Fisher traced from Augustine through the reformers and Pascal, to Schleiermacher and Newman, offered potentially valuable aid to any theologians less assured than Fisher himself. A religion that reemphasized the importance of faith as against reason was particularly well suited to an age of unprecedented scientific accomplishment. Clearly, religion could not long endure a climate in which the discovery of a bone fragment or a fossil stratum could threaten the entire fabric of Christianity. For some theologians, the situation seemed to call for jettisoning the mystical element in religion altogether, for working out a theism as rigorously logical as the logic of science itself. William James demonstrated another, and in the end more fruitful, approach, by offering a careful empirical assessment of the varieties of religious experience. James's work, in effect, gave scientific backing to the insights of Schleiermacher, and thus reinforced the retreat from metaphysics and the rise of theological empiricism.[37]

Darwinism alone did not give rise to the renewed theological emphasis on faith and feeling. George P. Fisher would have been profoundly influenced by Schleiermacher and Newman had Charles Darwin never lived or worked. Yet insofar as science explained more and more of the universe, and God was no longer needed to fill in the gaps, arguments from nature to God lost credence. And insofar as science seemed to pose a threat to religion, the appeal to experience offered an impregnable shield against naturalism. Those who wished could build on this basis an evolutionary theology that rejected many of the doctrines of traditional Christianity. But such modernism, which at times threatened to become less a faith than an ethic, never won the allegiance of more than a well-educated few. For most Christians in America, the reconciliation of Darwinism and religion left the old beliefs in all essentials intact.

NOTES

1. Henry Steele Commager, *The American Mind* (New Haven: Yale University Press, 1950), p. 167. For an overview of the religious situation after the Civil War, see the relevant chapters of Sydney Ahlstrom, *A Religious History of the American People* (New Haven: Yale University Press, 1972).
2. Charles Hodge, *What Is Darwinism?* (New York, 1874), pp. 47, 52, 175, 177.
3. Ibid., pp. 122–123.
4. Gray, *Darwiniana*, pp. 257–258.
5. James McCosh, *The Religious Aspect of Evolution* (New York, 1887), pp. xi–xii.
6. Joseph Le Conte, *Evolution, Its Nature, Its Evidences, and Its Relation to Religious Thought* (New York, 1897), especially Chapter 3.
7. Wright to Gray, June 26, 1875, cited in Dupree, *Asa Gray*, p. 363.
8. Wright, "Some Analogies Between Calvinism and Darwinism," *Bibliotheca Sacra*, 37 (1880): 54–55, 65–66, 68, 76.
9. Lyman Abbott, *The Theology of an Evolutionist* (New York, 1897), pp. 95, 96.
10. Ibid., p. 15.
11. Ibid., pp. 36 ff., 49, 72, 73, 75–76.

12. McCosh, *The Development Hypothesis—Is It Sufficient?* (New York, 1876), p.53.

13. Rev. J. H. McIlvaine, "Revelation and Science," *Bibliotheca Sacra*, 34 (1877): 260.

14. McCosh, *Religious Aspect*, p. 7.

15. Darwin, *Life and Letters*, 1: 279.

16. Ibid., 285.

17. Thomas Henry Huxley, *Lay Sermons, Addresses, and Reviews* (London, 1871), p. 303.

18. Thomas Henry Huxley, "Criticisms on 'The Origin of Species'," in *Darwiniana*, p. 82.

19. Gray, *Darwiniana*, pp. 57, 148.

20. Ibid., p. 152.

21. The argument from design was widely promoted as an empirical proof of God's existence. Actually, though the concept of design rested on empirical evidence—instances of biological adaptation— the force of the design argument rested on a nonempirical premise, on the claim, namely, that order in the universe is less probable than random disorder and therefore requires us to assume a cause for its existence. See James Ward Smith, "Religion and Science in American Philosophy," in *The Shaping of American Religion*, v. 1 of *Religion in American Life*, ed. by James Ward Smith and A. Leland Jamison, 4 vols. (Princeton: Princeton University Press, 1961), p. 420. Darwinism did not touch this premise at all.

22. Letter of Cardinal Newman, April 13, 1870, quoted in *Philosophical Readings in Cardinal Newman*, ed. James Collins (Chicago: Henry Regnery Co., 1961), p. 189.

23. *Hume's Dialogues Concerning Natural Religion*, ed. Norman Kemp Smith (London and New York: Oxford University Press, 1935), pp. 182–183.

24. Ibid., p. 185.

25. Gray did have a secondhand acquaintance with Hume, but he misconstrued the *Dialogues* altogether, taking as Hume's own the position favoring natural theology that Hume was in fact intent upon demolishing.

26. F. R. Tennant, "The Influence of Darwinism Upon Theology," *Quarterly Review*, 211 (1909): 431.

27. Newman Smyth, *Constructive Natural Theology* (New York: Charles Scribner's Sons, 1913), p. vii.

28. Ibid., pp. 2–3.

29. Ibid., pp. 2, 96.

30. "Louis Agassiz and Charles Darwin: A Synthesis," *Bibliotheca Sacra*, 73 (1916): 137–138.

31. Quoted in George P. Fisher, *Faith and Rationalism* (New York, 1879), pp. 89–90.

32. *Apologia Pro Vita Sua*, quoted in James Collins, *God in Modern Philosophy* (Chicago: Henry Regnery Co., 1959), p. 356.

33. A. Dwight Culler, *The Imperial Intellect: A Study of Newman's Educational Ideal* (New Haven: Yale University Press, 1955), pp. 267–268.
34. Ibid., p. 267.
35. Fisher, *Faith and Rationalism*, pp. 15, 38–39, 48, 16.
36. Ibid., pp. 34–35; George P. Fisher, *Manual of Natural Theology* (New York, 1893), p. 9; *Faith and Rationalism*, p. 98.
37. Other insights into the theological reaction to Darwinism can be found in Stow Persons's chapter, "Evolution and Theology in America," in his *Evolutionary Thought in America* (New Haven: Yale University Press, 1950) and in three essays in *The Shaping of American Religion*: Persons, "Religion and Modernity, 1865–1914"; James Ward Smith, "Religion and Science in American Philosophy"; and Daniel D. Williams, "Tradition and Experience in American Theology."

William James, 1842–1910. (Courtesy of The Bettman Archive, Inc.)

THREE

CAMBRIDGE METAPHYSICS: EVOLUTION, CHANCE, AND THE COSMOS IN JOHN FISKE, CHAUNCEY WRIGHT, C. S. PEIRCE, AND WILLIAM JAMES

HE RECONCILIATION OF SCIENCE and religion was the most sensitive and certainly the best-known aspect of the larger task of recasting contemporary philosophy in the light of Darwinism. In Cambridge, Massachusetts, in the years after 1860, a remarkable constellation of gifted men turned their analytical skills to the consideration of this larger task. These men, Chauncey Wright, C. S. Peirce, William James, John Fiske, Francis Ellingwood Abbot, and Oliver Wendell Holmes, Jr. among them, were accustomed to meet for serious discussions of science and philosophy in the informal setting of the "Metaphysical Club." They met in a philosophical atmosphere in which Concord Transcendentalism, fortified by later infusions of Hegelian idealism, clashed with the English empiricist tradition represented most conspicuously by John Stuart Mill. British empiricism was stronger than German idealism in the philosophical makeup of most of these men (Peirce later said that he alone of the group had come to philosophy through Kant), but they were by no means devoid of sympathy for the strengths of Kant and his successors. Indeed, they saw themselves as rethinking, with the aid of Darwin, the premises of the two schools, in the hope of working out a philosophy that would offer a satisfactory alternative to both.

Each of these men evolved, after his own fashion, some more or less comprehensive resolution of the various claims of Darwinian science, philosophy, and religion. All were committed to science; all wished to ensure complete freedom of inquiry to scientific investigation against the obstructionism of those theologians or metaphysicians who felt that science endangered faith or morals. At the same time, though they were uniformly critical of traditional theologies, all but Chauncey Wright gave allegiance to some form of liberal religious faith and viewed as an imperative task the demonstration of the compatibility of scientific knowledge and metascientific faith. John Fiske made religion the evolutionary fruit of science. Chauncey Wright, himself agnostic, contended for the irrelevance of science to faith. Charles S. Peirce, who shared Wright's belief in the neutrality of science, created a metaphysic, inspired by the gospels, of evolutionary love. William James demanded in the name of human freedom that science acknowledge the legitimate claims of faith. Their work, collectively, did much to clarify the nature of the relationship between what men know and what they believe.

John Fiske:
Apostle of Evolution to America

Though friends and philosophical sparring partners, two men more dissimilar than John Fiske and Chauncey Wright could scarcely be imagined—the one jovial, immense (in his mature years Fiske weighed nearly 300 pounds), incurably sentimental and optimistic; the other slender, unassuming, inclined to shyness and melancholy. Fiske, the successful popularizer and ardent Spencerian, was master of a lucid and effective prose style put to the service of a largely undistinguished body of ideas. Wright, a Darwinian almost unknown outside his own circle during his lifetime, concealed a powerful intellect in a thicket of diffuse prose. By all accounts a brilliant conversationalist, Wright never completed a book; only after his death were a number of his essays and review articles collected and published as *Philosophical Discussions* (1877). Fiske and Wright shared a common concern with evolution in all its bearings, scientific, philosophical, and moral.

John Fiske had intended in his younger years to become an academic. Gifted in languages and blessed with a highly retentive memory, he was perhaps more erudite than original. But that fact alone would scarcely disqualify a man from an academic career, and he would undoubtedly have been an effective teacher; the courses he did offer at Harvard seem to have been successful. For a number of reasons, however, including his heterodox views on religion, he never attained a permanent faculty position. Drained by the needs of a family which ultimately grew to six children, as well as by his own taste for good living, Fiske's finances were a constant source of anxiety to him. It may be that the continual pressure to write publishable pieces deflected Fiske from more serious research. It may equally well be, as his biographer claims,[1] that his talents were far more suited to popularization than to working on the frontiers of knowledge. At any rate, by taming the idea of evolution and then leashing it to an optimistic theism he achieved a greater, if less enduring, fame than all but a handful of his more academic contemporaries.

Born in Middletown, Connecticut, in 1842, John Fiske turned away in his teens from the Calvinism of his ancestors to the fairer prospect of English and French positivism. His heroes were numerous: the German Alexander von Humboldt, whose *Cosmos* was for Fiske "the Epic of the Universe," the English historians George Grote and Henry Thomas Buckle (together with philology, history was the field of Fiske's special competence), John Stuart Mill and George Henry Lewes, Sir Charles Lyell, Charles Darwin, Herbert Spencer, and the French sociologist August Comte (whom he later discarded). Always, however, Herbert Spencer stood out from the rest, and on discovering the prospectus of Spencer's *Synthetic Philosophy* in a Boston bookstore, Fiske hastened to subscribe. A letter to his mother explained that "I consider it my duty to mankind as a Positivist to subscribe; and if I had $2,000,000 I would lay $1,000,000 at Mr. Spencer's feet to help him execute this great work."[2]

After graduation from Harvard in 1863 Fiske took a law degree to satisfy his parents, and set up practice in Boston. But clients did not materialize, and Fiske's real interests did not in any case lie in the law. So he resolved to earn a living writing free-lance articles for national magazines like the *North American Review*, the *Atlantic Monthly*, and the *Nation*. There followed a period of financial insolvency, assuaged only by subsidies from Fiske's stepfather and in-laws. In 1869, however, Fiske received a temporary appointment to lecture at Harvard on the positive philosophy of Comte. Out of this appointment, so he optimistically presumed, would come both a book based on the lectures and the chance for a permanent profes-sorship. A book in two volumes did indeed appear in 1874, the *Outlines of Cosmic Philosophy*, Fiske's major philosophical work. But the Harvard appointment lapsed after two years, and with it faded Fiske's dream of an academic career. That dream was to evaporate altogether when Fiske failed to receive the history professorship left vacant by Henry Adams's resignation in 1877. Thereafter, writ-ing and lecture tours were Fiske's sole means of income. Many years were to pass before his income sufficed to balance his debts.

Fiske's interests were wide-ranging, embracing philology, philos-ophy, science, history, and religion. All these areas, he believed, could be brought under the aegis of evolution, and to this end he labored for the rest of his life. In so doing, Fiske followed Spencer rather than Darwin. It was Spencer who had founded the philosophy of evolution, he explained, while Darwin had merely investigated one particular aspect of it. After a luncheon with Dar-win, Fiske wrote to his mother that Darwin "impressed me with a sense of strength more than any other man I have ever seen." Still, "there is no doubt that Spencer is the profoundest thinker of all."[3] This attitude, as we shall see, marked one of the great differences between Fiske and Chauncey Wright.

Unlike Spencer, however, Fiske felt compelled to justify religion in the evolutionary scheme of things. He had cast off the shackles of "anthropomorphic theism" in youth, had even, in the full flush of Comtism, refused the minimal label "theist," but the religious im-pulse was not to be denied. In the *Outlines of Cosmic Philosophy*, Fiske satisfied himself that he had worked out the proper relation-ship between science and religion. "Though science must destroy mythology," he asserted, "it can never destroy religion; and to the astronomer of the future, as well as to the Psalmist of old, the heavens will declare the glory of God."[4]

Science, Knowledge, and Religion: A Cosmic Synthesis

The problem of religion as reflected in Fiske's work is as much epistemological as substantive, a question of method as well as of content. Contemporary science was forcing men to reflect on the processes of knowledge. How do we know? What do we know? What do we mean by valid knowledge, and what are its criteria? What is belief? In the absence of empirical verification, can belief be justified? These are the kinds of questions that evolution provoked among intelligent men. They were not entirely solvable—there are some questions which each generation must raise afresh. But for that very reason the problems with which Fiske dealt have a live air about them that the design argument lacks. Fiske's concerns coincided with those of his Cambridge friends, C. S. Peirce, William James, and Chauncey Wright, of whose circle Fiske was a regular member. Fiske was not himself a creative philosopher as these others were, but he did have a very competent grasp of the issues, together with the ability to give lucid exposition and a persuasive if somewhat superficial resolution of them.

To the essential question of what we can be said to know, Fiske and Wright actually returned rather similar answers, although Wright remained a positivist, wihle Fiske tried to penetrate beyond the realm of sense data to the Unknowable, the Noumenon of Herbert Spencer. Both Fiske and Wright believed that certain knowledge, as opposed to intelligent speculation or emotional commitment, can be attained only by the methods of science. Both held that scientific knowledge was relative and empirically verifiable, and that metaphysics was a matter of character or opinion but not of knowledge properly so called. Both rejected the idea that science and philosophy as different fields required distinctive methodologies. Thus Fiske, whose avowed aim—to "bring about a harmony between human knowledge and human aspirations"—caused him to deal with God as well as with science, had to confess that religious questions could never be settled "as scientific questions are settled. . . . We cannot expect . . . to obtain a result which, like a mathematical theorem, shall stand firm through mere weight of logic, or which, like a theorem in physics, can be subjected to a crucial test." Fiske proposed, instead, to try to see what conclusions about God and religion were most consonant with the findings of modern science.[5]

In his quest for a scientific theism, Fiske stayed close to the path already marked out by Herbert Spencer. Indeed, the *Outlines of Cosmic Philosophy* was not an attempt to construct a wholly new philosophy but a gloss on the philosophy of Spencer, together with an elaboration of those points, like the bearing of philosophy on religion, that Fiske felt the system required in the interests of completeness.

Anchoring his argument to the Spencerian dictum that "we are forever debarred from any knowledge of the Absolute, the Infinite, or the Uncaused," Fiske proceeded to demolish the epistemological basis for traditional theology. The process of cognition necessarily involves judgments of likeness, difference, and relationship, but these are elements totally foreign to an absolute deity. If religion cared to make its peace with science, Fiske declared, it would have to prune out the old anthropomorphic notions of God as loving father or omnipotent lawgiver or indeed as intelligence of any sort, and frankly confess the total inscrutability of the Absolute. Harsh surgery, perhaps, but necessary in the evolution toward a higher conception of deity. Fiske did not intend to leave erstwhile believers altogether bereft of the comforts of belief. He recognized that "upon the religious side of philosophy as well as upon its scientific side, the mind needs some fundamental theorem with reference to which it may occupy a positive attitude." Such a fundamental theorem he was prepared to supply, and not only to supply, but to certify as scientifically valid. It was this: *"There exists a POWER, to which no limit in time or space is conceivable, of which all phenomena, as presented in consciousness, are manifestations, but which we can know only through these manifestations."* The existence of God, divorced from any knowledge of Him, was to be the rock upon which science and religion might unite.[6]

Fiske knew, of course, that many would object to his denial that man can in any way know God. So he artfully outflanked the opposition by asserting that we worship not what we know, but what we do not know. Theology had always worked against itself. "Could the theologian have carried his point and constructed a 'science of Deity'; could the divine nature have been all expressed in definite formulas, as we express the genesis of vegetation or the revolutions of the planets, worship would have disappeared altogether. Worship is ever the dark side of the shield, of which knowledge is the bright side." Taking up a position athwart both sides, Fiske proposed as fit object for man's adoration the "wondrous Dynamis" eternally active in the universe.[7] (Not all who heard were convinced. "Great is Dynamis," derided one reviewer, "and John Fiske is Its Prophet.")

Fiske completed the *Cosmic Philosophy* as a young man wholly under the spell of Spencerianism. But the years passed and Fiske's juvenile romance with science ("O, my dear! there is nothing in this world like SCIENCE," he had written at the age of 22 to his fiancée) began to seem pale and unsatisfying. The happy reconciliation of science and religion with which he had concluded the *Cosmic Philosophy* might appeal to the intellect, but it said little or nothing to the heart. The heart's needs, meantime, had become more imperious. An essay written in 1876 gave vent to Fiske's dissatisfaction. Science, he wrote, could offer men only the vision of "a senseless bubble-play of Titan forces, with life, love, and aspiration brought forth only to be extinguished." But surely life was more than this:

> There are moments when one passionately feels that this cannot be all. On warm June mornings in green country lanes, with sweet pine-odours wafted in the breeze which sighs through the branches, and cloud-shadows flitting over far-off blue mountains, while little birds sing their love-songs, and golden-haired children weave garlands of wild roses; or when in the solemn twilight we listen to wondrous harmonies of Beethoven and Chopin that stir the heart like voices from an unseen world; at such times one feels that the profoundest answer which science can give to our questionings is but a superficial answer after all.[8]

Fiske's solution to these inner promptings took the form of an inferential warranty of religion based on science. In the beginning Fiske had not hesitated to clip the wings of religion rather severely. When he asserted that beyond the fundamental fact of the existence of God, science and religion had nothing to say to one another, since their modes of verification were entirely different, it was clear that his sympathies lay with the former. In 1871 he even suggested to a theologian that only natural selection could settle the controversy between the two fields. "The view which most thoroughly harmonizes with the general state of human knowledge in the future will of course prevail in the struggle for life." Even as late as 1877 Fiske was concerned over "the unpardonable sin of letting preference tamper with judgment."[9]

The Teleology of Evolution

Fiske did not maintain this position with entire consistency. Belatedly he came to see that religion, if it were to be at all meaningful, had to be a more luminous experience than the abstract worship of an unknowable force. But Fiske found it very difficult to justify religion on its own grounds. His youthful flirtation with positivism had left him permanently skeptical of nonscientific ways of knowing and anything that smacked of metaphysics. There lurked always beneath the assured surface of his writing the need to buttress faith with science, to show that religion was really the logical extension of certain scientific principles, and above all of evolution.

Thus Fiske became more and more emphatic about the teleological implications of evolution. He acknowledged that the *Cosmic Philosophy* had embraced only "an imperfect appreciation of the goal toward which the process of evolution is tending." That goal was man, whom Darwin had shown to be crown and glory of the world. It had become clear to Fiske in the years after 1874 that evolution not only transfigured man, but also suggested his immortality. In *The Destiny of Man* (1884), Fiske spoke of accepting the doctrine of immortality "not in the sense in which I accept the demonstrable truths of science, but as a supreme act of faith in the reasonableness of God's work."[10]

Fiske's final pronouncement on the subject, an address entitled "Life Everlasting," delivered in 1900, went well beyond "God's reasonableness." After disposing of all scientific objections, he reiterated and expanded an earlier argument that belief in an unseen world had arisen with the genesis of man and had remained strong ever since. From this he concluded that "the belief must be based upon an eternal reality, since a contrary supposition is negatived by all that we know of the habits and methods of the cosmic process of Evolution." Fiske looked forward with confidence to a new form of natural theology based on evolution. "The Nineteenth Century has borne the brunt, the Twentieth will reap the fruition."[11]

So, too, the larger question of religion as a whole could be put in perspective with the aid of evolution. For God did not mock—the universal intuition of religious awe must have an objective basis, since the study of evolution had shown just how internal perceptions were becoming more and more adjusted to external conditions. Religious feeling which had no foundation in reality would be an unseemly anomaly, a discontinuity in nature. Hence, "the lesson of evolution is that through all these weary ages the Human Soul has not been cherishing in Religion a delusive phantom. . . . Of all the implications of the doctrine of evolution with regard to Man, I believe the very deepest and strongest to be that which asserts the Everlasting Reality of Religion."[12]

Evolution the handmaiden of religion—indeed an unforeseen ending for one who had been the village infidel of Middletown. Still, Fiske had never denied the existence of God, had never been a true atheist. His faith, it would appear, never cost him anything. He did not have to be afraid of evolution; he had always known that "the results obtained from the study of man's spiritual and material nature are destined ultimately to coincide."[13] No wonder that a liberal theologian like Henry Ward Beecher, who had gone to school to Spencer and Fiske could confidently urge: "Subsoil the people with Spencer, Huxley, and Tyndall. . . . If the trellis of old philosophies is rotten and falling down, take it away and let us have a better. We can trim the vines of faith on the new one just as well."[14] No wonder that so many people, "perplexed and science-tossed," gratefully acclaimed the balm Fiske applied to troubled souls. And no wonder that in the end Fiske had nothing to say which would live on after his death. Fiske's easy optimism provoked wondrous visions, visions of a future "lighted . . . with the radiant colours of hope," when "peace and love shall reign supreme" and "strife and sorrow shall disappear."[15] But these visions we can no longer share, or if we share them we do so in the painful realization that before the glorious millenium we face an uncertain and dangerous interlude in a far from radiant world.

Fiske's serene confidence in the future was very much a product of his time and position, and despite its limitations it spoke to many troubled souls of his own day. He performed the genuinely necessary function of helping to ease the intellectual and spiritual transition to a Darwinian universe. The answers that he offered did not stand the test of time but can be respected for what they were—the honest responses of an innately religious and gifted, though not profound, mind to a thoroughly unsettling complex of scientific ideas.

The Dedicated Darwinian:
Chauncey Wright

Even as John Fiske was finding in evolution a welcome support for his religious intuitions, Chauncey Wright was appraising evolution and finding that it said nothing at all about religion. And he was perfectly content to let it go at that.

Like Fiske a native New Englander and graduate of Harvard, Wright was twelve years Fiske's senior. A lifelong bachelor, self-effacing and gentle but quick and formidable in debate, tough-minded and wholly unemotional in his pursuit of truth, Wright was in many ways the very antithesis of Fiske. The two remained nonetheless good friends who shared membership in the inner circle of Cambridge wit and intellect that C. S. Peirce later referred to as the "Metaphysical Club." Fiske has recorded how he and Wright walked back and forth between each other's gates late one evening after a session of the Club, until dawn put an end to their still-unfinished discussion. Wright was for several years the senior member of the Metaphysical Club; Peirce called him "our boxing master whom we—I particularly—used to face to be severely pummeled."[16]

Chauncey Wright accepted Darwinism with at least as much conviction and thoroughness as Fiske brought to Spencerianism. He had read Chambers' *Vestiges of Creation*, a farfetched attempt to establish a theory of evolution that preceded the *Origin* by some years, but remained sensibly skeptical. He was converted to evolution by a careful reading of Darwin in 1860. From that time forth his intellectual concerns revolved about Darwinism. Taking natural selection to be a true cause, he devoted himself to examining "the problems, physical and metaphysical, which the acceptance of this explanation presented."[17] The examination involved defending Darwin against his critics—especially St. George Mivart, an English Jesuit biologist—despite the fact that his own competence lay in mathematics and physics.

Darwin thought so highly of Wright's attack on Mivart that he asked Wright's permission to have it reprinted in England. Later Darwin requested Wright, "as your mind is so clear, and as you consider so carefully the meaning of words," to analyze in relation to the evolution of language the problem of "when a thing may properly be said to be effected by the will of man." Darwin was here touching on part of the central problem for evolutionary theory: just how much continuity existed between man and the lower animals. In response to Darwin's query, Wright wrote his best-known essay, "The Evolution of Self-Consciousness," in which he made his most important contribution to the body of Darwinian theory. While not fully answering Darwin's original request, Wright developed a naturalistic account of the appearance of new faculties like language and reason by supposing them to have arisen out of old faculties which, due to environmental change, were put to new uses. Thus he cut the ground from under the argument for "the 'supernatural' advent of the self-conscious soul" by demonstrating how self-consciousness, or reflection, could have arisen from the generalizing capacities of animals. At the same time, Wright did not wish to dispute the really profound distinction between human and animal consciousness; he disputed rather the cast of mind which would make that distinction absolute.[18]

Perhaps the central theme of Wright's philosophy is the idea of the neutrality of science. We have seen that John Fiske, while professing a kind of positivism about the limits of knowledge, eventually put science to work for faith. Not so Wright, who seems never to have suffered from metaphysical *angst* of any kind. On this point we have the independent testimony of both Fiske and William James. Wright's positivism, observes Fiske, "was an affair of temperament as much as of conviction; and he illustrates afresh the profound truth of Goethe's remark that a man's philosophy is but the expression of his personality."[19] James puts the case even more strongly: "Never in human head," he writes, "was contemplation more separated from desire. . . . Whereas most men's interest in a thought is proportioned to its possible relation to human destiny, with him it was almost the reverse. When the mere actuality of phenomena will suffice to describe them, he held it pure excess and superstition to speak of a metaphysical whence or whither, of a substance, a meaning, or an end."[20] Wright apparently did not share the usual philosopher's urge to get to the bottom of things. He was not at all convinced that there was a bottom. When a friend raised the problem of why we exist he replied, "Why, for nothing, to be sure! Quite gratuitously!"[21]

Thus prepared to contemplate life with equanimity, Wright consistently refused to put his science to the service of anything. Possibly taking a leaf from Asa Gray, who may have influenced his point of view, Wright insisted on the futility of all attempts to erect science into metaphysics. "True science," he affirmed, "deals with nothing but questions of facts. . . . " Scientific principles had no meaning beyond scientific boundaries. They meant no more and no less than what they had been formulated to mean.[22]

Fiske's idol, Herbert Spencer, pained Wright particularly. In 1865 he dealt Spencer a rather devastating blow in the pages of the *North American Review*. "Nothing justifies the development of abstract principles in science but their utility in enlarging our concrete knowledge of nature," observed Wright sternly. "The ideas on which mathematical mechanics and the calculus are founded, the morphological ideas of natural history, and the theories of chemistry are such working ideas—finders, not merely summaries of truth." (This notion of ideas as working hypotheses has been taken by some commentators to prefigure the pragmatism of Peirce and James.) In a later article Wright went on to deplore the inflation of evolution into a cosmic doctrine. Very likely, he wrote, evolution held true only of "the life of the individual organism" and related phenomena. And, in any case, careful thinkers would do well to heed "the too little regarded doctrine of Aristotle, which banishes cosmology from the realm of scientific inquiry . . . ."[23]

Positivism, Religion, and the Neutrality of Science

As a general rule of thought, Wright proposed that knowledge and faith be clearly distinguished. A thing could properly be said to be known only if it was amenable to concrete testing, or if it was a logical or mathematical truth. All other interpretations of reality belonged to the realm of faith, because they were unproven and unprovable. About this area of the unprovable Wright himself did not feel disposed to speculate; the only obligation he recognized was the obligation to remain open to fresh evidence. "Upon his chart of the Universe," wrote his friend Gurney, "the *terra incognita* of the not-proven that stretched between the firm ground of the proved and the void of the disproved, included some of the chief beliefs to which mankind has clung. . . . " Wright did not deny that truth might exist there; "he denied only that it lay within the range of man's experience, and therefore of knowledge in the sense in which he understood and used that term."[24] So, having sifted the arguments for the existence of God offered by reason, intuition, and revelation, and having failed to find hard evidence in any of them, he maintained a position of religious agnosticism. "The verdict of 'not proven,' " he wrote to a friend, "is the kind of judgment I have formed of these matters. . . . In fact, practical considerations determine that a state of suspended judgment on these themes is the state of stable equilibrium." (John Fiske had once written, "To the earnest inquirer the state of skepticism is accompanied by pain . . . .") Wright's judgment tended, however (though certainly not in any dogmatic way), to approach certainty—the certainty of nonbelief. "All the ends of life," he confided to his close friend, Grace Norton, "are, I am persuaded, within the sphere of life and are in the last analysis, or highest generalization, to be found in the preservation, continuance, and increase of life itself . . . ."[25]

Wright made it clear that he valued the kind of sentiment that lay behind traditional religion. Indeed, he suggested the positivist solution—reverence for "the interests of humanity"—as an alternative for those like himself who could no longer hold to orthodox forms of faith. He protested the entanglement of theological doctrine and moral precept which made it appear that morals disintegrated in the absence of formal religion. At the same time, Wright felt no evangelical compulsion to liberate the orthodox from their beliefs on grounds of intellectual doubt. He demanded of religion not that it forswear its traditional teaching but that it cease trying to make knowledge out of faith. His own position, as he noted in a letter to Francis Ellingwood Abbot, a liberal theologian and philosopher, "denies nothing of orthodoxy except its confidence; but it discriminates between the desirableness of a belief and the evidence thereof." A clear and honest distinction between science and religion would, Wright argued, put an end to the false incursions that each had in the past been inclined to make into the other's territory. Religion would stop trying to use science to prove God, and science would stop insisting on proofs of religion. It would then become apparent that no contradiction actually existed between them.[26]

For Wright, religion was not a matter of intellect in any case but a matter of spirit. To Abbot, who felt that he must give up the ministry because of his radical religious beliefs, Wright urged, "I hope that I have misunderstood you, and that you will be able to continue, as a religious instructor, to exemplify how irrelevant metaphysics really are to the clergyman's true influence. . . . To help to live up to the true ideals of life seems to me the noblest, if not the only, duty of the preacher." Religion was, as he put it elsewhere, "an affair of character, not of intelligence."[27]

Much has been made of Wright as a precursor of pragmatism in his doctrine of theories as working ideas which find truth. But he also shared with the pragmatists, James above all, that willingness to see reality piecemeal, that distaste for general systems (Wright called the philosophical systematizing of evolution "German Darwinism") which caused James to revolt against the "block-universe." In complete opposition to Fiske, Wright saw no necessary congruence between the laws of nature and the ethics of men. Ethical laws, he once argued, are "of a wholly different order" from cosmic laws, "neither contradictory to nor in conformity with those of the scientific cosmos."[28] So radical a bifurcation of reality, though hinted at by Darwin, was not characteristic of pragmatism, but the pluralistic spirit which inspired it was wholly characteristic.

There remain problems with Wright's antiseptic separation of knowledge and faith. If reason can correctly be exercised upon concrete evidence alone, if faith is made altogether a matter of sentiment and emotion, it seems difficult to escape from unrelieved subjectivism in questions of religious belief. Is feeling alone a trustworthy guide to religious judgments and moral choices? Wright had a partial answer to this question, in that the grounds for some decisions were accessible to critical, empirical examination. But the problem was not completely resolved. Wright's self-denying ordinance was certainly not likely to be acceptable in toto by the true believer of either side—religious or naturalist—who understandably felt that the intellect could rightfully address itself to nonempirical information.

Still, the disagreements that might arise at this point stem from Wright's positivist epistemology and not from the idea of scientific neutrality, an idea which was, after all, shared by the religiously orthodox Asa Gray. Wright's equation of true knowledge with scientific (empirical) knowledge lies at the heart of the problem about value judgments, but that equation need not be at issue here. What needs to be stressed is Wright's central role in the casting of an idea which became part of the pragmatic, and hence American, intellectual tradition. William James was to spend a good part of his philosophical and emotional energy battling what he considered the "anti-religious" and "nihilistic" qualities of Wright's thought. Nevertheless, both he and Peirce were in essential agreement with Wright about the need to distinguish between science and metaphysics. Indeed, Wright's distinction has remained very much a live idea right up to the present day. In its own time and place it was more than live, it was positively therapeutic. Unfortunately,

Wright never attained much of an audience during his lifetime. The other potential exponents of scientific neutrality were few and not yet effective: Gray, still encumbered by design, was unpersuasive; Peirce, unknown; and James, just beginning to write. In time, however, the idea would gain momentum, even as the monumental labors of Fiske and Spencer and Haeckel and Büchner, all confident of proving that science could yield the key to the cosmos, sank into semi-obscurity. We do not all, today, believe in metaphysics, though we do generally believe in science. But at least we can usually manage to tell the one from the other. Wright would not have asked more.

Peirce, Darwin and Evolution

Neither Fiske's theistic cosmology nor Wright's ascetic skepticism quite satisfied the requirements, at once scientific and humane, of the two founders of pragmatism, Charles S. Peirce and William James. Fiske's commitment to Spencerianism with its mechanical progress toward perfection, its disregard of the canons of scientific method, and its dogmatic finality, violated some of the cardinal principles of pragmatism. Both Peirce and James had been educated in science, and their pragmatic method was intended to banish from philosophical discourse the vagueness and imprecision that characterized so much of Spencer's "Synthetic Philosophy." At the same time, neither man could remain comfortable with the strict empiricism (James called it "nihilism") of Chauncey Wright— Peirce because it clashed with his logical doctrine of the reality of universals, and James because it denied validity to the duty (or as he later called it, the will) to believe.

Wright did, however, leave an indelible impression on the minds of his younger friends as an acute and wholly dispassionate seeker after truth, who curbed their own more ardent philosophical flights. He bequeathed them, in addition, his view of nature as incorrigibly rich and diverse, subject to no one interpretation or necessity, a view crystallized in his deft phrase, "cosmic weather." The same outlook was to reappear in James's pluralism and Peirce's tychism. Chance, freedom, indeterminism, possibility—such were the categories with which Peirce and James warded off the "block-universe."

Charles Sanders Peirce, son of the distinguished Harvard mathematician Benjamin Peirce, led a peculiarly isolated life—cut off because of personal idiosyncrasies from the academic world to which he aspired (except for a brief teaching career at Johns Hopkins and occasional lectures), temperamentally unfitted for any other form of remunerative employment, and, as a direct consequence, barred from most of the social and cultural, and indeed physical, amenities which ordinarily foster a productive intellectual life. (He once wrote to William James, "It is so cold in this room, 34°, that I can hardly write.")[29] And yet, though he published but one book, he managed to produce an impressive number of articles, lectures, and unpublished fragments of a projected work on the history of science, which reveal the searchingly original quality of his intellect. Virtually neglected in his own lifetime outside the small circle of his admirers in Cambridge (in this he resembles Chauncey Wright), Peirce was rediscovered only with the publication of his *Collected Papers* beginning in 1931. It is now clear that Peirce's role in the intellectual history of pragmatism, together with his other contributions to formal logic, especially symbolic logic and the calculus of probabilities, ensure him a secure place in the history of American intellectual life.

It is not always easy for the layman to get at Peirce's thought. Much of it belongs to the highly refined fields of symbolic logic and semantics and requires prior familiarity with those disciplines. Some of it demands a considerable mathematical finesse. But the obscurity of certain other sections of Peirce's work seems to be due to a quixotic unwillingness to write clearly. According to his friend, the philosopher Josiah Royce, Peirce appeared almost to fear lest mediocre minds, finding themselves able to follow his reasoning, might "form too high an impression of their own powers."[30] This is doubly strange in that Peirce valued clarity in writing, as in thought, so highly. He was given to scolding William James for just such lapses as he himself fell into: "When you write English," he complained, "I can seldom at all satisfy myself that I know what you are driving at."[31] Nevertheless, for our purposes we need not examine the darker corners of Peirce's system, for what directly concerns us here—Peirce's evolutionism and his notions of probability and chance—are among the more attainable of his ideas.

When Darwin's *Origin of Species* appeared, Peirce was in Louisiana on a surveying trip with the United States Coastal Survey.

He had graduated from Harvard the previous June and was shortly to return there for a master's degree and then a Sc.B. *summa cum laude* in chemistry. Peirce's thorough training in science, particularly chemistry, spectroscopy, stellar photometry, meteorology, and geodesy, form the background out of which evolved his views on the logic of science and scientific method, the tychistic nature of the universe, and the pragmatic theory of meaning.

Peirce accurately grasped the essential features of Darwin's theory of evolution. He realized that it involved the conjuncture of two factors—variation and natural selection—and that the former was, to all appearances, purely fortuitous. The fortuitous, or chance, aspect of the theory was what interested him most, for it made Darwin's theory one instance of the more general laws of probability. Peirce had early become convinced that the statistical interpretation of nature was fundamental to an understanding of the logic of modern science. Scientists, he believed, must abandon the expectation that individual events and elements could, in an ideally complete theory, be precisely determined. Such was the received tradition of classical physics, as exemplified, for example, in the work of the great English physicist James Clerk Maxwell. In Europe and America, however, the physicists Boltzmann and Gibbs, together with Peirce, had arrived at the view that this deterministic ideal was no longer tenable and would have to give way to a calculus of probabilities fixing the behavior, not of individuals, but of groups. The idea that "chance begets order," so Peirce observed, or, to put it another way, that "fortuitous events may result in physical law," was becoming "one of the cornerstones of modern physics."[32]

From this standpoint, Peirce turned his attention to Darwin and was able to see in natural selection an application of the statistical method to biology. "The Darwinian controversy," he wrote, "is, in large part, a question of logic. Mr. Darwin proposed to apply the statistical method to biology. The same thing has been done in a widely different branch of science, the theory of gases." As physicists could calculate the proportionate velocities and positions of the molecules of gases over the long run, without knowing the course of any individual molecule, so likewise "Darwin, while unable to say what the operation of variation and natural selection in any individual case will be, demonstrates that in the long run they will, or would, adapt animals to their circumstances."[33]

Only one so dry and abstract (Peirce thus characterized himself), and so wedded to the study of logic, could have called the controversy over Darwinism mainly logical. As a matter of fact, Peirce had his own reservations about Darwinism, and they were not entirely logical. As early as 1869, Peirce recorded his distaste for Darwinism: "It is not the sublimity of Darwin's theories which makes him admired by men of science, but it is rather his minute, systematic, extensive, strict, scientific researches which have given his theories a more favorable reception—theories which in themselves would barely command scientific respect." In 1893, long after most American scientists had been completely won over to Darwinism, Peirce remained aloof: "His [Darwin's] hypothesis," he asserted, "while without dispute one of the most ingenious and pretty ever devised . . . did not appear, at first, at all near to being proved; and to a sober mind its case looks less hopeful now than it did twenty years ago . . . ."[34]

The truth is that Peirce felt, as Philip Wiener puts it, "less than lukewarm" about Darwin's theory. Though enthusiastic about it as an instance of probability theory, he never believed that natural selection was sufficient to account for evolution. Rather, he viewed it as only one of three types of evolutionary process, the others being the Lamarckian (evolution through the inheritance of adaptive traits acquired through the efforts of individual organisms) and the cataclysmic (evolution through sudden large mutations).

Far worse than the scientific insufficiency of Darwinism, for Peirce, was its aesthetic and moral bankruptcy. He attributed its popularity "in large measure, to its ideas being those toward which the age was favorably disposed, especially because of the encouragement it gave to the greed-philosophy." According to Peirce, a true evolutionary formula would teach that all life and movement is growth, and that growth comes only from love, but Darwin had taught that progress occurs through "the animal's ruthless greed." Peirce remarked with distaste that Darwin ought to have taken for his motto, "Every individual for himself, and the Devil take the hindmost!" He added, "Jesus, in his sermon on the Mount, expressed a different opinion."[35] Such emotional philosophizing would not have appeared at all strange in the subjective, intensely personal world view of William James, but in Peirce, who castigated James roundly for sanctioning feelings and emotions as indicators of pragmatic truth, it seems rather out of place.

Peirce was, after all, the original formulator of the pragmatic rule of clarifying meaning by linking it to testable results. In the series of six articles that appeared in the *Popular Science Monthly* under the general title, "Illustrations of the Logic of Science," and, above all, in the most famous of the six, "How to Make Our Ideas Clear" (1878), Peirce gave pragmatism to the world. He meant it as an attempt to bring philosophy, which had languished under the rule of authority and dogma, into the shelter of scientific method. There it would be safe from those who would seize it to further some partisan doctrine, and there, its terms unambiguous and its propositions precise, it could flourish in a way unimaginable so long as philosophers continued to discourse in a metaphysical fog. "Consider," wrote Peirce, "what effects, that might conceivably have practical bearings, we conceive the object of our conception to have. Then our conception of these effects is the whole of our conception of the object." In other words, to determine the meaning of a concept, one must determine its conceivable practical efforts. If a person hears an object termed "hard," and wishes to know what hard means, he must put the hard object to the experimental test. He will then find that it can scratch other substances without itself being scratched, and can define hardness accordingly as the quality of not being scratched by many other substances.[36]

Peirce's scientific training and his desire to transform philosophy into a scientific discipline made him emphasize the ascetic and disinterested nature of true knowledge. Nothing could be further from the truth than the charge that pragmatism, at least as formulated by Peirce, was a philosophy of the useful. (The charge is somewhat more understandable when levelled at James). Indeed, Peirce tended to believe that on the really fundamental questions of life—questions of values and beliefs—philosophy could offer no guidance. "On vitally important topics reasoning is out of place . . . . In regard to the greatest affairs of life, the wise man follows his heart and does not trust his head. This should be the method of every man, no matter how powerful his intellect." Such a radical division of human powers was totally foreign to William James, nor would it have commended itself to the calmly rational Chauncey Wright. But Peirce was not ashamed to acknowledge himself a member of the party of sentimentalism, "the doctrine that great respect should be paid to the natural judgments of the sensible heart." It was one such judgment that motivated his hostility to

Darwinism as a "greed philosophy," though the question remains whether the relationship of Darwin's theory to certain individualistic economic and social doctrines is just grounds for criticism of the theory itself.[37]

Tychism vs. Scientific Determinism

Though Peirce did not approve of Darwin's theory, he was nevertheless an enthusiastic evolutionist after his own fashion. He had been forced to conclude for a number of reasons, he tells us, "that an evolutionary philosophy of some kind must be accepted." Nature demanded it: "The only possible way of accounting for the laws of nature and for uniformity in general is to suppose them results of evolution." Peirce took the Darwinian theory and used it as a springboard for some highly speculative metaphysical theorizing about the condition and development of the universe. Since Darwin had given evidence of the creative value of the idea that "chance begets order," Peirce bent this notion to the construction of a new version of Genesis:

> In the beginning—infinitely remote—there was a chaos of unpersonalised feeling . . . . This feeling, sporting here and there in pure arbitrariness, would have started the germ of a generalizing tendency. Its other sportings would be evanescent, but this would have a growing value. Thus, the tendency to habit would be started, and from this, with the other principles of evolution, all the regularities of the universe would be evolved. At anytime, however, an element of pure chance survives and will remain until the world becomes an absolutely perfect, rational, and symmetrical system, in which mind is at last crystallized in the infinitely distant future.[38]

Peirce did not claim that his "Cosmogonic Philosophy" was scientifically demonstrable, but he did argue that it was "in the general line of growth of scientific ideas," and that it might be verified in the future. An evolving universe, for Peirce, was perforce a universe of chance. His reasoning appears to have run somewhat along these lines: the most striking feature of our world is its sheer diversity and irregularity, notwithstanding the many uniformities which we designate as laws of nature. This diversity is incontestable; it is an observed fact. Either it has been present from the beginning of time, as the mechanists hold, or it has been in the making over time. But science tells us that all temporal systems show increased complexity in the course of time; they do not merely recapitulate past experience, they evolve in new ways. There must exist an agency which furthers diversity, and since it cannot partake of mechanical necessity, it must be purely spontaneous. Such is absolute chance (Peirce called his doctrine tychism after *tyche*, the Greek word for chance) and its role in our heterogeneous universe.[39]

Since Peirce believed that the process of evolution violated the basic premises of a mechanistic philosophy, he did not hesitate to take Herbert Spencer rather severely to task. Spencer's attempt to explain evolution mechanically was doomed for several reasons, not least of which was the fact that the reversibility of mechanical laws excluded any conception of an irreversible process like growth. What Spencer had written of evolution as mechanical force "is mathematically absurd and convicts him of being a man who will talk pretentiously of what he knows nothing about."[40]

If it was easy for Peirce to dispose of the scientific pretensions of Herbert Spencer, it was less easy to dispose of Spencer's philosophy of determinism, since Spencer's view was widely held by the scientific community of Peirce's day. Peirce formulated the basic position of mechanistic science precisely: it implied "that the state of things existing at any time, together with certain immutable laws, completely determine the state of things at every other time. . . . Thus, given the state of the universe in the original nebula, and given the laws of mechanics, a sufficiently powerful mind could deduce from these data the precise form of every curlicue of every letter I am now writing."[41] To Peirce's mind, such a position was not tenable, and he proceeded to demolish, one by one, the arguments commonly advanced in its favor: that determinism was a necessary postulate of scientific reasoning, that its operations had been empirically established by laboratory procedures, that the opposing hypothesis—that of spontaneity or chance—was unintelligible or inconceivable or impossible to verify. Peirce believed, too, that time was on his side, for recent developments in thermodynamics, particularly the kinetic theory of gases, were making it clear that in systems with numerous components, mechanical interpretation must give way to statistical. In other words, the precise determination of each individual particle must be jettisoned as a goal, at the same time that scientists could now chart with great accuracy the behavior of the system taken as a whole.

Peirce was aware that his reading of the significance of the statistical method was by no means universally accepted. Though he insisted that "I do no more . . . than follow the usual method of the physicists, in calling in chance to explain the apparent violation of the law of energy which is presented by the phenomena of growth," he added, "only instead of chance, as they understand it, I call in absolute chance." Peirce thus rejected the view held by Clerk Maxwell and by Darwin, among others, that chance was simply a cover term for the operation of laws of which men were still ignorant. He justified this rejection on the pragmatic ground that things which are ultimate for us, that is, things which do not permit further exact analysis, probably really are what they seem to be. "I believe," he wrote, "that in a broad view of the universe a simulation of a given elementary mode of action can hardly be explained except by supposing the genuine mode of action somewhere has place." And again, "We cannot help suspecting that the simulated violation of the law of energy [involved in the aggregation of identical molecules to form a chemical substance] has a real violation of the same law as its ultimate explanation."[42]

The Humanism of William James

Monistic by temperament, with a deep conviction that "we ought to begin by pressing the hypothesis of unity as far as we can," Peirce emerges as a strangely fragmented personality, preaching spontaneity and freedom but looking forward to "the crystallization of mind"; sternly scrupulous about the demands of scientific truth yet unwilling to follow the guidance of the intellect in the search for values; yearning for community while immured in a Pennsylvania farmhouse where he spoke to no one but his wife for days at a time. It would be hard to imagine a greater contrast of character than that between Peirce and his fellow exponent of the gospel of chance, William James. The two men were poles apart in temperament, in manner, in virtually every attribute that defines life-style. Peirce was a scientist and mathematician who looked to scientific method as the perfect model of the pursuit of truth. James, trained as a scientist but of a more empirical bent than Peirce, distrusted science whenever it threatened to ignore the immediate experience of life, especially the testimony of the emotions. He confessed himself, much to Peirce's dismay, hopelessly incompetent in mathematics. Peirce was a logician; James had little use for formal logic. Of James's doctrine of the will to believe, Peirce wrote severely that it "was a very exaggerated utterance, such as injures a serious man very much."[43] Peirce looked with favor upon the Absolute, and greatly admired the writings of James's Harvard colleague, the idealist Josiah Royce; James considered the Absolute intolerably despotic, and, while a warm supporter and friend of Royce personally, led the fight against idealism in the name of "radical empiricism."

Yet the two men maintained over many years a personal and intellectual friendship that bridged the differences between them. In a touching tribute written after James's death in 1910, Peirce exclaimed "[James's] comprehension of men to the very core was wonderful. Who, for example, could be of a nature so different from his as I. He so concrete, so living, I a mere table of contents, so abstract, a very snarl of twine. Yet in all my life I found scarce any soul that seemed to comprehend—naturally [not] my concepts, but the mainstream of my life better than he did."[44]

It was James, not Peirce, who made of pragmatism the world-famous American philosophy. James's pragmatism was not the same as Peirce's, however. Peirce had spoken of judging a concept by its "conceivably practical effects." James adapted this pragmatic maxim to read: "To develop a thought's meaning, we need only determine what conduct it is fitted to produce."[45] Conduct was not at all what Peirce had in mind by "conceivably practical effects"; his pragmatism was entirely intellectual and referred only to concepts, not to the possible behavior that they might inspire. Furthermore, Peirce limited his pragmatism to a rule for clarifying meaning. James expanded it to become a theory of truth as well. James spoke of truth as something that could vary from individual to individual and asked of an idea, "What concrete difference will its being true make in any one's actual life?" Peirce, far more austerely, took for his model of truth seeking the scientific community, and defined truth as "the opinion which is fated to be ultimately agreed to by all who investigate." Peirce excluded from philosophical consideration all the great questions of morality and religion. James directed his philosophy specifically to the consideration of these central human concerns. For all these reasons, Peirce eventually found it necessary to dissociate himself from the pragmatism of James and others by rechristening his offspring "pragmaticism."[46]

William James came by his intense humanism naturally. Raised under the benign and permissive, if eccentric, regime of his remarkable father, Henry James, Sr., James grew up in a milieu of wealth, culture, and intellectual stimulation in which it was taken for granted that ideas were important but people no less so. To the end of his days he retained a remarkable gift for friendship, a gift that even manages to impregnate the printed page with warmth and empathy.

James and Science

James came to the study of philosophy, like Peirce, from the standpoint of science; but in James's case the sciences were physiology and psychology. In 1890 James published his *Principles of Psychology*, a Darwinian classic that, among its other accomplishments, introduced the term "stream of consciousness" into American psychology. There is an unmistakable psychological residue even in the mature philosophy of James, an exquisite perception of the emotional and moral dimensions of human knowledge and a democratic unwillingness to accord higher status to one particular kind of knowing—scientific knowledge—just because of its claim to a monopoly on truth.

James deplored the arrogance and smugness of the scientific assumption that "there is something called scientific evidence by waiting upon which men shall escape all danger of shipwreck in regard to truth." Himself the least dogmatic of men (his student Santayana wrote of James, "I think it would have depressed him if he had had to confess that any important conclusion was finally settled"), James could not abide dogmatism in others, whether theological or scientific. But at the time and in the milieu in which he found himself, he considered it more urgent to attack the excesses of science than to confront the church. His audience of well-educated, middle-class Americans were, he believed, far less likely to suffer from superstition than from "paralysis of their native capacity for faith and timorous *abulia* in the religious field." They were undercredulous rather than overcredulous. In their behalf James did not hesitate to enter the lists against "a vision of 'Science' in the form of abstraction, priggishness and sawdust, lording it over all."[47]

James particularly deplored the common idea that science could be totally objective and disinterested, because he knew perfectly well that scientists, the best ones especially, were often emotionally involved in their work. Many of the greatest discoveries took place because the scientist *cared* about the outcome. "The most useful investigator, because the most sensitive observer, is always he whose eager interest in one side of the question is balanced by an equally keen nervousness lest he become deceived." Nor could scientists claim to be free of faith; they held to a set of beliefs that were as much a faith as medieval Catholicism. "The principle of causality, for example,—what is it but a postulate, an empty name covering simply a demand that the sequence of events shall some day manifest a deeper kind of belonging of one thing with another than the mere arbitrary juxtaposition which now phenomenally appears? It is as much an altar to an unknown god as the one that Saint Paul found at Athens. All our scientific and philosophic ideals are altars to unknown gods."[48]

The scientific mind that refused to believe or act without conclusive evidence was incarnated for James in the person of Chauncey Wright. In the ten years before his premature death in 1875, Wright was for James, as for Peirce, both mentor and sparring partner. James charged Wright with an agnostic paralysis of all action on unproven beliefs. Opposition to Wright's positivism—his unwillingness to believe anything more than the empirical evidence supported—called forth the initial statement in 1875 of James's doctrine of the will to believe. His argument, as expressed in mature form in the essay "The Will to Believe" of 1896, rested on a blunt and bold assertion: "Our passional nature not only lawfully may, but must, decide an option between propositions, whenever it is a genuine option that cannot by its nature be decided on intellectual grounds . . . ."[49]

Against the positivist asceticism that eschewed any belief on insufficient evidence, James vigorously defended the right of the moral and emotional element in man to pass judgment before the evidence was compelling. The English physicist Clifford, whom James called a "delicious enfant terrible," had written, "If [a] belief has been accepted on insufficient evidence the pleasure is a stolen one . . . . It is wrong always, everywhere, and for every one, to believe anything upon insufficient evidence." This was a notion James could not accept, because, as he pointed out, options, and above all moral options, did not always await—sometimes indeed precluded—the judgment of the dispassionate intellect. Failure to judge was itself a kind of judgment, a vote in the negative. "Skepticism . . . is not avoidance of option; it is option of a certain particular kind of risk. *Better risk loss of truth than chance of error,*—that is your faith-vetoer's exact position." Put to the test, James pointed out, suspension of judgment, or doubt, was often indistinguishable from active negation. The man who doubted that the room was growing cold would refuse to light a fire just as if the room were still warm. The man who refused to bail out a boat because he doubted whether his efforts would be successful was in fact helping to sink her. The man who did not intervene in a murder because it might be justifiable homicide was virtually abetting the crime. In some cases, indeed, belief was a necessary element in bringing about some new truth that would never have come without it: "How many women's hearts are vanquished by the mere sanguine insistence of some man that they *must* love him! he will not consent to the hypothesis that they cannot." Thus, "faith in a fact can help create the fact," and the agnostic rule was condemned as itself irrational.[50]

James saw his pragmatic method as mediating between the brute scientific empiricism of the English tradition and the rationalistic monism of the German tradition. He wished to salvage the factualism of the one and the idealism of the other and to blend them into a new philosophy that could "remain religious like the rationalisms, but at the same time, like the empiricisms, . . . preserve the richest intimacy with facts." Faithfulness to facts raised to the level of a world view eventually pointed James in the direction of "radical empiricism" and a pluralistic universe. By pluralism he meant a sense of the world as "strung-along" and "unfinished" rather than unified. Pluralism put its money on the empirical givenness of the world, which certainly appeared to be partly good and partly evil, partly pleasant and partly brutish, rather than wholly one or the other. Radical empiricism, James's mature metaphysics, looked to reality as a field of experience. James proposed, against idealists and abstract metaphysicians of all sorts, that philosophers restrict their discourse to things drawn from experience. But he also proposed, against skeptical empiricists of the Humean stripe, that experience be taken to include relations between things as well as the things themselves. That, surely, was the way a person experienced the world—in its couplings and uncouplings as well as in the isolated parts that went to make it up. Radical empiricism thus called on the data of psychology to help construct a true picture of things as they actually are, a "world of pure experience."

Freedom and Spontaneity in a Darwinian Universe

It was important to James intellectually to escape the "narrow, close, sick-room air" of monism. It was even more important morally. He simply could not live in a world where human freedom, if it existed at all, was nothing more than a momentary illusion. Determinism nullified morality. So ran his argument in "The Dilemma of Determinism," still a powerful piece of writing and one of James's most impressive expressions of the entire problem of determinism and chance.

In a letter to his friend and fellow philosopher, the Englishman Shadworth Hodgson, James put the matter succinctly: "I care absolutely nothing whether there be 'agents' [i.e., free actors] or no agents, or whether man's actions be really 'his' or not. What I care for is that my moral reactions should find a real outward application." If the world conformed totally to a system of "uniform law," as Hodgson urged, only two alternative and equally repugnant judgments on it could be made: "Either close your eyes and adopt an optimism or a pessimism equally daft; or exclude moral categories altogether from a place in the world's definition, which leaves the world *unheimlich*, reptilian, and foreign to man . . . ." For what, after all, did determinism claim? Simply "that those parts of the universe already laid down absolutely appoint and decree what the other parts shall be. The future has no ambiguous possibilities hidden in its womb; the part we call the present is compatible with only one totality. Any other future complement than the one fixed from eternity is impossible."

In such a world, a "daft" pessimism or optimism, at one extreme, or subjectivism, at the other, would be the only intellectually satisfying postures; for the evil that people experience would be a necessary part of the structure of things, and regret an exercise in futility. James posed the "dilemma of determinism": either admit that the universe suffers from "an incurable taint," or dismiss the idea that things are good or bad in themselves and judge them only in relation to their effects upon our own sensibilities. A few years earlier, James had written in similar vein to the French philosopher Charles Renouvier, "I believe more and more that free will, if accepted at all, must be accepted as a postulate in justification of our moral judgment that certain things already done might have been better done."[51]

The "dilemma of determinism" was an intensely personal dilemma for James. Highly sensitive, prone to nervous ailments that periodically disrupted his health, James was also immensely concerned about the place of moral views in a Darwinian universe. Both his spiritual and his physical well-being depended on the assurance that morality was a real component of the universe, and that man was free to act responsibly. That assurance was shaken when, as a young man, James studied physiology and medicine abroad. The late Victorian period was a time when the mechanistic approach in biology and medicine reached its zenith. For a time, James became nearly blind, and he underwent a spiritual crisis so severe as to occasion thoughts of suicide. His recovery dated from the day he read Renouvier's formulation of free will. As James recorded the event in his diary, the reading was a true conversion experience: "I think that yesterday was a crisis in my life. I finished the first part of Renouvier's second *Essais* and see no reason why his definition of free-will—'the sustaining of a thought *because I choose to* when I might have other thoughts'—need be the definition of an illusion. At any rate, I will assume for the present—until next year—that it is no illusion. My first act of free will shall be to believe in free will."[52] From this experience, James retained a special sympathy for the problems of "sick souls" whose mental health was in less than perfect equilibrium.

True free will, James believed, could exist only in a pluralistic universe, because it depended on the presence of real novelty in the world. Pragmatically, the concept of free will meant simply "the right to expect that in its deepest elements as well as in its surface phenomena, the future may not identically repeat and imitate the past." Thus "possibility" could become a basic category of human thought, and it could be affirmed that some decisions at least had not been determined from all eternity but were to be made in the here and now. According to James, monism denied possibility: "For monism, whatever is is necessary, and aught else is impossible, if the world be such a unit of fact as monists pretend."[53]

James hoped to reestablish the legitimacy of the notion of chance, for it was the presence or absence of chance, as he saw it, that was the crux of the whole problem of determinism. Others had tried to show that freedom was compatible with determinism, that free will could exist in a world in which the causal principle was absolute. James considered all such attempts so much sophistry. The issue was chance—you were either for it or against it; you were accordingly, either an indeterminist or a determinist, a freewiller or a necessitarian. The issue could not be straddled. He admitted that the reign of chance was a difficult pill for many of his friends to swallow. "What is it, they ask, but barefaced crazy unreason, the negation of intelligibility and law? And if the slightest particle of it exist anywhere, what is to prevent the whole fabric from falling together, the stars from going out, and chaos from recommencing her topsy-turvy reign?"[54]

To allay this kind of fear, James insisted that freedom was not license. A chance event, though not foreordained by its predecessors, did after all grow out of the soil of the past; chance was no bolt from the blue. To put it another way, a world of chance would not be distinguishable from the actual world of daily decision making that all men acknowledge. "In every outwardly verifiable and practical respect, a world in which the alternatives that now actually distract *your* choice were decided by pure chance would be by *me* absolutely undistinguished from the world in which I now live. . . . To *yourselves,* it is true, those very acts of choice, which to me are so blind, opaque, and external, are the opposites of this, for you are within them and effect them." But, urged James, if there is no way for me to distinguish your decisions from the operations of chance, should I not be permitted to call this world of your choices a world of chance for *me*? Loosen up the frame of the universe, he concluded, admit chance into the interstices of life. Reality will lose none of its meaning, and morality has everything to gain.[55] (Elsewhere in this same article James seems to have acknowledged the suspect nature of this argument by admitting that the determinist could with equal justice plead much the same case. A world of determinism would also be "absolutely undistinguished from the world in which I now live." But the moral argument remained, and it was the moral argument alone that James truly cared for.)

Where others had seen in Darwin a confirmation of determinism, James found support for his belief in the reality of human initiative. He seized on Darwin's theory of random variations, both as scientific confirmation of indeterminacy in the universe, and as fuel against the Spencerian view that organic changes arose passively in response to changes in the environment. A thorough Darwinian in his analysis of the human mind and emotions, James nevertheless preferred to stress the element of chance variation over that of natural selection when he used Darwin as a guide to social and moral theories. He pointed to the survival of certain precious human traits that could not be shown to have immediate survival value. These attested to the spontaneity and power of the active individual.

In an essay entitled "Great Men and Their Environment," directed against Spencer, James argued that the appearance of geniuses was an ultimate datum, a given, wholly analogous to the spontaneous variations with which Darwin worked. Environment alone could never sufficiently explain great men, as Spencer and his disciples (John Fiske among them) claimed. The most that it could do was to act upon the great man once he had come, and in so doing the environment became as much the modified as the modifier. Environment, in other words, exercised a selective function, not a causative one. It was wrong to speak of the "laws of history" as in any sense referring to events inevitable. Not that historical indeterminism was absolute: "Not every man fits every 'hour.' Some incompatibilities there are. A given genius may come either too early or too late. Peter the Hermit would now be sent to a lunatic asylum. John Mill in the tenth century would have lived and died unknown. Cromwell and Napoleon need their revolutions, Grant his civil war. An Ajax gets no fame in the day of telescopic-sighted rifles. . . . " Historical reality took shape rather at the intersection of two factors—the gifted individual, "bearing all the power of initiative and origination in his hands," and the social milieu, "with its power of adopting or rejecting both him and his gifts." Darwin's random variations, which Darwin believed to be in conformity to a strictly mechanical law beyond our ken, were thus converted by James into the foundation for a universe of moral freedom and individualistic initiative that Darwin might well have found difficult to recognize.[56]

Both James and Peirce, then, made use of Darwin to uncover spontaneity in nature. It was characteristic of James to concern himself above all with the moral and psychological dimensions of freedom, with *human* creativity and free will, just as it was in character for Peirce to devote himself to the logical and metaphysical implications. The difference was basic, and sprang in great part from the temperamental antithesis between the two men. They did, nevertheless, manage to agree on the fatal flaws of a mechanistic philosophy at a time when the influence of mechanism was at its zenith.

It would be idle to suppose that Americans as a whole ever subscribed to the notion of determinism—but then it would be idle to suppose that the average man of any time articulates a formal philosophy. For most people, there would have been a powerful dissuading force in the teaching of the churches. Unreconstructed Calvinism, it is true, continued to preach a form of predestination that was by definition deterministic. The American Calvinist divine who saw Darwin's theory as an analogue in the natural world of the divine drama of the chosen and the damned in the supernatural made a sound point. But by the last quarter of the nineteenth century his was distinctly a minority view. The evangelical impulse had won over the main body of American Protestantism to a belief in human free will. In any case, and apart from religion, the historian Henry Steele Commager believes that Americans "could not consistently accept determinism," because it belied their experience as a nation.

Having said this, it remains true that the specter of a law-bound universe, immense, impersonal, impervious alike to human striving and human desire, haunted the minds of a good many thoughtful Americans in the decades after 1865. A host of names comes to mind: Henry Adams and his brother Brooks, Lester Frank Ward and, at the other end of the political spectrum, William Graham Sumner, Jacques Loeb, Thorstein Veblen, and the novelists Jack London, Frank Norris, Stephen Crane, and Theodore Dreiser.

The science that underlay this determinism was post-Darwinian but preatomic. Scientists had not yet begun to grapple with the complexities of quantum physics. When they did, the certainties of Victorian determinism would dissolve into scientific and philosophic ambiguity. But in the meantime the weight of scientific evidence unmistakably favored the deterministic hypothesis. Only those few versed in the arcane language of statistical mechanics—a Peirce, a Boltzmann, a Gibbs—suspected that fissures might exist in the solid edifice of mechanism. But if Peirce was prophetic, no less so was William James, who insisted that the problem of freedom escaped the limits of scientific evidence altogether, and demanded of ideas that they satisfy man's moral, as well as his intellectual, nature.

Looking back some years later, John Dewey, the third member of the pragmatic triumvirate, confirmed James's conviction that scientific, like philosophical, principles are "altars to unknown gods." For, said Dewey, modern men believe that they have replaced superstition with sophistication in their dealings with the universe, but their sophistication can be fully as irrational as the credulity it replaces. "Our magical safeguard against the uncertain character of the world is to deny the existence of chance, to mumble universal and necessary law, the ubiquity of cause and effect, the uniformity of nature . . . . But when all is said and done, the fundamentally hazardous character of the world is not seriously modified, much less eliminated . . . ."[57] That nature is fundamentally hazardous was a heretical idea in the post-Darwinian intellectual climate. Men were still too new to science to abandon lightly the postulate of ultimate order. By the time the mainstream of intellectual life caught up with the prophets of chance, America would be well into the twentieth century.

NOTES

1. Milton Berman, *John Fiske: The Evolution of a Popularizer* (Cambridge, Mass.: Harvard University Press, 1961).
2. John Spencer Clark, *The Life and Letters of John Fiske*, 2 vols. (Boston and New York: Houghton, Mifflin Co., 1917), 1: 139.
3. Ibid., 1: 479.
4. John Fiske, *Outlines of Cosmic Philosophy, Based on the Doctrine of Evolution*, 2 vols. (Boston, 1874), 2: 416.
5. Ibid., 375, 378.
6. Ibid., 411, 415.
7. Ibid., 421, 422.
8. John Fiske, *The Unseen World, and Other Essays* (Boston, 1876), p. 56.
9. John Fiske, *Darwinism and Other Essays* (London and New York, 1879), p. 76.
10. John Fiske, *The Idea of God as Affected by Modern Knowledge* (Boston, 1885), p. xx; John Fiske, *The Destiny of Man Viewed in the Light of His Origin* (Boston, 1884), p. 116.
11. John Fiske, *Life Everlasting* (Boston and New York, 1901), pp. 86–87.
12. John Fiske, *Through Nature to God* (Boston, 1899), p. 191.
13. Review of W. E. H. Lecky, quoted in H. Burnell Pannill, *The Religious Faith of John Fiske* (Durham, N.C.: Duke University Press, 1957), p. 77.
14. Letter to E. L. Youmans, quoted in Fiske, *Edward Livingston Youmans*, pp. 201–202.
15. Fiske, *Destiny of Man*, p. 118.
16. Quoted in Philip P. Wiener, *Evolution and the Founders of Pragmatism* (New York: Harper & Row, 1965), p. 19. Wright's contribution to American philosophy is assessed in Edward H. Madden, *Chauncey Wright and the Foundations of Pragmatism* (Seattle: University of Washington Press, 1963).
17. James Bradley Thayer, ed., *Letters of Chauncey Wright, with Some Account of His Life* (Cambridge, Mass., 1878), p. 368.
18. Wright's article, "The Evolution of Self-Consciousness," appeared in the *North American Review* in April, 1873, and was reprinted in *Philosophical Discussions by Chauncey Wright with a Biographical Sketch of the Author*, Charles Eliot Norton, ed. (New York, 1877), pp. 199–266. Darwin's letter soliciting this essay is in *Life and Letters*, Francis Darwin, ed., 2: 343.
19. Fiske, "Chauncey Wright" in *Darwinism*, p. 108.
20. James, "Chauncey Wright," *Nation*, 21 (September 23, 1875): 194.
21. Letter of July 29, 1874 to Grace Norton, in Thayer, *Letters*, p. 274.
22. Letter of August 13, 1867 to F. E. Abbot in Thayer, *Letters*, p. 113.

23. Wright, *Philosophical Discussions,* p. 7.
24. Thayer, *Letters*, p. 381.
25. Letters of October 28, 1867 and July 29, 1874 in Thayer, *Letters*, pp. 133, 274.
26. Thayer, *Letters*, p. 103; Wright, *Philosophical Discussions*, pp. 40–41.
27. Letters of October 28, 1867 and February 10, 1869 in Thayer, *Letters*, pp. 135, 141.
28. Conversation of January, 1875 in Thayer, *Letters*, p. 328.
29. Ralph Barton Perry, *The Thought and Character of William James*, 2 vols. (Boston: Little, Brown & Co., 1935), 1: 420.
30. Josiah Royce in the *Journal of Philosophy, Psychology and Scientific Method,* 13 (1916), quoted in T. A. Goudge, *The Thought of C. S. Peirce* (Toronto: University of Toronto Press, 1950), p. 2.
31. Letter of July 23, 1905 in Perry, *William James*, 2: 433.
32. Charles Hartshorne and Paul Weiss, eds., *Collected Papers of Charles Sanders Peirce*, 6 vols. (Cambridge, Mass.: Harvard University Press, 1931–1935), 5: 364. (The accepted convention in references to these volumes is to cite the volume and paragraph number as just given.)
33. Ibid.
34. Wiener, *Evolution and the Founders of Pragmatism*, p. 77; Hartshorne and Weiss, *Collected Papers*, 6: 297.
35. Hartshorne and Weiss, *Collected Papers*, 6: 293. Philip Wiener makes the point about Peirce's ambivalence toward Darwinism in his *Evolution and the Founders of Pragmatism*, pp. 77–88.
36. Hartshorne and Weiss, *Collected Papers*, 5: 403.
37. Ibid., 1: 653; 6: 292.
38. Ibid., 6: 13; 6: 63, 6: 33.
39. Ibid., 6: 58; 6: 59, 6: 60.
40. Ibid., 6: 554.
41. Ibid., 6: 37.
42. Ibid., 6: 613.
43. Perry, *William James*, 2: 438.
44. Hartshorne and Weiss, *Collected Papers*, 6: 184.
45. William James, *Pragmatism* (New York: Longmans, Green & Co., 1907), p. 45.
46. Hartshorne and Weiss, *Collected Papers*, 5: 407; 5: 414.
47. William James, *The Will to Believe and Other Essays in Popular Philosophy* (New York: Longmans, Green & Co., 1911), p. x.
48. Ibid., pp. 21, 147.
49. Ibid., p. 11.
50. Ibid., pp. 8, 26, 54–55, 109.
51. Perry, *William James*, 1: 638; James, *Will to Believe*, pp. 150, 162ff.; Perry, *William James*, 1: 682.
52. Ibid., 323.
53. William James, *Some Problems of Philosophy* (New York: Longmans, Green & Co., 1911), p. 139.

54. James, *Will to Believe*, p. 153.
55. Ibid., p. 158.
56. "Great Men and Their Environment" in *Will to Believe*, pp. 225–227, 229–230, 232.
57. Quoted in Herbert Schneider, *A History of American Philosophy* (New York: Columbia University Press, 1946), pp. 554–555.

A New York street scene, from *Harper's Weekly,* 18 February 1860. (Courtesy of the San Francisco Public Library.)

FOUR

TAMING THE TIGER: DARWINISM IN SOCIETY AND SOCIAL THOUGHT

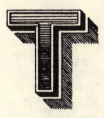

HROUGHOUT THE EARLY nineteenth century, America had been an intensely individualistic society. The old established institutions of church and bar and propertied aristocracy were losing their force. They did not disappear, though in some cases their vigor took new forms (as with the church, whose waning impact in the Congregationalist Northeast was offset by the tremendous energies of revivalism in the Midwest.) But they no longer exerted the coercive moral force that had made them the nuclei of communal authority in an earlier period. "In the America of the 1830s and 1840s," writes the historian Stanley Elkins, "there was no other symbol of vitality to be found than the individual, and it was to the individual, with all his promise, that the thinker, like everyone else, would inexorably orient himself." So it was that Ralph Waldo Emerson, greatest prophet of the nineteenth-century moral sensibility, exalted the virtue of self-reliance, the superiority of the individual to his society, and the supreme sufficiency of self. "In all my lectures," Emerson reflected, "I have taught one doctrine, namely the infinitude of the private man."[1]

In American society at large, the Emersonian exaltation of the individual struck a congenial chord. The self-conscious democracy

Ralph Waldo Emerson,
1803–1882. (Courtesy of
Culver Pictures, Inc.)

of the Jacksonian era was resolutely hostile to aristocracies and
establishments of all kinds, whether of wealth, of breeding, or,
indeed, of talent. Americans of the Jacksonian era congratulated
themselves upon their freedom from Old World bonds of caste and
privilege. They believed intensely in the natural right of the individual to make his way untrammeled by societal restrictions. When
Alexis de Tocqueville tried to describe the social philosophy
of the Americans in his *Democracy in America*, he used the term
"individualisme," a term adopted by his English translator with the
explanation that "however strange it may sound to the English ear"
there seemed to be "no English word exactly equivalent to the
expression." But if the word was unfamiliar, the attitude was not.
Democratic Americans, as Tocqueville depicted them,

> owe nothing to any man, they expect nothing from any man; they
> acquire the habit of always considering themselves as standing
> alone, and they are apt to imagine that their whole destiny is in
> their own hands.
>
> Thus not only does democracy make every man forget his ances-
> tors, but it hides his descendants and separates his contemporaries
> from him; it throws him back forever upon himself alone and
> threatens in the end to confine him entirely within the solitude of
> his own heart.[2]

Such emphatic individualism was not conducive to speculations about the social community. To the transcendentalists, intellectual custodians of their generation, society appeared to be an unusable abstraction, when it was not an actual obstruction to the pursuit of moral goodness. Emerson calling on man to retire from society in order to merge himself with nature, Thoreau complaining that "I was never molested by any person but those who represented the State," dramatize the uneasiness with which transcendentalists surveyed the institutions of their society. Their reservations were widely shared by Americans accustomed to look upon society as no more than a backdrop to individual exploit, and government as most successful when least obtrusive.

By a remarkable congruence, all the major streams of intellectual life seemed to flow in the same direction. Nineteenth-century religion, aflame with revivalism, preached the ability of the individual to save himself through conversion if only he would. The salvation of society lay in the cumulative effect of countless individual decisions for Christ. Nineteenth-century economic theory embodied the laissez-faire doctrines of the English classical economists Smith, Malthus, and Ricardo. Reacting against the heavy hand of state mercantilism, Smith and his successors urged exemption from restrictive governmental regulation for the rising class of industrial entrepreneurs. Classical economics assumed the existence of a natural economic order which flourished best when least disturbed, since the pursuit of gain by each individual inevitably furthered the greatest good of society. Though the individual "intends only his own gain," yet, wrote Smith, he is "led by an invisible hand to promote an end which was no part of his intention." In America, after about the mid-1830s, the doctrines of the British classical school were widely disseminated through influential college textbooks like Francis Wayland's *Elements of Political Economy*.

Nineteenth-century political theory, apart from the scattered utterances of communitarian theorists like Henry James, Sr., and the Fourierites, still took its tone from the writings of the Founding Fathers and above all from the Declaration of Independence, with its stress on the checks and balances whereby individuals could be safeguarded from governmental interference. The Lockean concept of society as a compact among free individuals living in a state of nature continued to rule the American mind. The election of Jackson in 1828 marked the victory of the Jeffersonian tradition of the negative state over the minority Federalist-Whig conception of the state as active promoter of the interests of the business community. Political theory henceforth until the Civil War would continue to extol the untrammeled individual and the minimal state. Indeed, Tocqueville argued that democracies by their very nature were hostile to a social ethic of commonality. For when relative equality of condition among men prevailed, the bonds that linked them together in mutual need dissolved. Democracy engendered individualism, "which disposes each member of the community to sever himself from the mass of his fellows and to draw apart with his family and his friends, so that after he has thus formed a little circle of his own, he willingly leaves society at large to itself." Democratic in origin, individualism was insidious in effect: "at first, [it] only saps the virtues of public life; but in the long run it attacks and destroys all others and is at length absorbed in downright selfishness."[3]

It is arguable that an intensely individualistic social philosophy was adequate to the needs of American life in the first half of the nineteenth century. America was a wide-open society of boundless opportunities and limitless growth. Its infant economy needed the spur of unfettered entrepreneurship. Its nascent cities had not grown large enough and noisome enough to disturb the national peace of mind. Its broad social accomplishments—temperance, women's rights, prison reform, improvement of the public schools—pointed to the effectiveness of private associations in improving society.

Social Growth:
The Erosion of Individualism

But in the years after Appomatox, society changed, and the old democratic individualism increasingly came to appear inadequate to the new conditions and the new ideas of the post-Civil War period. There was, in the first place, the troubling but manifestly central fact of the Civil War itself. If war were the ultimate outcome of the great American experiment in Lockean individualism, might that fact not betray a fatal flaw in the political premises of the Founding Fathers? American intellectuals began to cast around for usable materials to shape a new philosophy exalting the state rather than the individual. The war might after all be salutary, believed the militant Congregational theologian, Horace Bushnell, if it had the effect of curbing the dangerous American love of freedom and undermining the notion of government by consent. All governments were legitimate, Bushnell reasoned, so long as they earned the sanction of history: "It will almost always be felt that the government in power is in a sense historic, that it could not well be different from what it is. In that view, it will be accepted as a kind of Providential creation."[4] Bushnell's unhappiness with the philosophy of the Founders, his dissent from individualism, was echoed by other political theorists, men like Orestes Brownson, Francis Lieber, and Theodore Dwight Woolsey, who hammered home the dangers of Lockean contract theory and confirmed the need to develop a more solid foundation for the state.

But if the Civil War contributed to a developing sense of the bankruptcy of individualism, even more influential were the twin processes of industrialization and urbanization that were transforming the face of the nation. As the corporation became the trust, converting the economy into a marketplace of giants, impersonal, uncontrollable, so the great city replaced the small town as home for increasing numbers of Americans. And with the rise of the urban complex the nation faced a host of problems, not always entirely new, for cities had existed in the American landscape since colonial times, but of a scope and complexity altogether unprecedented. Society was becoming increasingly interdependent. Large-scale industrialization, together with the growth of new communication and transportation networks, meant that the old economic system of decentralization and relative autonomy for small-town producers was giving way to a tightly controlled system of large organizations with national markets. "The railroad, rural free delivery, the mail-order house, and after 1900, the interurban trolley and the automobile meant the decline of local independence." But the cities were in no condition to supply that larger sense of community which might have compensated the small towns for their forfeited independence. Unequal to the task of providing even essential social services for the increasing numbers attracted by their industrial opportunities, the cities could offer no solutions to the problem of community. They were, indeed, themselves the crux of the problem. Cities were drawing more and more people together into physical proximity, but by the 1880s and

1890s communal disintegration threatened. "The social organism has broken down in large districts of our great cities," wrote Jane Addams, a close observer of the Chicago scene. Technology had created interdependence; it had failed utterly to create community. "The Great Society created by steam and electricity may be a society," John Dewey observed, "but it is no community."[5]

Into the midst of this difficult transition from small-town to urban civilization dropped the message of Darwin and Spencer and their host of interpreters. To reflective Americans, it was readily apparent that the concepts of Darwin might lend themselves to social as well as biological speculation. As early as 1861, Charles Eliot Norton, the Brahmin conservative, had been moved to reflect on the likenesses between the Civil War and the war of nature, both painful, both costly in untimely death and untoward suffering, yet both essential to true progress. Taken simply at face value, Norton mused, Darwinian ideas tended to promote a harsh view of life: "Nature is careless of the single life. Her processes seem wasteful, but out of seeming waste, she produces her great and durable results. Everywhere in her works are the signs of life cut short for the sake of some effect more permanent . . . ."[6] Wastefulness, strife, warfare, suffering, death—these were, so Darwin himself had concluded, essential elements in the progress of organic life as a whole.

The conclusion was unsettling—not least to Darwin himself. In the *Origin*, Darwin contented himself with a large optimism which, ironically, echoed Paley. ("It is a happy world after all," Paley had exulted. "The air, the earth, the water teem with delighted existence.") "When we reflect on this struggle," Darwin reasoned, "we may console ourselves with the full belief, that the war of nature is not incessant, that no fear is felt, that death is generally prompt, and that the vigorous, the healthy, and the happy survive and multiply." And he concluded:

> from the war of nature, from famine and death, the most exalted object which we are capable of conceiving, namely the production of the higher animals, directly follows. There is grandeur in this view of life, with its several powers, having been originally breathed by the Creator into a few forms or into one; and that, whilst this planet has gone cycling on according to the fixed laws of gravity, from so simple a beginning endless forms, most beautiful and most wonderful have been, and are being, evolved.

Cosmic optimism, however, could not entirely dispel niggling doubts. In private, Darwin gave expression to bleaker views: "What a book a devil's chaplain might write," he exploded to Hooker, "on the clumsy, wasteful, blundering, low and horribly cruel works of nature!"[7]

So also Norton, who publicly maintained a posture of tough-minded acceptance of war and suffering, privately echoed Darwin's dismay: "In a large sense," he lamented, "the moral law prevails in the long run, and man, perhaps, slowly improves, but 'how blundering, wasteful and horribly cruel' seems the process!"[8]

Social Darwinism: Weeding Out the Weak

At the same time, some hardier souls were quite prepared to accept Darwin's account of nature at face value and apply it to human affairs. These hardy ones, the Social Darwinists, drew on Darwin and even more on Spencer to adapt the struggle for existence and survival of the fittest into a paradigm for the behavior of men and nations. In certain moods Darwin could himself give voice to some characteristic Social Darwinian anxieties. "We civilized men," he noted, "do our utmost to check the process of elimination; we build asylums for the imbecile, the maimed, and the sick; we institute poor-laws. . . . Thus the weak members of civilized society propagate their kind. No one who has attended to the breeding of domestic animals will doubt that this must be highly injurious to the race of man." But Darwin did not therefore give eugenic human breeding first place in his catalogue of values as some of his contemporaries did. He was too tenderhearted for that.[9]

Less tenderhearted was Herbert Spencer, who sternly adjudged that "fostering the good-for-nothing at the expense of the good, is an extreme cruelty," a "storing-up of miseries for future generations." Spencer was convinced that there was no surer path to ultimate woe than cosseting the unfortunate: "To aid the bad in multiplying, is, in effect, the same as maliciously providing for our descendants a multitude of enemies." Doubtless, individual altruism was all very well, but organized charity was intolerable: " . . . An unquestionable injury is done by agencies which undertake in a wholesale way to foster good-for-nothings; putting a stop to that natural process of elimination by which society continually

Baxter Street Court. Photograph by Jacob Riis, ca. 1890. (Courtesy of The Bettman Archive, Inc.)

purifies itself." Nor need one feel excessive pity for these under-privileged ones, the idlers, the imbeciles, the incompetent of every strain; for the most part, they brought their troubles on them-selves.[10] The same robust outlook on the international level pro-duced a school of theorists who justified war as the purifying agent among nations, a beneficial if rigorous tonic against the softening effects of effete civilization.

Social Darwinism spoke to the needs of several different groups in American society. Still, it may not have been quite so important an influence on the ethics of the Gilded Age as some historians have supposed. There can be no doubt, for example, that Social Darwinism in Europe often took the form of nationalism and militarism, but American society was only rarely congenial to its fiercer variants. Few, indeed, were the number of those in America willing to join the European voices raised in tribute to war, "not merely a necessary element in the life of nations but an indispensable factor of culture, in which a truly civilized nation finds the highest expression of strength and vitality."[11] Even among the few genuine militarists Darwinism tended not so much to initiate theory as to confirm ideas already established. In the words of Richard Hofstadter, "Neither the philosophy of force nor doctrines of *Machtpolitik* had to wait upon Darwin to make their appearance."[12]

Captain Alfred Thayer Mahan wrote his enormously influential *Influence of Sea Power Upon History* without benefit of Darwin. Mahan's arguments on behalf of a strong navy and a vigorous policy of expansion, cordially received by Theodore Roosevelt among others, rested on a close study of contemporary international relations and intimate familiarity with the great European military and naval theorists of the previous century. Reflection upon the lessons of history had led Mahan to a frank avowal of the supremacy of force in world affairs: "Force, the organized force of the community as the means of assuring its will, is and must remain the basis of social order so long as evil exists to be repressed." The use of force might at times appear coercive, Mahan conceded, but it was both natural and irresistible, and worked, in the main, for righteousness. "To such a view aggression, in its primary sense of onward movement, is inevitable. Those who will not move must be swept aside. They may be drawn into the movement by moral forces, as Japan has been; but if not, they must be brought despite themselves into external conditions favorable to their welfare and the general good, as has been done in India, in Egypt, and in the Philippines."[13] This virile imperialism, so apparently Darwinian in tone and temper, in reality owed nothing at all to the *Origin*.

So also with racism and the cult of the Anglo-Saxon that blossomed around the turn of the century. Darwinian concepts were brandished in support of ideas that had circulated long before 1859. In the United States popular racism dated back to the founding of the colonies and the introduction of black slaves. During the nineteenth century theories of racial determinism and white supremacy were given scientific foundation, so it was believed, by physiological studies differentiating the human species into groups on the basis of color, physique, or head shape. To this dubious anthropology Darwinism gave some support, emphasizing as it did the preservation of some species at the expense of others in the great struggle for life. It seemed plausible to view the Anglo-Saxon race as one of Darwin's fittest species, preeminently suited not only to survive but to furnish the main impetus to the progress of civilization.

At the same time Darwinism provided only ambiguous support for racist doctrine. For one thing, it discredited the notion of the separate and distinct origin of races, in favor of the evolution of races from a single source. This was discomfiting to racists, for, as Asa Gray noted, "the very first step backward [on the evolutionary scale] makes the Negro and the Hottentot our blood-relations."[14] For another thing, Darwinism did not answer the question of how traits were inherited (though Darwin did speculate, wrongly, as it turned out, about the mechanism of inheritance), and so could not establish the preponderance of heredity over environment, belief in which was crucial to racist ideology.[15] Indeed, many Darwinians, including Herbert Spencer, were also convinced Lamarckians, committed to the view that parents could transmit to their offspring traits acquired in their own lifetime. Such a view would be difficult to reconcile with the racist ideology of fixed and unchanging racial characteristics. Until Lamarckianism was scientifically disproven and an alternative theory of genetics supplied—developments which occurred well after 1900—Darwinism could only provide a set of rather vague though undeniably suggestive phrases and ideas to strengthen the ideology of race.[16]

Business Darwinism

The impact of Darwinism is often presumed to have been greatest on the business world. Richard Hofstadter's *Social Darwinism* disclosed to view the Darwinian social ethics of the Rockefellers, Hills, Carnegies, Vanderbilts, and Goulds, known collectively to history as the "robber barons." Along with the wit to capitalize on the unparalleled business opportunities of the Gilded Age, these men combined, so Hofstadter alleged, the ethics of the jungle. Of postbellum America Hofstadter wrote: "Its rapid expansion, its exploitative methods, its desperate competition, and its peremptory rejection of failure" made it "a vast human caricature of the Darwinian struggle for existence and survival of the fittest."[17]

There is some truth to this view, insofar as competition was intense, economic activity perilous, and the harshness of the industrial system unmitigated by any remedial public policy. But much the same thing could be said of early-industrial England in the first half of the nineteenth century. Some observers, indeed, have turned the tables on the chronology which gives Darwinism a causal role in the development of a predatory industrial ethic by speculating that the genesis of the *Origin* might be traced to Darwin's own knowledge of the rigors of British industrialism. Oswald Spengler, who described the *Origin* as "the application of economics to biology," remarked that it reeked of the atmosphere of the English factory. So also Nietzsche observed with distaste: "Over the whole of English Darwinism there hovers something of the suffocating air of over-crowded England, something of the odour of humble people in need and in straits."[18] These comments, though extreme, gain a certain plausibility when it is recalled that Darwin found the clue to the operation of natural selection in Malthus's essay on population. If it is true that Darwin generalized the insights of Malthus to include animals as well as human beings, then descriptions of the business world as a caricature of the Darwinian universe obviously invert the chronological sequence, even as the evils of unregulated industrialism predate the *Origin*.

Subsequent scholarship has cast doubt, in any case, on the picture of American businessmen as Social Darwinists who seized on the theories of Darwin and Spencer to cloak their rapacity. Evidence for that conclusion turns out to be remarkably scanty. There were, to be sure, a few businessmen who referred to their work in Darwinian terms, or who were familiar with Spencer's evolutionary philosophy, men like the publisher Richard R. Bowker, the textile manufacturer Daniel A. Tompkins, the sugar magnate Henry O. Havemeyer. The outstanding example is Andrew Carnegie, the steelmaster, a devoted disciple of Spencer. "Man was not created with an instinct for his own degradation," Carnegie learned from Darwin and Spencer. "From the lower he has risen to the higher forms, and there is no conceivable end to his march to perfection. His face is turned to the light; he stands in the sun and looks upward."[19]

But such men were few in number. A good bit of the material adduced as evidence for the Social Darwinian cast of American businessmen was in fact produced by intellectuals, social theorists, or publicists rather than by businessmen themselves. Such is the case with the well-known work of James H. Bridge, literary assistant successively to Herbert Spencer and Andrew Carnegie, who preached the benevolence of trusts as the industrial stage in which cooperation replaced competition. Bridge looked forward to a "rational industrialism," prefigured by the trusts, in which "we are to pass from the cruel egoism of old systems to the kindly altruism of the new."[20]

A careful search by Irvin G. Wyllie some years ago turned up remarkably little evidence of Social Darwinism among American entrepreneurs. It is hard to see how the case could be otherwise. A consciously Darwinian social philosophy would have required the kind of education few businessmen received in the late nineteenth century. Wyllie found that as recently as 1900, 84 percent of the businessmen included in *Who's Who in America* had received no education beyond high school. These men guided their businesses by a mixture of experience, observation, and native shrewdness; fretted at uncertainties, worried about slumps; and in general gave no evidence that they considered themselves the fittest to survive. They had, moreover, a rather well-developed social philosophy that did not coexist easily with Social Darwinism. Most businessmen believed that success came to those who mastered themselves, who triumphed over self-indulgence, sloth, intemperance, extravagance, and greed within their own bodies, rather than trampling over the bodies of their competitors. They might think of themselves as gifted or fortunate, but they were unwilling to view their success as purchased by the ruin of their fellow businessmen. Typically, businessmen did not view the world as a balancing scales whereon the rise of one signified the fall of others. To the contrary, successful men enhanced the opportunities for all. "Money getters," according to P.T. Barnum, "are the benefactors of our race." There were opportunities enough and to spare for the enterprising; Americans had no need to confront each other in a struggle for existence. To say all this is not, of course, to imply that all businessmen lived by a benign code of mutual goodfellowship, but simply to suggest that, whatever their practices, the theories of Social Darwinism had scant appeal for most of them.

Perhaps the strongest reason for the indifference of businessmen to Social Darwinism was the fact that they thought of themselves as Christians, in duty bound to observe the Golden Rule. Indeed, many middle-class citizens found Spencer initially repugnant because of the threat his philosophy posed to orthodox religion. Jack London, in his fictional guise as Martin Eden, hears Spencer derogated by his respectable host Judge Blount, and Blount's friend, Mr. Butler; as an ardent Spencerian, Eden is affronted: "To hear that great and noble man's name upon your lips is like finding a dewdrop in a cesspool."[21] Squaring Christianity with Darwinism was an enterprise that engaged some of the best and subtlest minds of the period, but certainly, on the face of it, the two systems appeared to conflict. Businessmen, as professing Christians, were unable to accept the harsh egotism of the Darwinian universe. That their conduct was, in fact, often less than Christian is self-evident; that it was consciously Darwinian is much less clear.[22]

One of the most sensible responses to the challenge of Darwinism to ethics came from Theodore Roosevelt. No softhearted philanthropist, Roosevelt did not shrink from competition and violence; but he protested vigorously the view that social progress was greatest where rivalry was keenest, that intense competition improved the species. If it were true that progress coincided with high birth and death rates—the best measures of the struggle for survival—then the greatest European races would be "the South Italians, the Polish Jews, and the people who live in the congested districts of Ireland." This sentence presumably spoke for itself, but Roosevelt spelled out the implications: "It is plain that the societies and sections of societies where the individual's happiness is on the whole highest, and where progress is most real and valuable, are precisely those where the grinding competition and the struggle for mere existence is least severe." Darwinism did not sanctify selfishness. "Undoubtedly, in the race for life, that group of beings will tend ultimately to survive in which the general feeling of the members, whether due to humanitarianism, to altruism, or to some form of religious belief proper, is such that the average individual has an unselfish . . . tendency to work for the ultimate benefit of the community as a whole."[23]

Turning to the business world, Roosevelt spoke for many businessmen when he ascribed success in business not to natural laws, or personal ruthlessness, or survival in the great race to get ahead, but to character. "No brilliancy of intellect," Roosevelt intoned, "no perfection of bodily development will count when weighed in the balance against that assemblage of virtues . . . which we group together under the name of character."[24] With this conclusion, evidence suggests, the majority of business men concurred.

Social Theory:
The Case Against Individualism

Americans of a more intellectual and articulate bent were not prepared to let the matter rest with a simple rejection of Social Darwinism. They could not afford to do so, since many of them were early and convinced adherents to the theories of Darwin, and some to those of Spencer as well. Men like John Dewey, the social psychologist James Mark Baldwin, the philosopher Josiah Royce, the sociologists Albion Small and Charles Horton Cooley, had to believe that it was possible to shape these theories to the needs of American social thought. To all these men it had become apparent that the old nineteenth-century individualism was no longer a viable intellectual tradition. Individualism had failed to meet the challenge of the cities. It seemed increasingly ill-suited to the facts of an industrial civilization. Complexity begot organization—the trust, the labor union—but society continued to limp along by the old rules of laissez-faire and every man for himself. "Our world, operated by individual motive," charged the anti-monopolist reformer Henry Demarest Lloyd, "is the country of the Chinese fable, in which the inhabitants went on one leg . . . . As gods we are but half-grown. For a hundred years or so our economic theory has been one of industrial government by the self-interest of the individual. Political government by the self-interest of the individual we call anarchy. It is one of the paradoxes of public opinion that the people of America, least tolerant of this theory of anarchy in political government, lead in practising it in industry. Politically we are civilized; industrially, not yet."[25]

The received wisdom of a simpler age could not stretch to fit the needs of the new situation, and it lent itself all too readily to the worst excesses of Spencerian Social Darwinism. "The man who should apply in his family or his citizenship this 'survival of the fittest' theory as it is practically professed and operated in business would be a monster, and would be speedily made extinct, as we do with monsters," asserted Lloyd. At its best, articulated by an Emerson or a Thoreau, individualism had spoken to noble instincts in the American soul. Emerson did not cease to touch the hearts of the new generation. William James fancied he saw a congruence between Emersonianism and Spencerian individualism that led him to hail Spencer's social theory as one that "breathes the purest English spirit of liberty, and his attacks on over-administration and criticisms on the inferiority of great centralized systems are worthy to be the textbooks of individualists the world over." James added, "I confess that it is with this part of his work, in spite of its hardness and inflexibility of tone, that I personally sympathize most."[26]

But James never fully grasped the magnitude of the need for a new social philosophy. Lloyd, who did, might be said to have spent a lifetime recasting Emerson into the new mold demanded by the times. Emerson remained for him a literary model and a moral sage, "the greatest of American minds and hearts." Lloyd would not sacrifice the individual, but "we can become individual only by submitting to be bound to others. We extend our freedom only by finding new laws to obey." The individual and society would forever be to some extent at odds. But the individual must no longer run amok; the balance must be redressed. "The happiness, self-interest, or individuality of the whole is not more sacred than that of each, but it is greater. They are equal in quality, but in quantity they are greater."[27] What was needed, then, was a theory of society and of the individual that would end the opposition between the two concepts, that would cease regarding one or the other of them as artificial, that would, in short, reintegrate man with his environment, using Darwinian concepts to refute the Social Darwinians.

"To tell us of the progressive sway of brotherhood in all human affairs is the sole message of history," exhorted Lloyd. The opposition case of tough-minded Spencerian individualism was being given its most cogent exposition, in the years of Lloyd's campaign against the trusts, from the Yale lectern of William Graham Sumner, first American sociologist and author of a deservedly classic little compendium of Social Darwinism, *What Social Classes Owe to Each Other*. Sumner taught that all mankind lived under the inexorable law of the struggle for existence. The struggle was two-fold: "first the struggle of individuals to win the means of subsistence from nature, and secondly . . . the competition of man with man in the effort to win a limited supply." This being so, men were not naturally brothers.

The Darwinian cosmos, Sumner insisted, had no room for sentimental notions about equality or natural rights. Men came into the world naked, powerless, with no claim whatever to the things of this world save that which they could make good by force. There was no such thing as a "natural right," and dogmas about the equal creation of men were nonsensical. Quite the contrary, all men were created unequal, for inequality was a law of nature. Man vied with man to win the rewards of nature, and victory went to the fit. Ever an ardent foe of socialism, Sumner stressed again and again the importance in a free society of making reward commensurate with effort. To this end governments were instituted, that a man might freely and exclusively dispose of what is his. The free man was responsible for his own and his family's welfare—and no one else's. Sumner warned that any attempt to tamper with nature's own system, to "take from the better and give to the worse," threatened social disaster: "Let it be understood that we cannot go outside of this alternative: liberty, inequality, survival of the fittest; not-liberty, equality, survival of the unfittest. The former carries society forward and favors all its best members; the latter carries society downwards and favors all its worst members."[28]

Sumner:
The Case for Individualism

The import of Sumner's social theory for government was a strict enjoinder to laissez-faire. In a passage redolent of Spencer, Sumner complained of the failure of the state, in its concern with "socialistic enterprise," to attend to its own proper business of maintaining peace and security. The modern world, according to Sumner, had passed out of a status society into a society of contract. "Contract, however, is rational—even rationalistic. It is also realistic, cold, and matter-of-fact. A contract relation is based on a sufficient reason, not on custom or prescription . . . . In a state based on contract sentiment is out of place in any public or common affairs." It followed, therefore, that the state should have nothing to do with humanitarian endeavors. Charity and philanthropy belonged to the private sector. "It is not at all the function of the state to make men happy." It *is* the function of the state to see that the conditions under which men as individuals pursue happiness are favorable. One could scarcely abbreviate Sumner's own summary of the functions of government. "At bottom," he wrote, "there are two chief things with which government has to deal. They are, the property of men and the honor of women. These it has to defend against crime." For the rest, the state ideally should embrace "a general and sweeping policy of non-interference." It is necessary to add, however, that Sumner drew back short of Spencer's inflexible hostility to the state—he favored public education and municipal sewage systems, and he even looked with apparent approval upon government regulation of life insurance. One must start with a presumption against government action—that was understood—but one must judge each case as a matter of expediency, not dogma.[29]

Like Herbert Spencer, Sumner deplored the well-meaning but ineffectual, and often downright harmful, efforts of do-gooders and "sentimentalists" to interfere in social problems. Such efforts could not succeed, for the ills of society were far too complex to succumb to easy solutions. "It would be hard," Sumner asserted, "to find a single instance of a direct assault by positive effort upon poverty, vice, and misery which has not either failed, or, if it has not failed directly and entirely, has not entailed other evils greater than the one which it removed."[30] The idea of an intricate net of social relations, each fiber linked in action and reaction with all the others into one sensitive whole, was a favorite notion of Spencerians. As a more complex vision of society than the mono-causationist theses of some nineteenth-century theorists like Henry George, it had much to recommend it, for it suggested that reality was rarely simple and that effects can not always be foreseen in their causes. Nor was it an easy position for reformers to refute, since it contained a good measure of truth. Sumner and Spencer were both convinced that acquiescence in the *status quo* was the true outcome of a sound sociology. Sociology offered an antidote to reform. Its function was not to plan utopias but rather "to enable us to make the best of our situation."

Another argument offered by Sumner against social action was that the recipients of it did not deserve help. The drunkard in the gutter belonged in the gutter. The pauper in the slum could "by moderate effort" leave it for an easier life in the country if he chose. Should we then shield the drunkard from nature's penalty for vice, or subsidize the stubborn refusal of the pauper to give up "the delights of the city"? In general, Sumner felt confident that misery and impoverishment flowed directly from vice. "Arbitrary interference and assistance" to relieve the unfortunate would only "offer premiums to folly and vice," thereby compounding the problem.[31]

The Forgotten Man

The sympathy Sumner refused to squander on the needy he bestowed instead on "the man who is never thought of," his famous "Forgotten Man." The forgotten man, neither plutocrat nor pauper, was a member of the great middle class, a laborer ready to do an honest day's work. He was "the clean, quiet, virtuous domestic citizen, who pays his debts and his taxes and is never heard of out of his little circle." It was the forgotten man who suffered from reform legislation, for it was he who lost out whenever a dollar of capital was diverted from the bank into charitable enterprise. Being quiet, industrious, and uncomplaining, the forgotten man remained invisible to us when in fact he was most worthy of our pity. "He works, he votes, generally he prays—but he always pays—yes, above all, he pays."[32]

The sole repository of hope for the future of America, according to Sumner, lay in the forgotten men of the land, each working at an honest trade, each frugally accumulating his little hoard of capital in the savings bank.

> The only two things which really tell on the welfare of man on earth are hard work and self-denial (in technical language, labor and capital), and these tell most when they are brought to bear directly upon the effort to earn an honest living, to accumulate capital, and to bring up a family of children to be industrious and self-denying in their turn.

The great fallacy of reformers was their conviction that by taking thought we can change the world. We cannot. The laws of nature are fixed. Great harm had been done in the past by the blundering of social thinkers. Indeed, "The greatest reform which could now be accomplished would consist in undoing the work of statesmen in the past . . . ." The world needed a science of society not as a spur to enterprise but as a spur to realism, a dispeller of illusions about what society ought to be, and a mirror of society as it really is.[33]

Sumner's skepticism of reform sprang from a thoroughgoing and wholly materialistic determinism. In a manner not unlike Thorstein Veblen's, he found the causes of social change in shifts in the environment and in the technological capacities of men. The things that would alter the human enterprise for better or for worse were "the great discoveries and inventions, the new reactions inside the social organism, and the changes in the earth itself on account of changes in the cosmical forces. These causes will make of it just what, in fidelity to them, it ought to be." There were laws of human as of physical nature, Sumner believed, and though we know very little of them yet, we cannot evade their operation. The "tide in the affairs of men" that Shakespeare described Sumner, too, perceived, but no man could ever take Sumner's tide at the flood; on the contrary, the tide took him:

> The great stream of time and earthly things will sweep on just the same in spite of us. It bears with it now all the errors and follies of the past, the wreckage of all the philosophies, the fragments of all the civilizations, the wisdom of all the abandoned ethical systems, the debris of all the institutions, and the penalties of all the mistakes. It is only in imagination that we stand by and look at and criticize it and plan to change it. Every one of us is a child of his age and cannot get out of it. He is in the stream and is swept along with it. All his sciences and philosophy come to him out of it. Therefore the tide will not be changed by us. It will swallow up both us and our experiments. It will absorb the efforts at change and take them into itself as new but trivial components, and the great movement of tradition and work will go on unchanged by our fads and schemes.[34]

Readers familiar with Spencer will find in Sumner many echoes of the master's voice. But Sumner did not parrot Spencer; he was always his own man. His indictment of state activity was somewhat more cautiously drawn than the Englishman's. He had no use whatever for the language of "natural rights" and for Spencerian metaphysics generally. But surely the most striking difference between the two is the temper they reveal—of optimism, on the part of Spencer, of pessimism only very slightly tinged with hope, on the part of Sumner. Though he later qualified his view somewhat, Spencer began his writing career as a believer in the eventual perfectibility of man and society. Professing that variety of evolutionism that saw history as a series of cumulative triumphs for the fit, he was committed to faith in human progress. Sumner was not so committed. Nature broods over Sumner's universe like a savage matriarch, bestowing boons and buffets with contemptuous indifference. She is a "hard mistress," an "opponent" against whom men strive for the means of subsistence. There are no gifts in this world; nothing is gotten without pain. Men "wrestle" with nature to "extort" from her what they need. Those who lack Sumner's own iron morality may feel that life in such an implacable environment can only be made tolerable by human solidarity and cooperation. Even Sumner weakened to the point of recommending "aid and sympathy, on account of the common participation in human frailty and folly." But let it be a private sympathy, and let it not take the form of charity. For the most part, each man must go it alone. In the bracing air of Sumner's individualism there is precious little place for fellowship. "He who would be well taken care of must take care of himself."[35]

Lester Frank Ward:
Anti-Sumner

Against the social philosophy of individual enterprise and governmental laissez-faire so crisply formulated by Sumner, the first major attack came from the sociologist Lester Frank Ward. Ward had arisen from the same stratum of society as Sumner—the poor but respectable working class. He was born in Illinois, the son of a mechanic and a clergyman's daughter. Poverty precluded much formal education, and his schooling was erratic. But despite the need to work from an early age, Ward would not be denied an education. He proceeded in his spare time to teach himself French, German, Latin, Greek, and the elements of physiology. After service in the Civil War, during which he was twice wounded, Ward entered government service as a clerk, meanwhile pursuing night courses at Columbian (now George Washington) University. He was graduated with a B.A. in 1869, then earned a law degree and finally an M.A. in 1872. Not content with even this clutch of degrees, Ward continued to study science, and especially botany, on his own until 1881, when he was made Assistant Geologist of the U.S. Geological Survey. Two years later he became Geologist, and in 1892, Paleontologist. By this time he had already published the two-volume *Dynamic Sociology*, the most important of his books and the basis for those that followed—*The Psychic Factors of Civilization* (1893), *Outlines of Sociology* (1898), *Pure Sociology* (1903), and *Applied Sociology* (1906). Not until 1906 did Ward have an academic post from which to disseminate his views; in that year he was called to occupy the chair of sociology at Brown University, a position he held until his death in 1913.

Biographical data are more than usually necessary to an understanding of Ward, for he lived his life over again in his work. In this respect he resembles Herbert Spencer more than William Graham Sumner. Childhood poverty left him with an enduring sympathy for the disadvantaged. He never forgot the "genuine satisfaction" with which he watched the poor boys in his classes " 'beat' the rich ones and 'go to the head.' "[36] It became an article of faith with him that nature had not apportioned intelligence according to social rank, and that Galton's studies of genius had grossly slighted "nurture" in favor of "nature." The self-acquired character of so much of his knowledge is, like his poverty, an important key to Ward's thought. At the superficial level of style, it made him a frequent captive to pedantry and its consequences—a laborious prose and a cumbersome nomenclature of Latin and Greek derivatives. It engendered a dangerous self-absorption, so that Ward felt only rarely the need to keep abreast of the work of other social theorists. ("Whether Ward wanted it to be so or not," wrote Albion Small, dean of the first generation of American sociologists, "his work was . . . always more insulated from that of men engaged on the same problems than was good for the author and his products.")[37] And not surprisingly, his comparative lack of formal instruction left him highly vulnerable to, and resentful of, professional criticism. These were the negative aspects. The gains were more important. By virtue of his own arduous experience, Ward could serve as a model of the value of education. He himself had risen through the power of the trained mind, from mechanic's son, to scientist and author, to professor. And he had no reason to think himself unique.

Was not his own career a capsule refutation of Spencerian fatalism? If one individual, by sheer determination, could lift himself up to a position where he might influence thousands, was it not nonsense to teach that man's lot was to suffer rather than to strive, to acquiesce rather than to effect?

Convictions like these motivated Ward as he set to work, in 1884, to appraise Sumner's book on social classes for the New York journal *Man*. He did so in the context of the gap he had previously identified between social theory and social practice. He had written: "The works of Adam Smith and Ricardo, of Pitt, Cobden and the two Mills, of Jean Baptiste Say and Michel Chevalier, and of the train of political economists who have followed these leaders, are, in the main, hostile to all those schemes of regulation which characterise the action of modern States."[38] Now he found in Sumner's book "a sort of final wail against the modern practices of states and people which run counter to these theories. The argument is simply the old cry: 'Laissez faire, laissez passer!' " Fresh from the writing of *Dynamic Sociology*, Ward suggested that Sumnerology had had its day and could no longer be considered a power in the land. Evidence refuted the argument of laissez-faire on all sides. Plainly the state did not bungle all its undertakings—witness the postal service—and people were not going to continue believing in the total incapacity of government. Ward pointed out, too, that Sumner was guilty of inconsistency in his attitude toward reformers, for they were themselves a natural product of society. "On his own theory, the author should let his deluded victims alone, should *laissez faire* . . . " Still, Ward concluded that Sumner's book would probably do more good than harm simply as a demonstration that "the laissez faire doctrin [sic], if it could be carried to a logical conclusion, would be nihilistic and suicidal."[39]

Ward dismissed Sumner with one book review, but he could not dismiss Herbert Spencer so easily, for Spencer was mentor as well as adversary. There are some interesting similarities between Spencer and Ward. Both had received an education largely independent of the usual channels, both labored to establish sociology at the apex of a classifying scheme of all the sciences, both believed in a kind of naturalistic monism (Ward once shed tears of emotion over "the great thought of unity and continuity," and planned to write a final book entitled *Monism The True Quietism, or the Continuity of Nature the only Faith that can satisfy the emancipated Soul*).

Neither man was willing to accept the world of things at face value, but insisted on categorizing, and pinning down, and relating everything to the largest possible frame of reference. Spencer tells us in his *Autobiography*, "It appears that in the treatment of every topic, however seemingly remote from philosophy, I found occasion for falling back on some ultimate principle in the natural order."[40] With equal unselfconsciousness, Ward noted that "I naturally consider everything in its relation to the Cosmos."[41] Aware that their thoughts soared above those of the average man, Spencer and Ward also shared a common dogmatism. What they said often had an air of being so self-evident that only the willfully blind could dispute it.

The "American Aristotle" took over from the "English Aristotle" a large part of his philosophical apparatus. He considered Spencer a master of synthesis, with a profound grasp of the natural sciences. Himself a distinguished botanist, Ward greatly admired Spencer's treatment of the general laws of biology. Like Spencer (and Darwin too, for that matter) Ward accepted the Lamarckian notion of the transmission of acquired characteristics, a theory which if proven correct would strongly buttress the case for universal education. It would be dramatic to imagine Ward pitting himself, as Dewey did, against the whole Spencerian mechanistic system. The truth is that Ward considered himself a disciple of Spencer, except for Spencer's social theories. But, of course, that break, for a sociologist, was the decisive one, since no amount of agreement about first principles or biological theories could offset a radical disagreement about social policy. Without deviating from the premise of a mechanical universe, Ward's powerful mind brought to bear upon Spencer's static sociology a devastating array of logical and scientific counterarguments. The ground that he covered no one ever again needed to retrace. Still, pioneer that he was, Ward did work with some rather old-fashioned equipment. Even after his lusty blows had shattered the walls of the fortress of laissez-faire, some of the debris remained behind to impede the raising of a more adequate structure. It fell to the pragmatists, John Dewey in particular, and to the social psychologists, to clear away these shards from the past.

Dynamic Sociology

Ward could not remember a time when he had not puzzled over "the deeper problems of nature and of man." His strenuous course of self-education had left him permanently impressed with the great difference between the educated and the uneducated person. Convinced that this difference was not inherent, he began to argue with friends the potency of environment as against heredity, and to ascribe to education a crucial role among the factors of environment. In 1869 Ward wrote out a plan of a book that would incorporate these germinating ideas, to be entitled *The Great Panacea*. "I was an apostle of human progress," he admitted, "and I believed that this could be greatly accelerated by society itself."[42]

Dynamic Sociology, as Ward retitled his treatise, was a compelling witness to his belief. "The real object of science," Ward argued, "is to benefit man. A science which fails to do this . . . is lifeless." But the sociology of Mill, Spencer, and Fiske did not pass Ward's test of life, and he wrote *Dynamic Sociology* to show how "the breath of life may be breathed into its nostrils."[43]

The trouble with social science, as Ward analyzed it, was that it had remained mired in the passively dynamic stage, the stage that "recognises only the changes wrought by Nature, unaided by Art." Before sociology could call itself a science it must break through to an actively dynamic stage, one in which "social phenomena shall be contemplated as capable of intelligent control by society itself in its own interest." It was imperative that the leap to a dynamic sociology be taken, and taken soon, lest civilization face the prospect of cultural decline: "The time must soon come when the control of blind natural forces in society must give way to that of human foresight, or the highest civilizations of the earth must reach their culminating point and commence their decline. . . . Thus far, social progress has in a certain awkward manner taken care of itself, but in the near future it will have to be cared for."[44]

Ward drew up a telling indictment of the bondage of contemporary social thought to laissez-faire. The theorists of laissez-faire assume, he pointed out, that the natural is always superior to the artificial, and that nature's way is therefore always best. But the alleged identity between the ways of nature and those of man is nonexistent: "There is no necessary harmony between natural law and human advantage." Nature operates on a scale of fantastic prodigality and waste. The octopus annually lays 50,000 eggs in order that one baby octopus may survive; the oyster spawns 2,000,000 embryos each season. Nature never checks population at the source, by diminishing fertility, but rather destroys the excess population after birth, with all the suffering that entails. Would anyone suggest this as a pattern for human emulation?[45]

Worse than the excessive waste of nature, perhaps, was the fierce competition she exacted. Ward believed that Spencer was absolutely correct in identifying competition and survival of the fittest as the fundamental law of nature, but he differed from Spencer in his estimate of the effects of this law. Spencer held competition to be beneficial because it weeded out the weak and preserved the fit. Ward insisted that, on the contrary, it inhibited rather than furthered the perfecting of the species. For proof he pointed to the practices of artificial breeding and nurture in agriculture, where controlled environments eliminated competition for survival and produced superior results.[46]

Ward inveighed against the faulty logic of those who argued that sociology was a domain of law like the physical sciences and yet denied that men could control these laws: "This laissez-faire school has entrenched itself behind the fortification of science, and while declaring with truth that social phenomena are, like physical phenomena, uniform and governed by laws, they have accompanied this by the false declaration and non sequitur that neither physical nor social phenomena are capable of human control . . . ." But the practical benefits of science come precisely from human control. "It is only through the artificial control of natural phenomena that science is made to minister to human needs; and if social laws are really analogous to physical laws, there is no reason why social science may not receive practical applications such as have been given to physical science."[47] Laissez-faire theorists had always been quick to point out the absurdities and failures of past legislation, as if that were reason enough to abandon social experimentation. But did they really believe that society could work out its own progress unaided?

> As well say to all inventors: Cease trying to control nature, let it alone and it will control itself; it will, if left undisturbed, work out, in its own good time, all the cotton-gins, reaping machines, printing-presses, and sand-blasts that are needed. Why not, because the first telegraph line and the first ocean cable failed, cry down the Wheatstones and the Fields, and say, Let these matters alone, they will regulate themselves?[48]

In "The Political Ethics of Herbert Spencer," Ward assembled an imposing list of measures and institutions that would require repeal were Spencer's creed ever put into practice. Gone would be all public works, such as harbors and roads and lighthouses, all postal service, all regulation of utilities, all public fire departments, public schools, health ordinances, and public sewage systems. Ward could not resist quoting Spencer on this final "climax of laissez-faire absurdity":

> Respecting sewage there would be no difficulty. Houses might readily be drained on the same mercantile principle that they are now supplied with water. It is probable that in the hands of a private company the resulting manure would not only pay the cost of collection, but would yield a considerable profit. But if not, the return on the invested capital would be made up by charges to those whose houses were drained: The alternative of having their connections with the main sewer stopped, being as good a security for payment as the analogous ones possessed by water and gas companies.

At this point Ward felt justified in concluding that Spencerian laissez-faire stood condemned by the verdict of realism as well as by logic.[49]

Man vs. Nature

Still, as a man of science, Ward could not content himself with verdicts rendered by realism and logic—he required the verdict of science as well. It annoyed him that the scientific description of man, by placing him squarely at the end of an evolutionary continuum with no seam or break, appeared to league itself with the passive fatalism of a Spencer or Sumner. "When I consider," he wrote, "the tendencies which are now so unmistakable, and which are so certainly the consequences of the protracted study, on the part of leading scientists, of the unquestionable methods of nature, I think I can, though holding precisely opposite opinions, fully sympathise with Carlyle in characterising the philosophy of evolution as a 'gospel of dirt'." The solution was certainly not to break the seamless web of nature and return mind to the metaphysicians. Ward, who took second place to no one in his adherence to a strictly naturalistic monism, insisted on the physical origin of mind. Science had shown the equivalence of mind with the brain, so that the study of mind was now a branch of biology. But granted the natural emergence of mind from matter, that emergence constituted an event of enormous significance in the history of evolution. Here was where Spencer and his school went off the track—by failing to recognize that "in the development of mind, a virtually *new power* was introduced into the world." Evolution taught continuity, but not uniformity. The introduction of the psychic factor meant that henceforth purpose and plan became a part of reality. Animals submitted to evolution; only man could guide it. "An entirely new dispensation has been given to the world. All the materials and forces of nature have been thus placed completely under the control of one of the otherwise least powerful of the creatures inhabiting the earth . . . . Nature has thus been made the servant of man."[50]

What did all this imply about the true relationship between the method of nature and that of man? Very simply that the relationship was one of complete opposition.

> Art is the antithesis of nature. If we call one the natural method we must call the other the artificial method. If nature's process is rightly named natural selection, man's process is artificial selection. The survival of the fittest is simply the survival of the strong, which implies, and might as well be called, the destruction of the weak. And if nature progresses through the destruction of the weak, man progresses through the *protection* of the weak.[51]

Turning from criticism to advocacy, Ward proceeded to elaborate what he liked to call the "method of collective telesis." Once assume that society can and ought to "adopt an aggressive reform policy guided entirely by scientific foresight," and the question remains—what must we do about it? To this question Ward returned a disarmingly simple response. We must institute a system of universal education. In a series of succinct theorems, Ward outlined his message:

A. Happiness is the ultimate end of conation.
B. Progress is the direct means to Happiness . . .
C. Dynamic Action is the direct means to Progress . . .
D. Dynamic Opinion is the direct means to Dynamic Action . . .
E. Knowledge is the direct means to Dynamic Opinion . . .
F. Education is the direct means to Knowledge . . . [52]

Thus, education became the starting point, the absolute and fundamental requisite to the institution of universal happiness. Let us attend properly to education, Ward urged, and the other steps will take care of themselves: "for applied sociology . . . there is really only one live problem, that of the maximum equalization of intelligence."[53]

Ward did not attempt to offer specific reforms. "I do not pretend," he wrote, "to be wiser than others in devising ways and means. And I am satisfied that the average intelligence of mankind is amply sufficient to work out, adopt, and carry into effect practical measures for the accomplishment of any clearly perceived and strongly desired end." He looked forward to a time when an educated and intelligent populace would choose as its representatives "scientific legislators" who would act on the deliberations of "true scientific sociologists and sociological inventors." In the meantime he shunned all efforts to enlist him in the ranks of active reform, insisting that he was writing science and not tracts. He had no more patience than Sumner with what he considered hasty measures of social reform that attacked only the symptoms and not the roots of distress.[54]

It is perfectly clear, nonetheless, from his letters as well as from his published works, that Ward spoke as a tribune of the people. For years he carried on a running battle with August Weissmann, chief of the neo-Darwinists, on behalf of Lamarck's notion of the inheritance of acquired characteristics. For, he wrote, once admit the neo-Darwinian hypothesis that acquired traits are not transmissible, and education benefits only the present generation. "If nothing that the individual gains by the most heroic or the most assiduous effort can by any possibility be handed on to posterity, the incentive to effort is in great part removed. . . . If, as Mr. Galton puts it, nurture is nothing and nature is everything, why not abandon nurture and leave the race wholly to nature?"[55] Ward, with his profound faith in the power of intellect to transform the environment on behalf of man, simply refused to accept this genetic equivalent of laissez-faire. To replace the "oligocentric" viewpoint of eugenics, with its conviction of the inferiority of the lower classes, he proposed to institute a science of eudemics, or "doctrine of the welfare of the masses."

The very last article Ward ever wrote was a paean of affirmation to this faith. "For an indefinite period yet to come," he noted, "society will continue to be recruited from the base." There were many who feared that this would lead to the inevitable degeneracy of the race. Was it possible to take any other view? "I think it is," Ward replied,

> and the only consolation, the only hope, lies in the truth that, so far as the native capacity, the potential quality, the 'promise and potency' of a higher life are concerned, those swarming, spawning millions, the bottom layer of society, the proletariat, the working

classes, the 'hewers of wood and drawers of water,' nay, even the denizens of the slums—that all these are by nature the peers of the boasted 'aristocracy of brains' that now dominates society and looks down upon them, and the equals in all but privilege of the most enlightened teachers of eugenics.[56]

William Graham Sumner, always skeptical of the democratic dogma, feared that democracy had been tried and found wanting; Lester Frank Ward was convinced that it had not yet been tried.

Dewey and the Hegelian Tradition

Ward's protest against the strictures of Spencerian social theory, powerful as it was, was not sufficient of itself to form the basis of the new morality demanded by Henry D. Lloyd. Technically, it was inadequate, as John Dewey pointed out, because it relied on an outmoded Lockean psychology. What Dewey wanted and did not find in Ward was "a theory of consciously organic activity." Dewey had begun to construct such a theory himself while still a Hegelian. His *Psychology*, published in 1887, had already demonstrated the active nature of the mind in experiencing sensations and translating them into knowledge. He argued then that though external stimuli are certainly necessary to move the mind to action, "the soul, when thus incited to action, responds to the stimulation with a characteristic production of its own, whose appearance, relatively to the physical phenomena, is a virtual creation; that is, cannot be in any way got out of them."[57]

Dewey's conception of mind acting creatively in response to external stimulus found strong support, once Dewey had turned away from Hegel to Darwin, in the Darwinian notion of the organism interacting with its environment. For as Dewey interpreted it, Darwinism meant that every structure and function of living things must be considered as "an instrument of adjustment or adaptation to a particular environing situation." Thought then, like any other organic activity, functioned to correlate organism and environment. But thought functioned actively—it transformed the situation in the process of adaptation. Dewey strenuously opposed the "spectator-theory of knowledge" that he attributed to the British empiricists, a theory that viewed thinking as a passive replication in the mind of the real, objective world "out there." Like William James, Dewey found in Darwinism support for his conviction that thought was a great deal more dynamic than Spencer and his empiricist forebears granted. When, in any problematic situation, doubt once initiated the process of thought (or inquiry as Dewey later preferred to call it), that thought could bring about a new, more satisfying situation in which organism and environment were once again in harmony. Thought, as James had said, helps to create truth; it does not simply subscribe to it.[58]

Ward's critique suffered, too, from the intensity with which any rebellious thinker has to assert his independence of his mentors. Significantly, in his review of Ward, Dewey remarks in passing that Ward took Spencer too seriously. Thus, Ward's radical disjunction between nature and art, the genetic and the telic, did not in the end serve the cause of the new social theory as well as Dewey's insistence on continuity. "Mind," Ward had written, "is . . . a natural product of evolution . . . " But if mind is natural, then Ward's separation of nature and man was unnecessary and even dangerous. Dewey, by contrast, emphasized that any vision of the cosmos that did not include man's transforming agency was only partial. When we say that man's intelligence transforms his environment, we do not mean that man is opposing or arresting nature. We mean rather that one element in nature, human intellect, acts to change another element, the world around it. The method of intelligent purpose does not war with the method of unconscious development; it completes it. The artificial is really only the natural raised to a higher power.

Dewey arrived easily at his conclusion about the ultimate oneness of the cosmos because he had served his philosophical apprenticeship in a school essentially unknown to Ward—the Hegelian. The philosophy of Hegel and his successors during the nineteenth century was in many respects the antithesis of the British empirical tradition. Indeed, much of the intellectual history of the late nineteenth century can be understood in terms of the confrontation between these two great philosophical systems. Hegel's philosophy, which began to be seriously studied in America in the 1860s, focused on the organic nature of reality as a unity—a whole in which man, nature, and history participated. Reality was unitary, but it expressed itself in process, flux, movement. Thus Hegelianism, while professing allegiance to an ultimate continuity, could nevertheless take account of activity and change.

History, a central category for Hegel, revealed the progressive manifestations of the Absolute in its quest for self-fulfillment. Among the instruments seized upon by the Spirit to play a part as vehicles in this enterprise were both individuals and institutions, but their value was by no means equal. Hegel believed that the individual, in and of himself, was rather a weak creature, entirely produced and shaped by his social environment. Institutions, above all the state, carried the World Spirit much farther in its course of self-realization. In Hegel's writings the state became "the divine on earth," a "higher ethical principle."

Hegel's theories offered a profound challenge to the individualism of the British empirical tradition. To those American academics, many of them educated in Germany, who were casting about after the Civil War for a more satisfactory grounding for social theory, Hegel seemed to provide a welcome alternative to Locke. It was good to learn that the individual was a social creation. It was useful to draw on a body of thought that magnified, rather than belittled, the state. One has only to juxtapose Sumner's strictures on government intervention because "the inadequacy of the State to regulative tasks is agreed upon, as a matter of fact, by all" with the political scientist John Burgess's doctrine that the state is "the human organ least likely to do wrong" to measure the distance between Spencer and Hegel.

Yet Hegel alone could never satisfy the needs of the new social philosophy. He dealt in metaphysics, while the American mind craved empiricism. Hegel's apotheosis of the state led to unpleasantly nationalistic effusions, as when Richard T. Ely, a young economist who offended orthodoxy by favoring state intervention in the economy, announced that "it is a grand thing to serve God in the State which he in his beneficent wisdom instituted, and that to betray a trust in the divine state is as heinous an offense as to be false to duty in the divine Church." James Mark Baldwin, a pioneer social psychologist, found Hegelianism a mixture of the useful and the extravagant. He did not like Hegel's emphasis on force as the foundation of social life. Nor did he savor Hegel's militaristic description of the process by which an individual achieves "self-recognition," a process Hegel epitomized thusly: "I cannot be aware of me as myself in another individual, so long as I see in that other another and an immediate existence: and I am consequently bent on the suppression of the immediacy of his. . . . The fight of recognition is a life and death struggle . . . ."[59] This was altogether too Prussian a version of the growth of self-consciousness to find favor with those American social theorists bent on refuting just that kind of anarchic egotism in the writings of the Social Darwinists.

What was needed, clearly, was a fusion of Germany and England so as to blend the best of both Hegel and Darwin. If Hegel was overly metaphysical and deductive, a scrupulous adherence to Darwin and empirical evidence would correct the balance so as to make the new social thought a science rather than a philosophy. If Darwinism had been perverted to support false theories of laissez-faire individualism, Hegelianism would supply the social and collective ingredient of reality. Within this framework a number of prominent American social scientists plied their skills toward the construction of a new theory of man and society. James Mark Baldwin, one of the earliest and most influential of these theorists, will serve as representative of the type.

James Mark Baldwin: Reconciler

Baldwin, professor of psychology at Princeton and Johns Hopkins, and interpreter of evolution to the nation at large, was a devout Darwinian who prided himself on his "confession [that] the net result . . . of my scientific work until now, is a contribution, whatever it may turn out to be worth, to the theory of Darwinism in the sciences of life and mind."[60] Like so many of the early generation of American social scientists (one thinks of Albion Small, G. Stanley Hall, and William Graham Sumner), Baldwin had turned away from a ministerial career, preferring to serve humanity as a social scientist; and, like them, he viewed social science as simply another way, more effective than religion, to establish moral truths. If to be scientific meant to be Darwinian, then Darwinism must somehow be harnessed to the construction of the ethical foundations of society. As a young man, Baldwin had studied under that sturdy Presbyterian moralist, James McCosh of Princeton, who never doubted that Darwinism could be safely reconciled with

Christianity. For Baldwin, who eventually abandoned the specific beliefs of Presbyterianism, that faith—transmuted only slightly into a conviction of the naturalness of ethical values—remained strong.

Baldwin was disturbed by the Spencerian account of the relationship between the individual and his society. Spencer, he felt, removed from man everything that was distinctively human; his constant reductionism was "like proving a bed of tulips to be onions by . . . nipping off the tell-tale blooms." In one of his best-known books, significantly entitled *Social and Ethical Interpretations in Mental Development*, Baldwin insisted that Spencer had failed to explain the discrepancy everyone experiences between right and wrong, between "acts which ought to be done and acts, equally impelling by physical or social impulsion, which ought not to be done." At the root of this failure lay Spencer's utter incomprehension of the social nature of personality. It was simply false to assert that men achieved personhood in splendid isolation. The sense of self was a social acquisition, achieved only through contact with others. There could be no opposition between the normal individual and his society. "Man," thundered Baldwin, "is not a person who stands up in his isolated majesty, meanness, passion, or humility, and sees, hits, worships, fights, or overcomes, another man, who does the opposite things to him, each preserving his isolated majesty, meanness, passion, humility, all the while, so that he can be considered a 'unit' for the compounding processes of social speculation. On the contrary, *a man is a social outcome rather than a social unit.*"[61]

Drawing on Hegel directly, and on German idealism as mediated by his good friend Josiah Royce, Baldwin elaborated a "dialectic of personal growth" to explain the development of personality. The child learned about himself by imitating others; he learned about others by experiencing himself. This give-and-take process operated at first within his own family, then gradually expanded to include his nurse, other children, the school, and ultimately "the broader fields of universal human interest." Even the ethical sense could be traced genetically. There existed, according to Baldwin, two images of self within each child—the "habitual self," assertive and aggressive, and the "accommodating self," open, imitative, sympathetic. Neither of these selves was capable of satisfactory ethical behavior: the habitual, because it lacked generosity; the accommodating, because it lent itself to capriciousness and maudlin sentimentality. The failure of these two selves to explain ethical behavior became evident whenever the child reluctantly obeyed an unpleasant command. His accommodating self would have been eager to comply; his habitual self would have refused to comply. Reluctant compliance signaled, then, the acquisition of a new image of the self—the ideal self, the self that fulfills the law, or, more simply, conscience.[62]

In this way Baldwin surmounted, at least to his own satisfaction, the naturalist theories of the origin of ethical behavior developed by Darwin and Spencer. He was willing, indeed eager, to accept the Darwinian explanation of the origin of morality. *"Morality has arisen because it is socially useful; that is the Darwinian account,"* Baldwin noted approvingly. "Once granted the origin of society by selective processes, with standards of group-utility replacing those of biological and individual utility, and the objection to Darwinism in ethics, on the ground of its individualism, completely disappears. The norms of social utility become the ideals of personal duty, which are unconditionally imperative to the individual." Morality was above all natural, and the dilemma of Thomas Henry Huxley, who thought human ethics were at war with nature, was no dilemma at all, but a false approach.[63]

Baldwin thought too much of his role as social scientist to relinquish morality to the intuitionists. Still, he was not prepared to give ethics over altogether into the custody of society. Society—the individual en masse—could be capricious, it could degenerate into a mob, "a lynching party, a corn-riot, a commune, a Chamber of Deputies, or a Jingo Senate." Society represented the mean, the average, the ethical sense of the multitudes. But occasionally there arose a "moral seer," one whose ethical sense outstripped the conscience of his generation. Society had produced him, but society could not contain him: "Who made social approval the measure of truth? What is there to eclipse the vision of the poet, the inventor, the seer, that he should not see over the heads of his generation, and raise his voice for that which, to all men else, lies behind the veil? The social philosophy of the school of Spencer cannot answer these questions."[64]

So, in the end, the individual retained his autonomy and dignity; but he was a new-model individual, unrecognizable to the Spencerians—a wholly socialized organism, who only developed into a person by a dialectic of give-and-take with the social environment that nurtured him. It was an attractive and optimistic vision—the ethical individual living in the benevolent state—and it quickly attracted disciples. Baldwin was not, however, a fully convincing seer. Pompous, pedantic, complacent, he served as medium to ideas he did not fully comprehend. After Baldwin it remained for other social theorists to free Baldwin's insights from the matrix of murky prose and dubious theory in which they were enmeshed, and to fill out the social theory of personality.

Prominent among these theorists was Charles Horton Cooley of the University of Michigan, another of those late nineteenth-century disciples of Emerson whose lifework was to fashion a social philosophy diametrically opposed to Emerson's. Cooley's personality was in many ways at odds with his work. He was, like Emerson, reserved and cold, uneasy in society and easily fatigued by social gatherings. If Emerson could write, "I was born cold. My bodily habit is cold," so also Cooley could record in his own journal, "I feel compunction at times for being so cold; in fact I have no intimate friends outside of my family." To entertain a visitor for as much as half a day caused him a night of sleeplessness.[65] Yet to this unsociable man, this intellectual recluse, we owe the pioneer statement of the organic interrelationship between the individual and society. "A separate individual," wrote Cooley on the first page of *Human Nature and the Social Order*, "is an abstraction unknown to experience, and so likewise is society when regarded as something apart from individuals. The real thing is Human Life, which may be considered either in an individual aspect or in a social, that is to say a general, aspect; but is always, as a matter of fact, both individual and general. In other words, 'society' and 'individuals' do not denote separable phenomena, but are simply collective and distributive aspects of the same thing . . . ."[66]

There could scarcely be a stronger statement of the organic unity of society. Though Cooley disliked metaphysics and had little formal acquaintance with it, his views had much in common with Hegelian idealism. The nature of social reality, for Cooley, was psychological. Society was not essentially structures or organizations or personal interactions; it was ideas: "Society . . . in its immediate aspect, *is a relation among personal ideas* . . . Society exists in my mind as the contact and reciprocal influence of certain ideas named 'I', Thomas, Henry, Susan, Bridget, and so on. It exists in your mind as a similar group, and so in every mind." Sociology must then rely primarily on trained imagination, rather than physical measurements or psychological tests, and Cooley concluded "that the imaginations which people have of one another are the *solid facts* of society, and that to observe and interpret these must be a chief aim of sociology."[67]

To this end Cooley developed two concepts which have become famous in sociological literature: the "looking-glass self" and the primary group. According to Cooley, the self, or the "I" of daily life, was necessarily a social self, developed as the individual grew in awareness of his differences from his fellows. An important aspect of how people felt about themselves was always how they thought other people felt about them.

> As we see our face, figure, and dress in the glass, and are interested in them because they are ours, and pleased or otherwise with them according as they do or do not answer to what we should like them to be; so in imagination we perceive in another's mind some thought of our appearance, manners, aims, deeds, character, friends, and so on, and are variously affected by it.
>   A self-idea of this sort seems to have three principal elements: the imagination of our appearance to that other person; the imagination of his judgment of that appearance, and some sort of self-feeling, such as pride or mortification.[68]

Individuals received their earliest training in selfhood in the primary group, nursery of human nature. By primary groups, Cooley meant "those characterized by intimate face-to-face association and cooperation," the most important of which were "the family, the play-group of children, and the neighborhood or community of elders." Within them, individuals achieved genuine humanity and were schooled in the primary ideals of loyalty, truth, service to others, kindliness, lawfulness and freedom.[69]

Cooley's socialization of the individual, both more solid academically and more pleasing aesthetically than the labored achievement of Baldwin, found in the sociological literature the lasting niche that was denied the work of the older man. Yet it should not be forgotten that Baldwin had pioneered the taming of the Spencerian tiger. Taking a new path, that of the mental development of children, he had undermined individualism by demonstrating that it never existed, that personality was an achievement, and a social achievement, not something donned at birth.

Here, then, was the new social theory called for by that ardent reformer Henry Demarest Lloyd when he sought "a book on 'Social Selection' showing how the institutional variations of society have been produced, and giving a scientific sanction to the processes of reform, and a scientific place to the idealizing faculty." Not that Baldwin or Cooley were themselves prophets of reform. Baldwin decried the "half-baked schemes of reform" put forward at the beginning of the twentieth century by "the so-called progressives, of whatever party." His own standard of political rectitude remained that sober and honest man, Grover Cleveland. Baldwin's friend and mentor Josiah Royce feared "ill-advised labor agitations" more than the "corporate misdeeds" which provoked them. Even Cooley, more generous and more open, was so averse to conflict and so committed to social harmony that he tended to imagine that reform was unnecessary. "The feeling between classes will not be very bitter," he believed, "so long as the ideal of service is present in all and mutually recognized. And it is the tendency of the democratic spirit to raise this ideal above all others and make it a common standard of conduct."[70]

Still, though not themselves interested in reform, these men forged the intellectual weapons of reform Darwinism. Lester Frank Ward had been the first sociologist to challenge Spencerian laissez-faire individualism, but his resources were not adequate to complete the task. Under Baldwin and Cooley and their colleagues, a judicious blend of Hegel and Darwin was made to harness Darwinian evolution to the service of the community. In Darwin, finally, lay salvation from Spencer. For Baldwin it was a passionate discovery: "Once let it be our philosophical conviction, drawn from the more general results of psychology and anthropology, that man is not two, an ego and an alter, each of which is in active and chronic protest against a third great thing, society; once dispel this hideous un-fact, and with it the remedies found by the egoists, back all the way from the Spencers to the Hobbeses and the Comtes—and I submit the main barrier to the successful understanding of society is removed."[71]

It has been said that the genius of America is its pragmatism, its willingness to follow the fact and eschew the theory. It has also been said that Social Darwinism was alien to the American spirit, and that it moved only those whose immediate interests were well served by it. The facts would seem to bely both these judgments. Americans accepted Darwinism, by and large, as an affair of intellect. They measured it with their minds, not their pocketbooks.

The American business community did, it is true, obey the precept of pragmatism, and continued to conduct its affairs, after Darwin as before, with small regard for finespun theory. But intellectuals took Darwinism with great seriousness from the first. They realized the challenge thrown up by Darwinian social theory to the fluid society of industrial America. Their contributions to the development of social theory, spurred on by that challenge, were great. They proposed not to abandon Social Darwinism but to tame it, to make it, at last, truly social. In this they achieved a dual success—the beginning of a sophisticated social science and the establishment of a collective theory of society. The United States had moved into the twentieth century; it now had a twentieth-century social philosophy.

NOTES

1. Stanley Elkins, *Slavery: A Problem in American Institutional and Intellectual Life* (Chicago: University of Chicago Press, 1968), pp. 34, 142.
2. Alexis de Tocqueville, *Democracy in the United States*, 2 vols. (New York: Vintage Books, Inc., 1954), 2: 105–106.
3. *Ibid.*, p. 104.
4. Quoted in George Fredrickson, *The Inner Civil War* (New York: Harper & Row, 1968), pp. 140–141.
5. Jean B. Quandt, *From the Small Town to the Great Community* (New Brunswick, N.J.: Rutgers University Press, 1970), pp. 15, 16, 25.
6. Quoted in Fredrickson, *Inner Civil War*, p. 75.
7. Charles Darwin, *On the Origin of Species*, p. 470; Francis Darwin and A. C. Seward, eds., *More Letters*, 2 vols. (London, 1903), 1: 94.
8. *Letters of Charles Eliot Norton*, with biographical comment by his daughter, Miss Sara Norton, and M. A. DeWolfe Howe, 2 vols. (Boston: Houghton Mifflin Co., 1913), 2: 336.
9. Charles Darwin, *The Descent of Man*, pp. 133–134.
10. Herbert Spencer, *The Study of Sociology* (New York, 1874), pp. 344–345, 346.
11. Von Bernhardi, *Germany and the Next War*, quoted in Richard Hofstadter, *Social Darwinism in American Thought*, p. 197.
12. *Ibid.*, p. 171.
13. Alfred Thayer Mahan, *Armaments and Arbitration* (New York: Harper & Bros., 1912), pp. 10, 117.
14. A. Hunter Dupree, *Asa Gray*, p. 296.
15. John Higham, *Strangers in the Land: Patterns of American Nativism 1860–1925* (New York: Atheneum, 1970), p. 136.

16. See the rather scant evidence of new departures in racial theory influenced by Darwinism in Thomas Gossett, *Race: The History of an Idea in America* (Dallas: Southern Methodist University Press, 1963), Chapters 7 and 8.

17. Hofstadter, *Social Darwinism*, p. 44.

18. Himmelfarb, *Darwin*, p. 418.

19. Quoted in Hofstadter, *Social Darwinism*, p. 45. But see the very definite limitations on Carnegie's Social Darwinism contained in Joseph Frazier Wall, *Andrew Carnegie* (New York: Oxford University Press, 1970), esp. pp. 316–347.

20. James H. Bridge, ed., *The Trust: Its Book* (New York: Doubleday, Page & Co., 1902), p. xxxxv.

21. Jack London, *Martin Eden,* p. 298.

22. This summary of the influence of Social Darwinism on businessmen draws on Irvin G. Wyllie, "Social Darwinism and the Businessman," *Proceedings of the American Philosophical Society,* 103 (October, 1959), 629–635; Edward C. Kirkland, *Dream and Thought in the Business Community* (Ithaca, N.Y.: Cornell University Press, 1956), pp. 13–14, 18; and Richard M. Huber, *The American Idea of Success* (New York: McGraw-Hill Book Co., 1971), pp. 64–74.

23. Theodore Roosevelt, "Social Evolution," *The Works of Theodore Roosevelt* (New York: Charles Scribner's Sons, 1923–1926), 14: pp. 110, 112–113, 123.

24. Theodore Roosevelt, "Character and Success," *Outlook,* 64: 725.

25. Henry Demarest Lloyd, *Wealth Against Commonwealth* (New York, 1894), p. 496.

26. Ibid., p. 495; William James, *Memories and Studies*, pp. 140–141.

27. Lloyd, *Wealth Against Commonwealth*, pp. 527, 506, 496.

28. William Graham Sumner, *The Challenge of Facts and Other Essays*, ed. by Albert Galloway Keller (New Haven: Yale University Press, 1914), p. 25.

29. William Graham Sumner, *What Social Classes Owe to Each Other* (New York, 1883), pp. 25, 35, 101; Sumner, *Earth-Hunger and Other Essays*, ed. by Albert Galloway Keller, (New Haven: Yale University Press, 1913), pp. 287, 271f.

30. William Graham Sumner, *War and Other Essays*, ed. by Albert Galloway Keller (New Haven: Yale University Press, 1913), p. 186.

31. *Challenge of Facts*, p. 169; *War*, p. 185.

32. William Graham Sumner, *The Forgotten Man and Other Essays*, ed. by Albert Galloway Keller (New Haven: Yale University Press, 1918), pp. 480, 491.

33. *War*, p. 186; *Social Classes*, p. 118; *War*, pp. 209–210.

34. *War*, p. 209.

35. *Social Classes*, pp. 158, 81.

36. Some autobiographical comments are given in Lester Frank Ward, *Applied Sociology* (New York: Ginn & Co., 1906), pp. 105–106, 127–128.

37. Albion W. Small, "Fifty Years of Sociology in the United States," *American Journal of Sociology*, 21 (1915–1916): 751.

38. "Politico-Social Functions," *Glimpses of the Cosmos*, 6 vols. (New York: G. P. Putnam's Sons, 1913–1918), 2: 336.

39. "Professor Sumner's Social Classes," *Glimpses of the Cosmos*, 3: 305.

40. Herbert Spencer, *An Autobiography,* 2 vols. (London: Williams and Norgate, 1904), 2: 5.

41. *Glimpses of the Cosmos*, 1: xx.

42. Ibid., 3: 147, 172.

43. Lester Frank Ward, *Dynamic Sociology*, 2 vols. (New York, 1883), 1: vii.

44. *Dynamic Sociology*, I, vi, 706.

45. *Dynamic Sociology*, II, 86.

46. "The Psychologic Basis of Social Economics," *Glimpses of the Cosmos*, 4: 357–361.

47. "Politico-Social Functions," *Glimpses of the Cosmos*, 2: 352.

48. *Dynamic Sociology*, I, 53.

49. "The Political Ethics of Herbert Spencer," *Glimpses of the Cosmos*, 5: 61–62.

50. "Mind as a Social Factor," *Glimpses of the Cosmos*, 3: 367–370.

51. "Mind as a Social Factor," p. 371.

52. *Dynamic Sociology*, 2: 108–109.

53. Ward, *Applied Sociology*, p. 314.

54. Ward, *Applied Sociology*, p. 296.

55. "Neo-Darwinism and Neo-Lamarckism," *Glimpses of the Cosmos*, 4: 291.

56. "Eugenics, Euthenics, and Eudemics," *Glimpses of the Cosmos*, 6: 397.

57. John Dewey, *Psychology* (New York, 1887), p. 43.

58. Quote from Morton White, *The Origins of Dewey's Instrumentalism* (New York: Columbia University Press, 1943), p. 144. See generally Dewey's *Essays in Experimental Logic* (Chicago: University of Chicago Press, 1916) and *Logic: The Theory of Inquiry* (New York: Henry Holt & Co., 1938).

59. *Hegel's Philosophy of Mind*, quoted in James Mark Baldwin, *Social and Ethical Interpretations in Mental Development* (New York, 1897), p. 504 fn.1.

60. James Mark Baldwin, *Darwin and the Humanities* (Baltimore: Review Publishing Co., 1909), p. ix.

61. *Social and Ethical Interpretations*, pp. 307, 87. An acute account of Baldwin is given in R. Jackson Wilson, *In Quest of Community* (New York: John Wiley & Sons, 1968), pp. 60–86.

62. *Social and Ethical Interpretations*, pp. 34–55.

63. *Darwin and the Humanities*, pp. 612, 65.

64. *Social and Ethical Interpretations*, pp. 157–158.

65. Edward C. Jandy, *Charles Horton Cooley* (New York: The Dryden Press, 1942), pp. 42, 47.

66. Charles Horton Cooley, *Human Nature and the Social Order* (New York: Charles Scribner's Sons, 1902), p. 1.

67. *Human Nature and the Social Order*, pp. 84–85, 86, 87.
68. *Human Nature and the Social Order*, p. 152.
69. Charles Horton Cooley, *Social Organization* (New York: Charles Scribner's Sons, 1909), pp. 23, 24.
70. R. Jackson Wilson discusses the social stance of Josiah Royce and Baldwin in *In Quest of Community*, pp. 79–81, 163–164, 169–170. Jean Quandt, *From the Small Town to the Great Community*, explores at greater length the tenuous political liberalism of some important Progressive intellectuals at the turn of the century.
71. *Social and Ethical Interpretations*, p. 88.

Henry Brooks Adams, 1838–1918. Drawing by Samuel Laurence, 1868.
(Courtesy of The Bettman Archive, Inc.)

FIVE

HISTORY, SCIENCE, AND HENRY ADAMS

 HAVE FAITH; NOT PERHAPS in the old dogmas, but in the new ones; faith in human nature; faith in science; faith in the survival of the fittest. Let us be true to our time, Mrs. Lee! If our age is to be beaten, let us die in the ranks. If it is to be victorious, let us be first to lead the column. Anyway, let us not be skulkers or grumblers." So spoke Nathaniel Gore in Henry Adams's novel *Democracy*.[1] Adams never himself achieved the robust faith of his literary creation. Faith in science he certainly lacked; faith in the survival of the fittest, always weak because he had absorbed the anti-Darwinian bias of Agassiz at Harvard, gave way at last altogether; faith in human nature he could claim only to the extent of a fixed expectation that the great mass of humanity would prove unworthy of trust.

Adams's pessimism about the future of mankind was truly cosmic. Yet he was no mere crank, raging blindly and indiscriminately at the modern age. Realizing with a clarity shared by few of his Brahmin associates that science was in the process of dissolving their familiar universe and reshaping it into something new and strange, Adams could not content himself either with deploring the process or with ignoring it. Painfully, at an age when most men would have declared themselves too old for reeducation, Adams undertook to come to grips with the great transforming ideas of nineteenth-century science and, with their aid, to interpret what he saw of history and life. His efforts have been rather generally criticized, both by scientists and by historians, but it speaks well for Adams that he was sensitive enough to raise questions about the troubling effect of science on the modern world, questions that our own age has scarcely been successful in putting to rest. It may be instructive, then, to examine Henry Adams's reaction to the new scientific discoveries of his time, not because he was typical (an Adams could not be typical), but because he was thoughtful. And being thoughtful, he eschewed easy solutions.

The Scientific Education of Henry Adams

According to his brother Brooks, Henry Adams had a hereditary aptitude for science. His grandfather John Quincy Adams had been greatly interested in the promotion and diffusion of scientific knowledge, and, as Secretary of State, had written a lucid and erudite treatise on weights and measures. If Henry inherited an aptitude for science, however, it did not manifest itself in his undergraduate years at Harvard, where most of the scientific courses made little or no impression on him. The exception was a lecture course by Louis Agassiz, which seems to have given Adams a lifelong suspicion of evolutionary theories in general, and of uniformitarian evolution, or evolution by gradual slow changes, in particular. One of Agassiz' most famous contributions to geology was his theory of the glacial period as a catastrophic break from the previous geological epoch, and this theory of catastrophism could in no way be reconciled with the gradualism of Darwinian evolution.

The nascent interest in geology planted by Agassiz flowered during the years that Adams spent in London as private secretary to his father, the American minister to Great Britain. These were the years of the Civil War, when friends of the Union cause in England were few in number. One frequent visitor to the American legation was the great geologist Sir Charles Lyell, whose *Principles of Geology* had paved the way for public acceptance of the uniformitarian thesis propounded by Darwin. Through Lyell, Adams was initiated into the tremendously stimulating world of English science. Adams's sojourn in England coincided with the years when Darwinism was shaking the intellectual establishment, and when men like Herbert Spencer and Henry Buckle were trying to do for the social sciences what Darwin had done for biology. So intrigued was Adams by the beckoning vistas of science, that a letter of 1863 to his older brother records "serious thoughts of quitting my old projects of a career, like you. My promised land of occupation, however, my burial place of ambition and law, is geology and science."[2]

Lyell had promised to introduce Henry Adams to Darwin himself should Darwin ever come to town. Darwin never came, so Adams was forced to uncover for himself the secrets of the *Origin of Species*. It was, he would have us believe, a congenial revelation for one who had been "a Darwinist before the letter; a predestined follower of the tide." Perhaps. But when Adams undertook to publicize the tenth edition of Lyell's *Principles*, newly published, through the medium of an essay in the *North American Review*, his faith in Darwinism had already begun to weaken. The obstacle was precisely the one a disciple of Agassiz might be expected to balk at: the glacial period. On the uniformitarian principles of Lyell and Darwin, the period of glaciation could not be considered a break in the evolutionary scheme. To Adams, it looked like a chasm. "If the glacial period were uniformity, what was catastrophe?"[3]

A second difficulty concerned Pteraspis, the ganoid fish and earliest known vertebrate, which had lived and swum in the Silurian period, so Lyell informed Adams. But earlier than Pteraspis no trace of vertebrate fossil structure had been found, nothing but a few shellfish. Where then was evolution? Where uniformitarianism? Years later, recalling these early perplexities, Adams still found no reason to recant his heresy of disbelief in "natural selection that did not select—evolution finished before it began—minute changes that refused to change anything during the whole geological record—survival of the highest order in a fauna which had no origin—uniformity under conditions which had disturbed everthing else in creation . . . ."[4]

The years after Adams's initiation into English science were years, first, of free-lance political writing and reform in Washington; then, of teaching medieval history at Harvard and editing the *North American Review*; and finally, of writing the magnificent *History of the United States of America During the Administrations of Thomas*

Jefferson and James Madison. It was not until after 1890 that Adams found the time and inclination to resume his scientific education. He was both persistent and diligent after his own fashion, under the guidance of Samuel Langley, director of the Smithsonian Institution and his personal Virgil in the alien world of contemporary science. To Langley he doubtless owed his acquaintance with the work of the great Yale physicist Josiah Willard Gibbs, although William Jordy has shown at some length how superficial Adams's knowledge of Gibbs really was. Adams's library contained, in addition, works of Wilhelm Ostwald and Ernst Haeckel, two giants of European science; and he knew the work of Hermann von Helmholtz, one of those, like Lord Kelvin, who had helped establish the Second Law of Thermodynamics. Of at least equal importance to Adams were a number of works on the philosophy of science— those by John B. Stallo, Henri Poincaré, Ernst Mach, and Karl Pearson enormously influenced Adams's views on the nature of science. Numerous marginal annotations testify to the care with which Adams absorbed this massive infusion of science. Whether his understanding of what he read went beyond the intelligent layman's (and some of his comments are remarkably shrewd), whether he used his material with a proper regard for its intrinsic meaning and not simply to prove a point of his own, it is undeniable that Adams concluded his education with a good deal more scientific expertise than most cultivated gentlemen of his day could boast.

The Quest for a Science of History

Adams began his quest to solve the riddle of the universe as a rather conventional, if brilliant, scientific historian of the late nineteenth-century Rankean variety. The German historian Ranke and those whom he influenced, it will be recalled, insisted on obtaining accurate and objective data, sifted with the greatest care for authenticity, and presented with as little interpretation from the historian as possible in order that the facts might "speak for themselves." In this spirit Adams sought, as he tells us in his *Education*, "to satisfy himself whether, by the severest process of stating, with the least possible comment, such facts as seemed sure, in such order as seemed rigorously consequent, he could fix for a familiar moment a necessary sequence of human movement."[5] The "severest process of stating" involved putting the narrative on an "exact basis," and this in turn demanded of the historian a close reliance on unvarnished source materials rather than on his own colorful or dramatic narrative power. The historian's duty, said Adams, was "only to give a running commentary on the documents in order to explain their relation."[6] In this way the historian would approximate, as it were, the laboratory isolation of the scientific experiment, merely setting up the factual apparatus and letting the sequence of events work itself out, before the very eyes of the reader, without further interference on his part.

Scientific history, by the same token, proscribed the pointing out of conclusions, on the theory that conclusions would emerge in the act of setting forth the facts. Since Adams's time it has, of course, become a commonplace of historiography that the historian's active control of his material is not lessened by refusal to spell out conclusions; it is simply concealed. The very selection and ordering of historical data involve definite assumptions about their interpretation on the author's part.

But Adams's scientific aspirations went beyond method. In germ in the *History*, and full-blown in the later essays, appears his conviction that history conforms to precisely the same general laws as those operative in the physical universe at large. Even as a young man Adams had voiced his conviction about the essential continuity of things. "My philosophy teaches me, and I firmly believe it," he wrote to his brother Charles in 1863, "that the laws which govern animated beings will be ultimately found to be at bottom the same with those which rule inanimate nature, and, as I entertain a profound conviction of the littleness of our kind, and of the curious enormity of creation, I am quite ready to receive with pleasure any basis for a systematic conception of it all."[7]

Adams was 25 when he recorded this bit of philosophy, but it was not until his fifty-fifth year that he saw fit to disclose it publicly for the benefit of his fellow historians, in his presidential message to the American Historical Association, together with a few of the implications of a truly scientific history. "Those of us who read Buckle's first volume . . . and almost immediately afterwards, in 1859, read the *Origin of Species*," Adams reminisced, " . . . never doubted that historians would follow until they had exhausted every possible hypothesis to create a science of history." Since that time, Adams conceded, skepticism about the possibility of scientific history had probably grown, but the effort could not be abandoned. "Science itself would admit its own failure if it admitted that man, the most important of all its subjects, could not be brought within its range."[8]

The reduction of historical complexity to one great historical law—such was the challenge, and it was a challenge not only to historians but to all the entrenched institutions of society, for Adams assured his peers that any science of history must be predictive, must "fix with mathematical certainty the path which human society has got to follow." Since it was not possible that this path should be acceptable to all the conflicting interests of society, some would inevitably be hostile to its establishment. At this point Adams retreated to the ironical safety of the elder statesman, who would not himself have to deal with such difficulties as might arise. His own generation could "take the same attitude that our fathers took toward the theories and hypotheses of Darwin." It was up to the younger professors to establish their fledgling science in the teeth of hostile interests, and Adams finished by commending to them consideration of the situation's "serious dangers and responsibilities."[9]

If Adams gave over in print the quest for a science of history, in private he had no such intention. Relapsing into the official silence he affected after the suicide of his wife in 1885, he devoted himself to assimilating the basic conclusions of nineteenth-century science. Somewhere, in some learned book or in one of the annual Smithsonian reports sent to him by his friend Samuel Langley, he would surely come across the grand generalization that would unify history. Years passed, years of incessant travel and loving cultivation of numerous friendships (for within his select coterie of friends, the aloof and impenetrable public mask fell away, revealing a warm and genuinely sensitive personality). In 1904 *Mont St. Michel and Chartres* appeared, and in 1907 *The Education of Henry Adams*, both in privately printed editions distributed to friends. And all the while, as he confessed in the latter book, "a historical formula that should satisfy the conditions of the stellar universe weighed heavily on his mind." Such a formula had to be essentially mechanical, for history was thought, and thought was a force precisely like other forces, and obeyed the same laws. "The motion of thought had the same value as the motion of a cannonball seen approaching the observer on a direct line through the air. One could watch its curve for five thousand years."[10]

By 1904, according to Adams's testimony in the *Education*, a "dynamic theory of history" was already taking shape in his mind. Based on the premise that reality was force, it viewed history as the continuous interaction between the forces of nature and the force that is man. Men commonly thought of themselves as exercising mastery over nature, when in fact the reverse was true: "The forces of nature capture man." These forces shaped the course of history into a succession of discontinuous phases, each phase dominated by a particular kind of force. In earliest times, the dominant force had been the occult, institutionalized in religion. Over thousands of years men had lived and worked under the primary stimulus of occult force. Then, sometime between 1400 and 1700, a momentous change had taken place with the development of Renaissance science, which ushered in a new mechanical phase of several hundred years. Adams, born into the phase of mechanism, had lived long enough to feel himself hustled into yet another epoch, the electrical, presided over by the brooding genius of the dynamo. What would come next, he hardly dared conceive; the present was distressing enough: "Power leaped from every atom, and enough of it to supply the stellar universe showed itself running to waste at every pore of matter. Man could no longer hold it off. Forces grasped his wrists and flung him about as though he had hold of a live wire or a runaway automobile."[11]

Energy was accelerating; observation told that much. But observation could not reveal the rate of acceleration, though a law specifying that rate was crucial to a scientific theory of history. For the essence of science was prediction, and prediction rose on wings of law. Adams had recourse to the "law of inverse squares" on the (not wholly serious) grounds that the visible acceleration of thought during the nineteenth century resembled the law of squares, which, furthermore, also governed the curve of the vaporization of water. "The resemblance is too close to be disregarded, for nature loves the logarithm, and perpetually recurs to her inverse square." And, furthermore, it was convenient! Squaring the 300 years of the mechanical phase gave the rather formidable total of 90,000 years to the religious phase. By the same token the electrical phase could only endure for about seventeen and one-half years, that is, the square root of 300; and the final, or ethereal phase (when thought would float increasingly removed from empirical reality), for four years, bringing thought "to the limit of its possibilities" in 1921. Adams could see two possible outcomes once the ethereal stage had been reached. One would be simply "the subsidence of the current into an ocean of potential thought, or mere consciousness," resulting in a stationary social state. The other would be the prolongation of thought as a "universal solvent," with man still continung "to set free the infinite forces of nature, and attain the control of cosmic forces on a cosmic scale." In this case the result would be anything but stationary—it might well be more like the change from caterpillar to butterfly, or from radium to electrons.[12]

Thus, pen in hand and tongue at least partially in cheek, Henry Adams lectured his brother historians on the meaning of physics for history. Nor was his lecture complete. Even as he awaited a requested critique of his paper from Professor Henry Bumstead, who happened by good luck to have been a student of Willard Gibbs, he was hard at work on his final legacy to the historical profession and to the world. Less cryptic and also less brilliant than the "Rule," less capriciously eclectic in its profusion of scientific lore, more doggedly directed to a single end, the "Letter to American Teachers of History" also revealed more of the Adams temperament and sensibility.

History and Thermodynamics

"A Letter to American Teachers of History" opens with a discussion of the Second Law of Thermodynamics as formulated by William Thomson, Lord Kelvin. Physicists had long been familiar with the First Law of Thermodynamics, which asserted that energy could neither be created nor destroyed but remained always a constant amount. This was the very well-known law of the conservation of energy. It had once stirred John Tyndall, probably the most famous English physicist of his time, to memorable rhapsodic heights:

> This law [wrote Tyndall] generalises the aphorism of Solomon, that there is nothing new under the sun, by teaching us to detect everywhere, under its infinite variety of appearances, the same primeval force. To nature, nothing can be added; from nature nothing can be taken away; the sum of her energies is constant. . . . Waves may change to ripples and ripples to waves,—

magnitude may be substituted for number, and number for magnitude,—asteroids may aggregate to suns, suns may resolve themselves into florae and faunae, and florae and faunae melt in air,—the flux of power is eternally the same. It rolls in music throughout the ages, and all terrestrial energy,—the manifestations of life as well as the display of phenomena, are but the modulations of its rhythm.[13]

But the First Law, while evidently inspirational, had begun to appear incomplete. Though none of the new physicists could match Tyndall for eloquence they felt compelled to add an all-important qualifier, the Second Law of Thermodynamics, to the First Law: if the quantity of energy remained constant, its availability for work, its potential usefulness, tended always to decrease. As Thomson succinctly wrote, "there is at present in the material world a universal tendency to the dissipation of mechanical energy."[14] Energy did not disappear; it simply changed into a form less useful to man. The best-known example of the dissipation of energy was the working of a steam engine, which could never reverse its operations, since that would require a colder body to give up heat (for work) to a warmer one.

Taken as a cosmic process, the Second Law offered a very dismal prospect indeed—that of the heat death of the universe, when "the solar radiations shall at length fall powerless upon the earth, and all nature shall be locked in the icy embrace of solid matter," as an American paleobotanist and sociologist described it.[15] The prognosis rested on the assumption that the universe was a closed system, since the Second Law was limited in its operation to closed systems; but that assumption once granted, few physicists would have denied the grim conclusion. If human history, like cosmic history, obeyed the Second Law, its future was all downhill.

Branching out from Kelvin and thermodynamics, Adams pursued the downward path in geology and paleobotany, paleozoology and anthropology, sociology and psychology. One of the most useful clues he found in the pursuit was the conception of reason as a degraded form of will. "Thought comes as the result of helplessness," the Frenchman Lalande had announced, and Adams seized on the suggestion. He bolstered it with a generous quotation from Henri Bergson, the French philosopher, on the suppression of intuition by intelligence. "Consciousness in man," Bergson wrote, "is chiefly intelligence. It might have been,—it seems as though it ought to have been,—intuition too. . . . In reality, in the humanity of which we make part, intuition is almost completely sacrificed to intelligence . . . ."[16] Thought, then, was "truncated Will"; its products, "the last traces of an instinct now wholly dead or dying," testified yet again to the universality of the Second Law.[17]

What are we to make of the Adams version of scientific history? It has been suggested that Adams's work was never intended to be taken seriously, least of all by the author himself, that his essays are an extended joke whose point is lost if taken seriously. Certainly there is a large element of playfulness and even raillery in the historical essays, but William Jordy has rightly pointed out that without some intelligible level of meaning, the joke of meaninglessness becomes feeble. Furthermore, Adams took history seriously—he could scarcely have written the nine volumes of the *History* (even if he later labeled it a failure) had he not been truly engaged by the historian's craft. His concern lest history become anachronistic in a world increasingly directed by science was genuine. Adams was bitter, assuredly—bitter at science for claiming so much and knowing so little of what really counted; bitter at historians for remaining complacent literary hacks in the face of the gigantic intellectual upheavals of his day. But it would have been curiously misdirected strategy to have aimed a dissertation on the meaninglessness of scientific history (which is the way some critics have interpreted these essays) precisely at the very group least likely to worship at the feet of science. For in respect to any fundamental laws of history analogous to the laws of science, Adams's brother historians remained overwhelmingly skeptical. Adams himself did not trust science, but he knew enough to realize that it was even then shaping the future of his world. If he carried scientific nonsense to extremes in his essays, it was only partly to give vent to his growing dissatisfaction with the metaphysical failures of science; this dissatisfaction he had already expressed in the *Education*, and even in *Mont St. Michel and Chartres*. Adams intended much more to point up, by exaggeration, the intellectual gap between the world of the scientist and the world of the historian, and to suggest that the latter had better get acquainted with the former.

Had Adams known that posterity would judge his writings to be utterly paradoxical he would have been delighted. Adams cherished paradoxes, to the point of branding as "failure" a life which by any ordinary criterion would have been judged brilliantly creative. If he failed in the world of affairs, it was perhaps in not achieving the presidency like his two distinguished forebears—which only a member of the Adams dynasty could consider failure. More seriously, he failed to make a new synthesis of science and humanism that would serve to reintegrate the scattered fragments of learning which passed, or so he believed, for education in his own day. But, again, this flaw in his achievement could only be reckoned as failure on some scale larger than life. Can it even be claimed that the rival strengths and wisdoms of the scientific and the humane disciplines have been reconciled to everyone's satisfaction in our time? That he saw as much as he did see of the future of science and of our need to adapt to it—and some of his prophecies, read today with the benefit of hindsight, are astonishingly suggestive—ought to be accounted credit enough. And so they are, in one sense. Yet here, again, paradox rears its head, for Adams was not wholly sincere in his cultivation of science. His expertise was always guided by a polemic purpose. It was well that Adams allowed his youthful flirtation with science to languish, for he did not have the disinterested eye of the professional scientist. He was never truly interested in science as an end in itself, or in research that issued only in tentative or partial conclusions.

The example of Darwinism will show how Adams sharpened his scholarship toward previously defined ends. We have seen Adams's growing skepticism about the validity of the Darwinian account of nature, but this skepticism was only partially created by the insufficiency of the geological record. What really aroused Adams's scorn was the incorrigible (as he saw it) optimism of Darwinian and Spencerian theories of evolution. His own researches in the years after 1890 uniformly suggested the pessimistic conclusion that man was rushing toward physical, mental, and social calamity. For years Adams had been assembling a file of newspaper clippings illustrative of human decay—"falling off of the birth rate;—decline of rural population;—lowering of army standards;—multiplication of suicides;—increase of insanity or idiocy;—of cancer;—of tuberculosis;—signs of nervous exhaustion;—of enfeebled vitality;—'habits' of alcoholism and drugs;—failure of eye sight in the young;—and so on, without end . . . ."[18]

His mind full of these intimations of impending social doom, Adams was greatly excited to have found in Kelvin and his Second Law scientific corroboration of decadence. "I'm sorry Lord Kelvin is dead," he lamented to his closest English friend, Charles Milnes

Gaskell. "I would travel about a thousand million miles to discuss with him the thermo-dynamics of socialistic society. His law is awful in its rigidity and intensity of result." Darwin versus Kelvin: such, in symbolic form, was the scientific argument about the future of the universe, and it was with something akin to relish that Adams pitted these two towering figures against each other. "The violent contradiction between Kelvin's Degradation and Darwin's Elevation was so profound,—so flagrant,—so vital to mankind, that the historian of human society must be supposed to have watched with agonized interest the direction which science should take . . . ." Let no one suppose that Adams in fact watched with agonized interest: he *knew* who had the right of things, and it was not Darwin. A letter more accurately reflects his feelings: "Kelvin was a great man," he wrote, "and I am sorry I did not know enough mathematics to follow him instead of Darwin who led us all wrong. Our early Victorian epoch was vastly *naif*!"[19]

If science was useful as confirmation of intuition, it was also useful, at another level, as symbol. The passage of history from Chartres to the twentieth century had been a passage from faith to reason, from unity to multiplicity, from intuition and art to science. Modern civilization, whether for good or ill (and Adams was not persuaded it was wholly for good), was irrevocably scientific. Science, then, could function as symbol of contemporary culture. The dynamo especially fascinated Adams, and came to embody for him the sheer power and magnitude of modern science. First confronted by the dynamo at the Chicago Exposition in 1893, Adams resumed his study of it at the Great Exposition in Paris in 1900. There he could "sit by the hour over the great dynamos, watching them run noiselessly and as smoothly as the planets, and asking them with infinite courtesy where in Hell they are going . . . ?" He came to look upon the machines as pure force, "ultimate energy," the twentieth-century counterpart of the Virgin, who had been in the twelfth century "the greatest force the Western world ever felt." As the one represented "unity, simplicity, morality," so the other represented "multiplicity, contradiction, police." From the Virgin to the dynamo—such had been the path of energy in the making of the modern world, such must be the account of the historian, for it was the historian's job "to follow the track of the energy; to find where it came from and where it went to; its complex source and shifting channels; its values, equivalents, conver-

South entrance to the Electricity Building at the World's Columbian Exposition, Chicago. Drawing by H. D. Nichols, from *Harper's Weekly*, 22 April 1893. (Courtesy of the San Francisco Public Library.)

sions." Even now, Adams mused, the huge wheels might be spinning man with ever greater velocity into a new phase of human history.[20]

Adams had always had an intuitive, and for the most part pessimistic, feeling for the transforming imprint of science on modern life. As early as 1862, when he was only 24 and the technological revolution was still in its infancy, he wrote in a prescient paragraph to his brother Charles, "I tell you these are great times. Man has mounted science, and is now run away with. I firmly believe that before many centuries more, science will be the master of man. The engines he will have invented will be beyond his strength to control. Some day science may have the existence of mankind in its power, and the human race commit suicide by blowing up the world." Some forty years later Adams had not revised his sense of impending disaster. To his brother Brooks he confided his sense of an approaching "ultimate, colossal, cosmic collapse; but not on any of our old lines. My belief is that we are like monkeys monkeying with a loaded shell; we don't in the least know or care where our practically infinite energies come from or will bring us to." On the basis of a similarly foreboding prophecy, which included the prediction that "explosives would reach cosmic violence," it has even been suggested that Adams first envisaged the atomic bomb.[21]

Science as support for instinct; science as symbol; and, eventually, science as metaphysics—the new metaphysics which should decide once and for all, with mathematical formulae and abstruse calculation, everything that the old philosophy had failed to resolve. Adams admitted whimsically to Brooks to "having always had a weakness for science mixed with metaphysics. I am a dilution of a mixture of Lord Kelvin and St. Thomas Aquinas." The preoccupation with ultimate questions, and the demand that science produce ultimate answers, resulted in a very unscientific impatience with anything less than certitude as well as in a disdain for modest facts as opposed to sweeping generalizations. The *Education* records that "the details of science meant nothing: he wanted to know its mass."[22]

Unfortunately, it turned out that the mass could not be taken for granted. When Adams turned to the science of the new twentieth century for authoritative responses to his queries about the nature of reality, he found no answer. In the days of Darwin, scientists had been confident of what they knew. They had "sailed gaily into the supersensual," certain that they would find there a reflection of the

Victorian—possibly even of the divine—harmony and order. But Adams now read Karl Pearson's *Grammar of Science* in which "suddenly . . . science raised its head and denied." No longer could men claim to read law in nature. The laws men read, according to Pearson, existed only within themselves—outside was chaos: "In the chaos behind sensations, in the 'beyond' of sense impressions, we cannot infer necessity, or order or routine, for these are concepts formed by the mind of man on this side of sense impressions."[23]

Pearson, however, was an Englishman, and Adams reflected that English thought had after all "always been chaos and multiplicity itself." So Adams pictures himself turning "with confident hope" to Germany, since "German thought had affected system, unity, and progress." He plunged into Ernst Haeckel, that stalwart of nineteenth-century materialism, and into the physicist Ernst Mach. The results did not reassure; even Haeckel seemed unsure of what matter really was, while Mach denied matter completely.[24]

In desperation, Adams continued his intellectual hegira to Paris, where "he felt safe. No Frenchman except Rabelais and Montaigne had ever taught anarchy other than as path to order. Chaos would be unity in Paris even if child of the guillotine." But it was not to be. Adams read the mathematician Henri Poincaré and discovered that truth or falsity were less important attributes of an idea than convenience. It made no sense to ask whether Euclidean geometry was true or false. One should rather ask whether it was useful. Mathematics was only a "particular system of symbols." Adams read no more; there was no longer room for doubt. It was quite clear that France could not give him the reassurance he professed to seek. Nor was there anywhere else to turn. Science had no answer for multiplicity.[25]

So runs the public account of Adams's disillusionment with science, as recorded in the *Education*. But the *Education* is notoriously opaque about the real Adams. It should be savored and appreciated, but not necessarily believed. It is extremely doubtful if Adams ever entrusted himself as wholeheartedly to the tutelage of science as he would have us imagine. It is at least equally doubtful whether his consternation at the metaphysical retreat of science was unfeigned. Adams rather enjoyed, while pretending to deplore, the growing uncertainty of post-mechanistic natural science. He could never quite forgive Darwin and Haeckel and the other Victorian savants their air of imparting certified truth to an ignorant world.

"Forty years ago," he recalled to his friend Gaskell—one can almost hear the note of sardonic glee—"our friends always explained things and had the cosmos down to a point, *teste* Darwin and Charles Lyell. Now they say that they don't believe there is any explanation, or that you can choose between half-a-dozen, all correct."[26]

Already by 1903 he had begun to assemble a collection of perplexed scientists—those who had lost the faith, who no longer believed, as the Darwinians had believed, in the simplicity of nature. Kelvin was one of Adams's prize specimens, for he admitted frankly "that neither he nor his antagonists know what they mean." It was a fatal admission. "Every generalisation that we settled forty years ago, is abandoned," declared Adams with that quixotic mixture of melancholy and satisfaction that characterized his attitude toward the discomfitures of modern science.[27] In a lighter vein, he made sport of the scientists' admission of ignorance about the nature of matter and motion:

> Dear Me!
> What can matter be?
> Dear me!
> What can motion be?
> Playing all alone
> By their little selves?
> First motion dances
> Then matter advances
> Then both prances
> All by their selves—
> Dear me![28]

Faith and Reason:
The Search for Balance

If science failed to reassure the inquirer after cosmic order; if there was, after all, no structure, no final meaning to the universe, why then did Adams invest such a remarkable amount of time and energy in constructing a scientific account of history? The motive forces within Henry Adams were various and complex, but the answer seems to be that Adams continued to believe in the need, and indeed, the duty, to "run order through chaos" to the best of his ability for so long as he lived, despite the "supersensual chaos" lurking without. To give up the quest for order, even when order might prove illusory, was cowardice. "As long as he could whisper, he would go on as he had begun, bluntly refusing to meet his creator with the admission that the creation had taught him nothing except that the square of the hypothenuse of a right-angled triangle might for convenience be taken as equal to something else. Every man with self-respect enough to become effective, if only as a machine, has had to account to himself for himself somehow, and to invent a formula of his own for the universe, if the standard formulas failed."[29]

In the Middle Ages men had been able to account for themselves by constructing the splendid Gothic spire of intuition and emotion that was religion. In those days unity had seemed self-evident, and art, quickened by an openness to the spirit, had flourished. Adams knew full well that for himself such a solution was no longer possible. His was a modern mind, and "the modern mind," as Jordy has written, "could not intuit truths." To commit oneself in the twentieth century to the assurances of religious intuition would be to escape into illusion. But Adams could not believe that the matter-of-factness of contemporary culture nourished men's spirits as it fed their minds. The fact is that Adams experienced an inner dialogue of unusual sharpness between the opposing principles of reason and intuition, science and art, rationality and aesthetics.

The Adams family had traditionally displayed a certain Puritan adherence to the rational, and a corresponding mistrust of the instinctual, in man. Noted for their powers of intellect, Adams men refrained from giving free rein to emotion. Henry Adams had been raised in this spirit of emotional asceticism, and he could not wholly shake off the ancestral ways. (His artist friend John LaFarge periodically admonished him, "Adams, you reason too much!" To which Adams could only reply that it was the fault of his having been born in Boston. "The mind resorts to reason for want of training, and Adams had never met a perfectly trained mind.") Still, nothing could entirely suppress a vein of deep emotionalism in Adams's makeup. If he remained aloof and reserved in public, or outside his circle of friends, he displayed a warm affection toward his bevy of real and acquired "nieces," was adored by children, with whom he could romp unaffectedly, and confessed to adoration of his dear friend Mrs. Cameron. At rare intervals he permitted this banked passion to erupt into his writings, as in the episode of his sister's tragic death from tetanus, recounted in the *Education*, or in his letter to Elizabeth Cameron recalling the golden years of the 1870s when his wife still lived: "Swallow, sister! sweet sister swallow! indeed and indeed, we really were happy then."[30]

As with his personal, so with his intellectual life—the rational, identified with science, came into conflict with the intuitive. Over the years Adams came to believe, or at least to profess, that intelligence in man really represented the degradation of instinct, and hence that thought was a mode of knowledge inferior to intuition. The intellectual arrogance of science irritated him enormously, since he believed it could encompass only a very narrow segment of human experience. Adams had first sounded this note of skepticism about the grander claims of science in his Class Day address at Harvard. There he declared that his studies had taught him that "though man has reduced the universe to a machine, there is something wanting still; that there are secrets of nature which have puzzled chemist and philosopher even in these days of science, and which still wait for a solution . . . ." It was the declaration of one seeking to make room in the tidy mechanistic universe of science for some irrational tag end of human experience. Great was Adams's pleasure whenever he came across the admission of a renowned natural scientist like Lord Kelvin that science could not after all put man any farther along the road to ultimate truth. Hardly less great was his satisfaction in finding many of his arguments already tailor-made for him by the neo-vitalists, of whom the most distinguished was probably the French philosopher Henri Bergson. Though Berson failed to "amuse" him because of his attempt to reconcile science and philosophy ("I like metaphysics and I like physics," Adams had remarked, "but I don't much care to reconcile them, though I enjoy making them fight"), he did corroborate Adams's own argument about "the superiority of Instinct over Intellect."[31]

When he felt most pugnacious, Adams even denied that science was wholly rational. For if scientists could entertain doubt about the foundations of their belief, if they were all "plainly forced back on faith in a unity unproved and an order they had themselves disproved," then science was scarcely very different from religion. In Adams's second novel, *Esther*, the scientific protagonist, Strong, says as much: "Mystery for mystery science beats religion hollow. I can't open my mouth in my lecture-room without repeating ten times as many unintelligible formulas as ever Hazard [the minister] is forced to do in his church." Later on in the story Strong waxes even more emphatic. "There is no science," he assures the heroine Esther, "which does not begin by requiring you to believe the incredible. . . . I tell you the solemn truth that the doctrine of the Trinity is not so difficult to accept for a working proposition as any one of the axioms of physics."[32]

With convictions such as these, one might have expected Adams to reject science altogether and become a pure instinctualist on the order of Nietzsche. It would have been a consistent position for one who alternately deprecated science as the embodiment of the degraded faculty of reason, and mocked it for its reliance on unproven and esoteric axioms. But consistency never ranked as high as paradox on Adams's personal list of virtues. By paradox, one could reveal science as at once rational and incredible. By paradox, one could deplore, even as one exhausted one's mental resources to promote, the intellectual hegemony of modern physics and biology.

What emerges from a study of Adams is a picture of a man harboring within himself a number of mutually contradictory traits. Both by personality and by training he was prey to perpetual vacillation between the principles of reason and unreason, science and art, rationality and aesthetics. On the one hand there were his rationalistic background and family heritage, the habits of a lifetime of scholarship, the intellectual stimulus of the modern, scientific *Weltanshauung,* all pointing him toward reason and its incarnation in science. On the other hand there was his aesthetic, acutely sensitive personality, appalled by the empty vistas of mechanistic science and utterly convinced that life must hold something more, pointing him toward intuition and its incarnation in art. Adams possessed, as he himself once said, a "balanced" mind, in which the two principles jostled one another in uneasy tension.

It is not surprising that a mind so constructed would feel particular affinity with a time when faith and reason had arrived at an accord. Adams discerned such a time in the Middle Ages, during the period of the Gothic Transition, and he lovingly enshrined it in the pages of *Mont St. Michel and Chartres.* Chartres Cathedral had been built during the Transition period in medieval art and architecture: "The Transition is the equilibrium between the love of God—which is faith—and the logic of God—which is reason. . . .

One may not be sure which pleases most, but one need not be harsh toward people who think that the moment of balance is exquisite. The last and highest moment is seen at Chartres, where, in 1200, the charm depends on the constant doubt whether emotion or science is uppermost."[33]

Adams saw no reason to believe that the triumphant integration of Chartres would be achieved again. Men had lost the capacity to wonder; the universe itself had changed. Faith and simplicity had bowed, definitively, before science and multiplicity. One need not approve the transformation. One must, however, acknowledge it and, if wise, come to terms with it. Stripped of illusions, men faced a future of explosive violence and anarchy. A lifetime of education led, then, to this: failure, and the acceptance of failure. The old education had failed; the old man had failed. Would the new man, capable of handling the upsurge of anarchic forces, appear in time? Adams did not know, nor did he venture an opinion. His task was completed with the analysis. The rest, as he says, was silence, for "silence, next to good temper, was the mark of sense."

NOTES

1. Henry Adams, *Democracy: An American Novel* (New York, 1880), pp. 78–79.
2. Ernest Samuels, *The Young Henry Adams* (Cambridge, Mass.: Harvard University Press, 1948), p. 150.
3. Henry Adams, *The Education of Henry Adams* (Boston and New York: Houghton Mifflin Co., 1927), p. 227.
4. Ibid., p. 399.
5. Ibid., p. 382.
6. Quoted in William H. Jordy, *Henry Adams: Scientific Historian* (New Haven: Yale University Press, 1952), p. 10. On Adams's early quest of scientific accuracy in history, see Jordy, pp. 6–22.
7. Worthington Chauncey Ford, ed., *A Cycle of Adams Letters*, 2 vols. (Boston: Houghton Mifflin Co., 1920) 2: 90.
8. "The Tendency of History," in Henry Adams, *The Degradation of the Democratic Dogma*, ed. Brooks Adams (New York: The Macmillan Co., 1919), p. 126.
9. "Tendency," in *Degradation*, pp. 129, 132, 133.
10. Adams, *Education*, pp. 376, 457.
11. Ibid., pp. 474, 494.

12. "The Rule of Phase Applied to History," in *Degradation*, pp. 308f.
13. Quoted in "A Letter to American Teachers of History," in Adams, *Degradation,* pp. 144–145.
14. Ibid., p. 141.
15. Lester Frank Ward, *Dynamic Sociology,* 1: 166–167.
16. "A Letter to American Teachers," in Adams, *Degradation*, pp. 203, 204–205.
17. Ibid., pp. 205f.
18. Ibid., pp. 186–187.
19. Worthington Chauncey Ford, ed., *Letters of Henry Adams*, 2 vols. (Boston and New York: Houghton Mifflin Co., 1930–1938), II: 518; "A Letter to American Teachers" in Adams, *Degradation*, pp. 162–163; Ford, *Letters*, 2: 519.
20. Quoted in Ernest Samuels, *Henry Adams, The Major Phase* (Cambridge, Mass.: Harvard University Press, 1964), p. 226; Adams, *Education*, p. 388; Harold Dean Cater, ed., *Henry Adams and His Friends* (Boston: Houghton, Mifflin Co., 1947), p. 558; Adams, *Education,* p. 389.
21. Ford, *Cycle*, I: 135; Cater, *Henry Adams,* pp. 529, 559.
22. Ford, *Letters*, 2: 392; Adams, *Education*, p. 377.
23. Adams, *Education,* p. 452, Pearson quote p. 451.
24. Ibid., p. 453.
25. Ibid., p. 454f.
26. Ford, *Letters*, 2: 407.
27. Ibid.
28. Quoted in Samuels, *Henry Adams, The Major Phase*, pp. 306–307.
29. Adams, *Education*, p. 472.
30. Ibid., p. 370; Ford, *Letters*, 2: 638.
31. Samuels, *Young Henry Adams,* p. 50; Ford, *Letters,* 2: 524.
32. Henry Adams, *Esther: A Novel* (New York, 1884), pp. 191, 199.
33. Henry Adams, *Mont St. Michel and Chartres* (Boston and New York: Houghton Mifflin Co., 1933), pp. 317–318.

Thorstein Veblen (1857–1929). Painting by Edwin Burrage Child, 1934. (Courtesy of the Yale University Art Gallery. Gift of the associates of Mr. Veblen.)

SIX

THORSTEIN VEBLEN: DARWINIAN, SCEPTIC, MORALIST

Y 1898 DARWINISM HAD largely ceased to be considered an alien cancer on the body of American intellectual life. It had been scrutinized, sifted for useful ideas and methods, and incorporated in one way or another into the general stock of most academic disciplines. To at least one close student of the matter, however, there was a flagrant exception: "Why is economics not an evolutionary science?" inquired Thorstein Veblen, with no little exasperation.[1]

By "evolutionary science" Veblen meant, as we shall see, one that fulfilled what he believed to be the methodological canons of post-Darwinian natural science. Economics had remained for a surprisingly long time impervious to the phrases and doctrines of Darwinism—in part, perhaps, because the field was still dominated by clerics, who would not welcome a theory both godless and purposeless. More fundamentally, as Richard Hofstadter has suggested, economics already possessed a set of categories—competition, free trade, the invisible hand—corresponding to the Darwinian ideas of natural selection and survival of the fittest that were the chief attractions of Darwinism for social theorists. Most economists in the Gilded Age were apologists for the established order, writes Hofstadter, and for their purposes Adam Smith had at least as much to offer as Darwin.[2]

It is certainly permissible to look at Darwinian doctrine as a kind of recapitulation of classical economics, not only because the parallels are persuasive, but also because Darwin found in the economist Thomas Malthus the clue that led him to formulate his theory of natural selection. But Darwin did diverge from the "invisible hand" thesis in one important respect—he stressed struggle and conflict. To orthodox economists, accustomed to preach the natural harmony of interest among all classes in society, such notions could only have been distasteful, for, as Marx realized in his enthusiastic response to the *Origin*, the idea of an inherent struggle for existence was potentially radical. Although in the end Darwinism was tamed to serve the existing order perfectly, economists may have been wise, from their point of view, to regard it with reserve at first.[3]

At the hands of Thorstein Veblen, the neglect of Darwinism by economists was rectified, and with a thoroughness that fully compensated for previous indifference. Veblen was a complete Darwinian, committed not alone to the doctrines, but also to the methods of Darwinism. At the University of Chicago, in the years 1898–1906, he worked out a devastating critique of orthodox economics, and then defied traditional academic boundaries altogether to elaborate a general theory of cultural and social evolution. Always aloof, Veblen attracted few followers in his lifetime. His classroom manner was forbidding, his domestic life, which included from time to time women who were not his wife, sufficiently irregular to keep him from winning a permanent academic position. His writing style, which could rise to moments of genuinely witty epigrammatic utterance, at times bogged down in ponderous, almost Teutonic, prose. For all these reasons Veblen's voice was heeded by few of his contemporaries. But gradually his brilliance and originality won Veblen a devoted following. By the 1930s he had become a vogue, and at the present time he is regarded as probably the most seminal mind in American economics.

Veblen's Darwinism: Theory and Method

I have said that Veblen was the complete Darwinian. Of all the figures considered in this book, Veblen most frequently made use of Darwinian terminology, of evolution as the key to understanding existing institutions, of process and cumulative sequence as the heritage of post-Darwinian science. It is immediately apparent to even the most casual reader that Veblen accepted the theory of evolution and its specific Darwinian explanation without question. Not all of the details were entirely clear in his mind—in *The Theory of the Leisure Class*, for example, he offers a hypothesis of selective variation among a few relatively durable ethnic types as the mechanism of social evolution. But he hastens to add: "This conception of contemporary human evolution is not indispensable to the discussion. The general conclusions reached by the use of these concepts of selective adaptation would remain substantially true if the earlier, Darwinian and Spencerian, terms and concepts were substituted."[4] The idea of adaptation, however it might occur, was crucial to Veblen's entire scheme of cultural evolution.

The concepts of Darwinism did not, however, exhaust the fruitfulness of that source for Veblen. He also championed what he took to be the methods of Darwinism. It was the economists' failure to make their discipline over into a contemporary post-Darwinian science that aroused Veblen's impatience in 1898. If we follow the step-by-step analysis Veblen adopted in laying bare the sins of his colleagues, we can better understand the nature of his discontent.

It has been alleged, Veblen begins, that the distinctive feature of modern science is its realism, that is, its dependence on facts. But the historical school of Austrian economists has been fully as insistent on data-gathering as any advanced science, and yet has come no closer to creating an evolutionary discipline. Factual rigor alone is not enough. Veblen here makes his first point: "Any evolutionary science . . . is a close-knit body of theory", not merely an assemblage of data worked up into a narrative account.[5]

But what sort of theory is required? A theory of process, certainly, and yet theories of economic process, even developmental theories, existed in the literature of classical economics, and yet did not suffice to render classical economics evolutionary. Veblen goes a step further in his analysis: pre-Darwinian sciences differ from post-Darwinian sciences in the fundamental philosophical preconceptions from which they rise. Here is the point Veblen wishes to make—that criteria have changed, or, as he puts it, "the analysis does not run back to the same ground, or appeal to the same standard of finality or adequacy, in the one case as in the other."[6]

If we now inquire how these standards differ, Veblen responds that modern science has adopted "the notion of a cumulative causation" involving a strict adherence to causal relationships. "The great deserts of the evolutionist leaders—if they have great deserts as leaders—lie, on the one hand, in their refusal to go back of the colorless sequence of phenomena and seek higher ground for their ultimate syntheses, and, on the other hand, in their having shown how this colorless impersonal sequence of cause and effect can be made use of for theory proper, by virtue of its cumulative character." Classical economists, on the contrary, go beyond the sequence of cause and effect to search out an underlying "spiritual" factor, a tendency to normality considered to be "natural law" in action. Veblen believed that Darwinian science had no place for imputed norms or tendencies of any sort; science was the study of cumulative causation, but it could never assume any particular direction in the processes under scrutiny. Above all—and here classical economics had sinned most grievously—a true science must never establish an a priori criterion like normality, and then label everything that failed to fit that preconceived category as a "disturbing factor."[7]

Veblen's case becomes a bit clearer when we see how he applied this analysis to the writings of Marx. Veblen admired much in Marxian economics—nor is this surprising considering the substantial similarities between his own work and Marx's—but he objected vigorously to the Hegelianism of Marx insofar as it contravened the Darwinian ban on teleology. Marx had taken over from Hegel the idea of history as a necessary progression toward a final goal—in Marx's analysis to be reached through the mechanism of a conscious class struggle. The interpretation of history as progress toward a defined goal, "the classless economic structure of the socialistic final term," violated Veblen's criterion of "colorless impersonal sequence." It referred facts back to a preconceived master scheme, and was therefore alien to Darwinism. Darwinism, Veblen affirmed, "is a scheme of blindly cumulative causation, in which there is no trend, no final term, no consummation. The sequence is controlled by nothing but the *vis a tergo* of brute causation, and is essentially mechanical. The neo-Hegelian (Marxian) scheme of development is drawn in the image of the struggling ambitious human spirit: that of Darwinian evolution is of the nature of a mechanical process."[8]

Once pruned of goals and trends, economics was to become a discipline based on cumulative causation, a "genetic account of the economic life process." By this Veblen meant that economics must become far more historical than it had been, more concerned with "the origin, growth, persistence, and variation of institutions, in so far as these institutions have to do with the economic aspect of life either as cause or as effect." Evolutionary economics would try to "know and explain the structure and functions of economic society in terms of how and why they have come to be what they are . . . "[9]

Genetic inquiry implied, in Veblen's mind, a fundamental broadening of the subject matter of economics to take account of human agency. For in the course of cultural evolution it was men who changed, primarily; and changes in material objects occurred only because of previous changes in men. "It is in the human material that the continuity of development is to be looked for; and it is here, therefore, that the motor forces of the process of economic development must be studied if they are to be studied in action at all. Economic action must be the subject-matter of the science if the science is to fall into line as an evolutionary science."[10]

The Pragmatic Case
Against a Hedonistic Psychology

Why had economists failed to make their discipline a science of human action? Principally because in their professional capacity they did not believe men could act! Veblen charged that the hedonistic psychology handed down from the English utilitarians had blocked the growth of an evolutionary economics by treating men as passive and inert. One of Veblen's more famous passages describes hedonistic man: "The hedonistic conception of man is that of a lightning calculator of pleasures and pains, who oscillates like a homogeneous globule of desire of happiness under the impulse of stimuli that shift him about the area, but leave him intact. He has neither antecedent nor consequent. He is an isolated, definitive human datum, in stable equilibrium except for the buffets of the impinging forces that displace him in one direction or another. Self-imposed in elemental space, he spins symmetrically about his own spiritual axis until the parallelogram of forces bears down upon him, whereupon he follows the line of the resultant. When the force of the impact is spent, he comes to rest, a self-contained globule of desire as before."[11]

Over against this hedonist psychology which put man at the mercy of the elements, Veblen placed the results of the "later psychology," by which he meant the work of Dewey and James. The new psychology demonstrated that man's essence is to do, not to be done to. Man is active, he has impulses that seek outlets. "He is not simply a bundle of desires that are to be saturated by being placed in the path of the forces of the environment, but rather a coherent structure of propensities and habits which seeks realisation and expression in an unfolding activity." Veblen noted with approval the pragmatic assertion that "knowledge is inchoate action inchoately directed to an end; that all knowledge is 'functional'; that it is of the nature of use. This, of course, is only a corollary under the main postulate of the latter-day psychologists, whose catchword is that the Idea is essentially active."[12] The new psychology was just what Veblen needed to build up a Darwinian account of social evolution on the basis of the interaction between men's habits and the institutional environment.

These then were the essential building blocks of Veblen's evolutionary economics: the idea of cumulative causation, expressed as the thesis that "each new situation is a variation of what has gone before it and embodies as causal factors all that has been effected by what went before";[13] the genetic mode of inquiry; and the new pragmatic social psychology. Despite Veblen's eagerness to turn economics toward more fruitful endeavors and despite his concern with scientific method, he did not work out a detailed methodology or, indeed, any methodology at all beyond vague exhortations to genetic inquiry. Elementary problems of method— what kinds of data to gather, how best to process and organize material, what rules of validation to follow—apparently did not concern him at all. More surprisingly, he failed to address the larger problems raised by his advocacy of a new economics: what specifically did he mean by a causal sequence, and how did he propose to certify the existence of any given cause-effect relationship? How does a causal account differ from a narrative account? What actually distinguishes science from other intellectual enterprises? Given the assumption (Veblen's own) that the "canons of validity" in any field of knowledge are an outgrowth of the contemporary "scheme of life" and change necessarily with changes in the general culture, why is it useful to rail against prevalent economic doctrine? For doctrine can change only with changes in the "consensus of habits of thought current in the community." Presumably Veblen meant to suggest some sort of cultural lag among economists. Perhaps, too, he would have argued that gadflies like himself could sting their fellows into realizing their backwardness. But these conjectures were not explored by Veblen himself.

If Veblen failed to develop an evolutionary methodology, he also failed to develop a comprehensive evolutionary theory to explain in detail how institutions evolve in the cultural environment and what sorts of interaction occur between economic activity and institutional structures. Veblen was something of an intellectual butterfly, and he often lacked the patience to elaborate his ideas into a coherent system. But he teemed with fragmentary insights, and these can be pieced together to suggest the outlines of a Veblenian scheme of cultural evolution—what might be called a "pre-theory" of culture change.

Social Evolution—
Process and Prospect

In the beginning, we must assume a Darwinian social universe, characterized by a struggle for existence and selective adaptation on the part of human character and human institutions. Veblen's use of the term "institution" is slippery, but he means roughly a particular way of thinking, "a habit of thought," so widespread throughout a culture that it has become part of the common intellectual equipment of the participants in that culture. Institutions may take on concrete form, as, for example, when the concept of private property is written into codes of law. They are the basic carriers of social change, mediating between the individual and the thrust of the environment, for it is by means of institutions that individuals strive to come to terms with the circumstances in which they find themselves. But the circumstances are constantly changing, and therefore the institutions—being responses to environmental stimuli—change too. A process of interaction ensues, in which changes in environment evoke changes in institutions, which in turn call forth new changes from the environment, "and so on," as Veblen says, "interminably."[14]

What of the human material that has created this institutional matrix? In the midst of change, it changes too, but only partially and reluctantly. Veblen believed that the essential components of human nature, what he referred to with deliberate vagueness as "instincts" or "proclivities," were stable over time. "The typical human endowment of instincts," he wrote, " . . . has . . . been transmitted intact from the beginning of humanity . . . ." Still, it was not possible for man to live in an environment of constant change and himself remain altogether unchanged. Veblen asserted that while the underlying nature of man, in the cave or in the city, was identifiably the same, its manner of expression—"the ways and means, material and immaterial, by which the native proclivities work out their ends"—did change, and change drastically. Cultural development involved three factors in mutual interaction: individual personalities, institutions, and the environment. The primal stream of human nature might flow on impervious to the tides of history, but the habits of life through which this stream was channeled were forever shifting.[15]

They did not shift quite fast enough, however. Veblen depicted men as perennially engaged in a race to keep abreast of their altered surroundings, and perennially failing to do so. The perfect "adjustment of inner relations to outer relations" that Spencer had defined as social equilibrium could never actually be attained, since the institutions through which men tried to come to terms with the present had themselves been handed down from the past.

> Institutions are products of the past process, are adapted to past circumstances, and are therefore never in full accord with the requirements of the present. In the nature of the case, this process of selective adaptation can never catch up with the progressively changing situation in which the community finds itself at any given time; for the environment, the situation, the exigencies of life which enforce the adaptation and exercise the selection, change from day to day; and each successive situation of the community in its turn tends to obsolescence as soon as it has been established.[16]

With this quotation we come to the heart of Veblen's famous concept of cultural lag, which is defined as the inevitable gap between the realities of the present situation and the past-dominated minds of the men who must meet them. The cleverest men, the most flexible men, can never entirely shake off the burden of history. They cannot quite square reality with heredity.

Veblen's theory, it will be seen at once, was inherently pessimistic about the likelihood of a good fit between institutions and environments. In his own words, "The law of natural selection, as applied to human institutions, gives the axiom: 'whatever is, is wrong.' "[17] Veblen saw no reason to imagine that human adaptation was improving, and some grounds for suspecting that it was growing worse. For "in so slowbreeding a species as man, and with changes in the conditions of life going forward at a visibly rapid pace, the chance of an adequate adaptation of hybrid human nature to new conditions seems doubtful at best. . . . As the matter stands, the race is required to meet changing conditions of life to which its relatively unchanging endowment of instincts is presumably not wholly adapted, and to meet these conditions by the use of technological ways and means widely different from those that were at the disposal of the race from the outset."[18]

Intelligence counted for something, no doubt, in the attempt to bring human habits and institutions up to date. But Veblen was not disposed to stress the creative force of intelligence. Civilizations, as he saw it, rose or fell not because they were endowed with more or less intelligence, but because they had the right instincts. At crucial junctures in history, civilizations had heretofore "chosen variously, and for the most part blindly, to live or not to live, according as their instinctive bias has driven them." But the right combination of good (i.e., community-enhancing) instincts and institutions flexible enough to be reshaped without social upheaval was not easily come by. Veblen concluded: "History records more frequent and more spectacular instances of the triumph of imbecile institutions over life and culture than of peoples who have by force of instinctive insight saved themselves alive out of a desperately precarious institutional situation, such, for instance, as now faces the peoples of Christendom."[19]

Veblen and Dewey:
Habits of Thought vs. Creative Intelligence

Veblen's skepticism about the future, which became even more marked in the years after World War I, sets him apart from John Dewey, Albion Small, William I. Thomas, and the other members of the so-called Chicago school, all of whom entertained a more sanguine view of man's ability to cope with his world. Although he artfully employed Spencerian categories to most un-Spencerian ends in his book on the leisure class, his view of the relationship between organism and environment was actually more Spencerian than Deweyan. Veblen described the human personality more behavioristically than did Dewey—as a "complex of habits of thought" reacting to environmental stimuli. "Habit" was one of the great concepts of the pragmatists as well, but the pragmatists never suggested, as Veblen nearly did, that habits overruled intelligence.

Dewey's phrase, "creative intelligence," his conviction that "mind, whatever else it may be, is at least an organ of service for the control of environment in relation to the ends of the life process,"[20] were notions foreign to Veblen. Veblen did not stress intelligence. "Under the Darwinian norm," he wrote, "it must be held that men's reasoning is largely controlled by other than logical, intellectual forces . . . ." One of his major objections to Marx's system was its assumption of a rational calculation of interest on the part of the workers, when in truth "the conclusion reached by public or class opinion is as much, or more, a matter of sentiment than of logical inference . . . ."[21] Nor did the Deweyan idea of controlling the environment for human ends find a place in Veblen's scheme, which interpreted social change rather as human response to "the pressure exerted by the environment." Most of the initiative, apparently, resided in the environment: "The evolution of society," Veblen asserted, "is substantially a process of mental adaptation on the part of individuals under the stress of circumstances which will no longer tolerate habits of thought formed under and conforming to a different set of circumstances in the past." And he added, "The readjustment of institutions and habitual views to an altered environment is made in response to pressure from without; it is of the nature of a response to stimulus."[22] The environment exercised "pressure" and "coercion" and "constraining forces" upon men's habits of thought, which only then, "tardily and reluctantly," abandoned their archaic forms. Veblen's mind, in sum, was less likely to create than to conform.

It would be foolish to claim that Veblen denied a role to human intelligence. He embedded it into the very definition of instinct, so that he could write, "all instinctive action is intelligent in some degree." He objected strongly to the idea that all knowledge was "pragmatic," that is, "designed to serve an expedient end for the knower," and insisted on the importance of disinterested inquiry, or idle curiosity, as the wellspring of science. Still, Veblen seems to have inherited something of the skeptical naturalism of his Yale mentor, William Graham Sumner. Man for Veblen was in great part a pawn of his environment, forever a step behind, forever forced to change by intolerable pressure from without.

Contrast this view with Dewey's confident affirmation of the instrumental role of mind in man's interaction with his environment. Ideas for Dewey are tools, transforming, creative tools that can initiate change as well as respond to it. Man has it within his power to make an "intelligent selection and determination of the environments in which we act." The universe is not fixed, and our efforts count for something in advancing the "moving unbalanced balance of things." Thus Dewey can conclude that the particular function of mind is, as Schneider paraphrases it, "to redirect activities by an anticipation of their consequences. Mind is simply nature feeling her way, groping in her own darkness by her own light. . . . In short, the career of the human mind has a significance for nature as well as for man."[23]

Darwinian theory had suggested to both Veblen and Dewey the provocative notion of man as an organism in transaction with his surroundings, neither a "spectator," in Dewey's vocabulary, nor a "homogeneous globule" oscillating under "the buffets of the impinging forces," in Veblen's. But Darwin had not made clear whether or to what extent the transaction proceeded on equal terms. Did the environment determine men's thoughts, or was it possible that thought could, to some degree, determine the environment? William James made his own preference clear in an essay of 1890 in which he argued that spontaneous variations occurred altogether independently of the process of natural selection, so that new ideas or mutant fancies that might arise from time to time were simply "flashes of genius in an individual head, of which the outer environment showed no sign."[24] Without recourse to such specifically Darwinian terminology, Dewey, too, ratified the constructive power of thought. It was perhaps the core of his philosophy. But Veblen remained skeptical to the last: man acted, but he acted tardily; man adjusted, but he adjusted himself, not his environment. The world did not lay itself open at Veblen's feet; whether for temperamental or intellectual reasons, he was never able to summon the vigorous optimism of his pragmatic colleagues.

157

Still, beneath all the differences of mood and perspective there was an underlying identity of method between Veblen and Dewey, and the method identified them as intellectual kin more surely than the mood divided them. Both Veblen and Dewey were firm advocates of genetic inquiry. Veblen's first book, *The Theory of the Leisure Class*, was subtitled *An Economic Study in the Evolution of Institutions*. In article after article Veblen sketched out evolutions and temporal developments, endeavoring to explicate the present by exposing its origins. The attempt made a great deal of sense, given his theory of social development as cumulative adaptation by men and institutions to the impact of environmental change. For each individual's "methods of life today are enforced upon him by his habits of life carried over from yesterday and by the circumstances left as the mechanical residue of the life of yesterday."[25] Clearly, residues and old habits carried over from the past can only be understood in the context of that past.

I say "clearly," and yet this group of social theorists came to the genetic method with a sense of liberation that suggests that history had not previously been greatly prized as an instrument of inquiry. Dewey asserted that the *Origin of Species* by "laying hands upon the sacred ark of absolute permanency, in treating the forms that had been regarded as types of fixity and perfection as originating and passing away,"[26] ushered in a revolutionary new mode of thinking. That mode was historical. Veblen insisted that the characteristic questions of modern science were: "What takes place next, and why? Given a situation wrought out by the forces under inquiry, what follows as the consequence of the situation so wrought out? or what follows upon the accession of a further element of force?"[27] It may be difficult for us today to recapture the genuine feeling of release from "formalism" and deductive abstraction that animated these assertions, but that is doubtless because of the extent to which they have entered into the makeup of our own thought. In their time, these assertions seemed genuinely fresh.[28]

The genetic, or historical, method was essentially simple—it proposed to elucidate what is by what has been. The careful tracing out of the course of an institution or belief or cultural complex was held to be the key to its present incarnation. Thus development became the central concept, and if the method foreswore (as, according to Dewey, it must) probing for "absolute origins and absolute finalities," nevertheless the diligent genetic analyst would re-trace the path of his quarry as far back as possible. He believed that history was continuous and that light could be thrown on the complexities of contemporary customs or institutions by examining them in their embryonic simplicity.

In an early article on ethical theory, John Dewey laid down the claim for the indispensability of what he called "evolutionary method." Dewey asserted that the experimental method in science itself partook of the genetic, because it examined "the exact conditions, and the only conditions, which are involved in [a phenomenon's] coming into being." In a similar way, history revealed the process of becoming in areas where experiment was impossible. The two methods were precisely analogous: "History is for the individual and for the unending process of the universe, what experiment is to the detached field of physics. . . . History offers to us the only available substitute for the isolation and for the cumulative recombination of experiment."[29]

Implicit in Dewey's advocacy of genetic method—and he elsewhere makes it explicit—is the notion that a thing can be understood only when it is seen as embedded in its environment and therefore wholly relative to a particular time and place. That kind of relativism is, of course, a basic element in the heritage of Darwinism, which focused attention on the intricate interplay between organisms and environments and regarded behavior as adaptive response to a given situation. It follows, according to Dewey, that the ethical theorist of genetic bent would view a moral idea as "essentially an attitude that arises in the individual in response to the practical situation in which he is involved. It is the estimate the individual puts upon that situation. It is a certain way of conceiving it or interpreting it with reference to the exigencies of action." Pinned in this fashion to a particular locus, moral ideas and customs and beliefs of all kinds could be judged and graded on performance. "The point of the genetic method," Dewey continued, "is then that it shows relationships, and thereby at once guarantees and defines meaning. We must take the history of any intuition or attitude of moral consciousness in both directions: both *ex parte ante* and *ex parte post*. We must consider it with reference to the antecedents which evoked it and with reference to its later career and fate. It arises in a certain context, and as a reaction to certain circumstances; it has a subsequent history which can be traced. . . . Now when we see how and why the belief came about, and also know what else came about because of it, we have a hold upon the worth of the belief which is entirely wanting when we set it up as an isolated intuition."[30]

The Leisure Class as Cultural Relic

At about the time that Dewey's analysis of the uses of history appeared, Veblen was demonstrating his own prowess with the genetic method in *The Theory of the Leisure Class*, published in 1898. Veblen offered, as a fundamental thesis, the proposition that the leisure class in contemporary Western civilization had originated in barbarism: "The evidence . . . indicates that the institution of a leisure class has emerged gradually during the transition from primitive savagery to barbarism; or more precisely, during the transition from a peaceable to a consistently warlike habit of life." Veblen first unveiled the leisure class in full bloom during the higher barbarian culture, and then worked his way back through middle and lower barbarism to primitive savagery, the earliest phase of cultural development and the only one without a leisure class. Two features were peculiar to this primitive phase of life— first, a relative lack of discrimination or invidious distinction between economic classes or occupations, and second, peaceful conduct, with relatively little resort to aggression. The dominant mentality of these primitive savages was "an unreflecting, unformulated sense of group solidarity" that militated against competition and self-seeking and expressed itself in "truthfulness, peaceableness, good-will, and a non-cumulative, non-invidious interest in men and things."[31]

Into this Eden the serpent intruded in the form of ownership, originally the ownership of women and later the ownership of goods. Why the institution of private property arose, Veblen does not make entirely clear, but once extant, it converts the struggle for existence "from a struggle of the group against a non-human environment to a struggle against a human environment." In other words, men stop vying with nature to vie among themselves. They struggle for possession of goods. In early barbarism, the competition takes the form of exploit, or the seizure of booty by aggression, and the successful man is the man who has accumulated the most "trophies of the chase or of the raid." Honor becomes equated with

Fifth Avenue Critics, Etching (10¹/₁₆″ × 12³/₈″) by John Sloan, 1905. (Collection of the Whitney Museum of American Art.)

force: "A honorific act is in the last analysis little if anything else than a recognized successful act of aggression; and where aggression means conflict with men and beasts, the activity which comes to be especially and primarily honourable is the assertion of the strong hand."[32]

Where worth attaches primarily to strong-arm tactics, other forms of acquisition are ipso facto less honorable. Productive employment or personal service in the employ of another are looked upon as ignoble pursuits so long as the predator remains a culture hero. At this point the stage is set for the appearance of a leisure class, since the necessary invidious distinction among occupations, with its concomitant hierarchy of status, has become fully developed. In the phase of high barbarism, as for example in Europe during the Middle Ages, the leisure class may be seen at its fullest development. Caste distinctions are very strong, the upper classes are exempt from productive work, and the lower classes are strictly barred from leisure-class occupations.[33]

According to Veblen's stage-theory of cultural development, mankind had long since emerged from barbarism into "the modern peaceable stage of pecuniary culture." The distinctively predatory habits of the leisure class had by no means disappeared, but they had been transmuted in the shift: "devastation," or the "predilection for physical damage that characterises the barbarian," had given way to "the less obtrusive pecuniary virtues; such as providence, prudence, and chicane." In both cases, however, the typical individual acted in a manner that was solely self-regarding. The ideal pecuniary man, like the ideal barbarian, displayed an "unscrupulous conversion of goods and persons to his own ends" together with "a callous disregard of the feelings and wishes of others and of the remoter effects of his actions . . . ."[34]

Having traced the evolution of the leisure class to modern times, Veblen proceeded to demonstrate its obsolescence. Predatory habits served the interests of the community so long as those interests were bound up with hostility to other communities, so long, that is, as groups had to struggle among themselves for the means of existence. But modern civilization had advanced beyond competition to cooperation. In the modern world the success of one community redounded to the benefit of all. Such a world demanded a different set of habits from ferocity and fraud. It required rather "honesty, diligence, peacefulness, goodwill, an absence of self-seeking, and an habitual recognition and apprehension of causal sequence." These were the traits that best served the collective interest of the modern industrial community. They were also traits markedly absent from the intellectual makeup of the leisure class, for that class was engrossed solely in "pecuniary employments," those having to do with ownership and acquisition and therefore furthering the predatory aptitudes. "Industrial employments," all those that dealt directly with production, by contrast tended to foster the virtues suitable to modern life in the minds of the men engaged in them, the members of the working class. The institution of a leisure class was therefore a cultural atavism, breeding archaic habits and antique dispositions: "The institution acts to lower the industrial efficiency of the community and retard the adaptation of human nature to the exigencies of modern life."[35]

The Engineers and the Price System

Veblen's distinction between industrial and pecuniary employments in *The Theory of the Leisure Class* was an early expression of perhaps the best-known of his dualisms—the dualism between industry and business, between productivity and profit, between the technicians and the captains of industry. Since Veblen believed that technology, "the state of the industrial arts," shaped culture in the most fundamental way, this cleavage described a basic, indeed *the* basic, aspect of modern industrial society. Veblen pointed out that the business entrepreneur in the twentieth century had ceased to exercise the active supervision that had formerly aligned him with industry rather than business.

> Half a century ago it was still possible to construe the average business manager in industry as an agent occupied with the superintendence of the mechanical processes involved in the production of goods or services. But in the later development the connection between the business manager and the mechanical processes, has on an average, grown more remote; so much so, that his superintendence of the plant or of the processes is frequently visible only to the scientific imagination. . . . His superintendence is a superintendence of the pecuniary affairs of the concern, rather than of the industrial plant; especially is this true in the higher development of the modern captain of industry.[36]

The businessman no longer concerned himself with production, but with profit. His activities, while lucrative, were by no means necessarily "serviceable to the community." Indeed, in response to the exigencies of the price system, businessmen customarily resorted to industrial sabotage, by way of artificial controls on production, in order to maintain high levels of profit. "The mechanical industry of the new order is inordinately productive. So the rate and volume of output have to be regulated with a view to what the traffic will bear—that is to say, what will yield the largest net return in terms of price to the business men who manage the country's industrial system."[37] Attendant upon this obsession with profit were a cluster of other character traits—conservatism, acquisitiveness, predation, disingenuousness, ferocity—typical of the captain of industry. In his guise as impartial and objective academician, Veblen may have dealt Social Darwinism the severest blow of all by revealing the business inefficiency of the entrepreneurs.[38] Other social critics had excoriated their greed, their ruthlessness, their inhumanity, but Veblen alone dared to attack the one facet of their reputation that had been considered unimpeachable—their indispensability. Were businessmen rational, far-sighted, efficient, venturesome? On the contrary, insisted Veblen, businessmen were anachronisms, relics of an earlier stage of civilization, saboteurs who retarded, rather than advanced, technological development. Success in the business world waited upon guile:

> The successful man under this state of things succeeds because he is by native gift or by training suited to this situation of petty intrigue and nugatory subtleties. To survive in the business sense of the word, he must prove himself a serviceable member of this gild of municipal diplomats who patiently wait on the chance of getting something for nothing; and he can enter this gild of waiters on the still-born pecuniary gain, only through such apprenticeship as will prove his fitness. To be acceptable he must be reliable, conciliatory, conservative, secretive, patient, and prehensile.[39]

If the captain of industry was the archetype of greed, the engineer in Veblen's scenario was the archetype of productivity. Little touched by pecuniary ambition, the engineers, technicians, and workmen who actually ran the factories came insensibly under the discipline of the machine process. The machine process inculcated habits of thinking in quantitively precise ways, in terms of measurable cause and effect and regularity of sequence. It eradicated anthropomorphisms and replaced them with the laws of material causation, ignoring the traditionally true, beautiful, and good. Finally, the discipline of the machine process strengthened the native instinct of workmanship, that hereditary bias toward economy, efficiency, craftsmanship, and serviceability that had been handed down from the days of savagery.

Veblen consistently refused to admit that these conclusions were in any way judgmental. His writings are full of disclaimers to that effect. The straight-faced, scholarly manner and the gravely academic prose that he adopted did give a certain plausibility to these disclaimers. Thus he could demonstrate the "wastefulness" of conspicuous consumption and yet insist that "waste" was merely a technical term referring to expenditure that "does not serve human life or human well-being on the whole." A moment's thought, however, suggests that "the serving of human life or human well-being on the whole" is for most people precisely the end of man as a social creature. Again, Veblen soberly reckons up the various types of "waste and obstruction," including outright sabotage, that he claims are essential to the working of the price system and then adds blandly: "There is, of course, no blame, and no sense of blame or shame attaching to all this everyday waste and confusion that goes to make up the workday total of businesslike management. All of it is a legitimate and necessary part of the established order of business enterprise, within the law and within the ethics of the trade."[40]

Few readers are likely to be taken in by these elaborate professions of neutrality. The cumulative impact of words like ferocity, waste, obstruction, predation and disingenuousness, on the one hand, as against workmanship, serviceability, cooperation, and peacefulness, on the other, is too massive to be denied. Veblen was above all a moralist, and though he could not be overly sanguine about the future of civilization, he offered both diagnosis and prescription.[41] Modern civilization was sick unto death, Veblen believed, suffering from the dominance of a business culture. Should that dominance not soon be overthrown, "the date may not be far distant when the interlocking processes of the industrial system shall have become so delicately balanced that even the ordinary modicum of sabotage involved in the conduct of business will bring the whole to a fatal collapse."[42]

Technology, Veblen insisted, was the common property of civilized peoples, not the preserve of the privileged few, and those trained to master it were instructed at community expense. Since the economic health of the community hinged on the smooth functioning of the industrial system, these production specialists were, in effect, "keepers of the community's material welfare," and the community—rather than the financiers—had a right to their allegiance. Veblen admitted that the engineers had hitherto remained content with the full dinner pail, and manifested no disposition to revolt. But he looked to them for leadership in the revolution—if there was to be a revolution: "Any question of a revolutionary overturn, in America or in any other of the advanced industrial countries, resolves itself in practical fact into a question of what the guild of technicians will do."[43]

The Values of Veblen

Nothing short of a complete overthrow of business hegemony would break the grip of the vested interests on society. On this point Veblen was emphatic, and he consistently derided lesser palliatives like middle-class reform. He viewed with a skeptical eye the motives of the "contingent of well-to-do irregulars." These ladies bountiful went out "to humanize the poor" by teaching them the elements of upper-class culture. Their solicitude resulted, Veblen observed dryly, in "a substitution of costlier or less efficient methods of accomplishing the same material results." Reform, in any case, was laughably ineffectual, consisting of "meritorious endeavors to save mankind by treating symptoms."[44]

For socialism Veblen felt a great deal more sympathy. The question has often been asked whether Veblen was a socialist. Assuredly he was, by his own definition of socialism as the belief "that the mechanical exigencies of the industrial system must decide what the social structure is to be." In practice this meant the abolition of the system of ownership, or private property. The machine process, as Veblen understood it, was weakening the hold of shibboleths about private property on those who came under its discipline. The matter-of-fact, materialistic habits of thought inculcated by the machine fostered "ineptitude for an uncritical acceptance of institutional truths." Among these institutional truths was numbered the sacredness of private property. Hence, "the machine industry, directly or indirectly, gives rise to socialism . . . ."[45]

Sympathy for the goals of socialism did not blind Veblen to its vagaries. Broad similarities exist between his own system of thought and that of Marx, yet he was an acute and unsparing critic of Marxian socialism. He castigated American socialists for wishful thinking and called their expectation of the imminent conversion of the proletariat "a faith prompted by their own hopes rather than by observed facts or by the logic of events." Personally, Veblen remained aloof from organized causes or creeds of any kind. The drift of his thought is clear enough, however, and if it was not toward the socialism of an organized political party, it certainly looked to an overthrow of the vested interests and a new industrial order based on the abolition of private property.

Students of Veblen have referred to some of his more utopian ideas collectively as a faith, or even a theology. The terminology is just. Ludicrous as it may seem, this dour, tough-minded Darwinian cherished a sentimental vision of the potentialities of humankind, once freed from imbecile institutions. Human nature, innately decent and good, had been overlaid, so Veblen believed, by a multitude of barbaric contrivances like ownership, patriarchy, the price system, and the nationalistic state. In a state of nature man was peaceful, cooperative, and industrious. He worked to secure the interests of the community at large, not his own selfish concerns, and he did not feel the destructive lust of ownership. So long as savage men lived in harmony with one another, as they had done until the advent of ownership and a regime of competition, they continued to be characterized by peaceableness and goodwill. Veblen expressed the same point of view in a more precise, though scientifically dubious, way in *The Instinct of Workmanship and the State of the Industrial Arts,* where he enumerated several instincts—above all the instinct of workmanship and the parental bent—that "conduce directly to the material well being of the race." These humane instincts became warped and repressed by the weight of alien institutions under a regime of pecuniary competition, but they did not altogether disappear, for Veblen was convinced that the instinctual inheritance of humanity was essentially fixed and unchanging.

Perhaps the most surprising formulation of Veblen's conviction of the basic decency of mankind is an essay entitled "Christian Morals and the Competitive System." Veblen regularly debunked the pretensions of the Christian church as a formal institution. A hilarious note appended to the chapter on "Manufactures and Salesmanship" in *Absentee Ownership* makes the case for the church as supersalesman, and "the Propaganda of the Faith" as "quite the largest, oldest, most magnificent, most unabashed, and most lucrative enterprise in sales-publicity in all Christendom." Likening the selling of religion to the selling of "the familiar soap-powders, yeast-cakes, lip-sticks, rubber tires, chewing-gum, and restoratives of lost manhood," which share with religious faith a basis in "unreasoning fear, aspiration, and credulity," Veblen goes on to point out that the church has never actually delivered the goods advertised—i.e., heaven and hell. (This is just as well, since hell-fire would not be welcomed by the ultimate consumers, and the Kingdom of Heaven ought not to be, "being presumably something of a dubiously gaudy affair, something in the nature of three-rings and a steam-calliope, perhaps.") Such complete failure to deliver the goods, while retaining the credulity of the consumers, stood for Veblen as a monument to the art of effective salesmanship.[46]

But Veblen did not extend his barbed wit to Christian morality. The Christian church might be decadent; Christian morality was not. To the contrary, so intimate was the relationship between that morality and western civilization that its suppression would occasion a cultural revolution of the first magnitude. Veblen located the core of the "Christian animus" in two principles—nonresistance (or humility or renunciation) and brotherly love (the impulse to mutual service). Of these, brotherly love was the more important, as well as the more deep-seated, trait. Veblen did not hesitate to trace it back to the peaceable savage culture of earliest times, back indeed to "the ancient human instinct of workmanship, which approves mutual aid and serviceability to the common good." Part of the original character endowment of human nature, brotherly love cropped out again and again in human history whenever "the pressure of conventionality [was] removed or relieved." Veblen inclined to believe that this trait was growing stronger, and he concluded with a prophecy that exhibits overtones of pious wish: "Except for a possible reversion to a cultural situation strongly characterized by ideals of emulation and status, the ancient racial bias embodied in the Christian principle of brotherhood should logically continue to gain ground at the expense of the pecuniary morals of competitive business."[47]

Mordant as his appraisal of contemporary society and its immediate prospects might be, then, Thorstein Veblen—in this, if in nothing else, at one with his Progressive contemporaries—nourished the vision of an essentially sound human nature, developed under savagery, manitained beneath an overlay of barbarisms, and ready to spring forth anew under the gentle ministrations of the machine. Events tested that faith, particularly the debacle of World War I and its uneasy settlement. Veblen grew increasingly shocked, outraged, alienated. His skepticism sharpened. Yet he never repudiated the logic of *The Theory of Business Enterprise,* which had shown how the machine discipline "cut away that ground of law and order on which business enterprise is founded," so that in the long run the price system was doomed. In 1921 Veblen analyzed the revolutionary potential of American society, ascertained that revolution could only come from the technicians and engineers, and concluded that the danger of an overturn was slight. But he was careful to qualify this conclusion with two words that, reiterated perhaps four or five times, took on an air of subdued menace: there was, he said, no danger to the vested interests "just yet." With luck, there might be.[48]

The teleology Veblen banished from economics reemerged full-blown in his cosmic anthropology. Veblen had censured Marx severely for viewing history as progress toward a final goal. He had avowed allegiance to a Darwinism in which "there is no trend, no final term, no consummation." A softer strain nevertheless belied the crusty, morally neutral Darwinian guise. His inner eye illumined rather more by faith than by science, Veblen contemplated the triumph of the machine and the victory of the golden rule.

NOTES

1. Thorstein Veblen, "Why Is Economics Not an Evolutionary Science" (hereafter cited as "Economics and Evolution"), in *The Place of Science in Modern Civilization and Other Essays* (New York: B.W. Huebsch, 1919), p. 56.
2. Richard Hofstadter, *Social Darwinism*, pp. 144–145.
3. Joseph Spengler comments on the "natural harmony" bias of classical economists in his essay "Evolutionism in American Economics, 1800–1946," in Stow Persons, ed., *Evolutionary Thought in America*, pp. 212–213.
4. Thorstein Veblen, *The Theory of the Leisure Class* (New York: Vanguard Press, 1928), pp. 217–218.
5. Veblen, "Economics and Evolution," in *Place of Science*, p. 58.
6. Ibid., p. 60.
7. Ibid., p. 61.
8. Veblen, "The Socialist Economics of Karl Marx and His Followers," in *Place of Science*, pp. 436–437.
9. Veblen, "Gustav Schmoller's Economics," in *Place of Science*, pp. 265, 267.
10. Veblen, "Economics and Evolution," in *Place of Science*, p. 72.
11. Ibid., pp. 73–74.
12. Ibid., p. 74; "The Place of Science in Modern Civilization," in *Place of Science*, p. 5.
13. Veblen, "The Limitations of Marginal Unity," in *Place of Science*, p. 242.
14. Veblen, *Theory of the Leisure Class*, p. 191.
15. Thorstein Veblen, *The Instinct of Workmanship and the State of the Industrial Arts* (New York: B. W. Huebsch, 1914), pp. 18, 19.
16. Veblen, *Theory of the Leisure Class*, p. 191.
17. Ibid., p. 207.
18. Veblen, *Instinct of Workmanship*, pp. 35–36.

19. Ibid., pp. 24–25. One can suggest, as I do at a later point, that the thrust of Veblen's argument about the benevolent effects of the machine discipline on men pointed to a future utopia of social solidarity and still recognize that, anxious perhaps to preserve his sardonic objectivity, Veblen professed strong skepticism about the future of man. For the argument that Veblen was a disguised utopian, see David W. Noble, "Dreiser and Veblen: The Literature of Cultural Change," *Social Research,* 24 (1957): 313–329. See also the chapter on Veblen in Daniel Aaron, *Men of Good Hope: A Story of American Progressives* (New York: Oxford University Press, 1961), especially pp. 214–216.

20. John Dewey, "Interpretation of Savage Mind," *Psychological Review*, 9 (1902): 219.

21. Veblen, "The Economics of Karl Marx," in *Place of Science*, p. 441.

22. Veblen, *Theory of the Leisure Class*, pp. 195, 197, 192–193.

23. Schneider, *A History of American Philosophy*, p. 556.

24. James, "Great Men and Their Environment," in *Will to Believe,* p. 253.

25. Veblen, "Economics and Evolution," in *Place of Science*, p. 75.

26. John Dewey, "The Influence of Darwin on Philosophy," in *The Influence of Darwin on Philosophy* (New York: H. Holt & Co., 1910), pp. 1–2.

27. Veblen, "The Preconceptions of Economic Science" in *Place of Science*, p. 84.

28. The revolt against deductive logic and other "formalisms" is analyzed in Morton White, *Social Thought in America: The Revolt Against Formalism* (Boston: Beacon Press, 1957).

29. John Dewey, "The Evolutionary Method as Applied to Morality," *Philosophical Review*, 9 (1902): 108–109, 113.

30. Ibid., pp. 364–365, 359.

31. Veblen, *Theory of the Leisure Class*, pp. 219, 224.

32. Ibid., p. 17.

33. Ibid., pp. 1–2.

34. Ibid., 240, 237.

35. Ibid., pp. 227, 244.

36. Veblen, "Industrial and Pecuniary Employments," in *Place of Science*, pp. 291–292.

37. Thorstein Veblen, *The Engineers and the Price System* (New York: B.W. Huebsch, 1921), p. 8.

38. This point is made by Daniel Aaron in his chapter on Veblen in *Men of Good Hope*.

39. Quoted in Daniel Aaron, *Men of Good Hope,* p. 224.

40. Veblen, *Theory of the Leisure Class*, p. 97; *Engineers and the Price System*, p. 109.

41. The strongly normative strain in Veblen's writings is emphasized by both Morton White and Daniel Aaron.

42. *Engineers and the Price System*, p. 57.

43. Ibid., p. 115.
44. *Theory of the Leisure Class*, pp. 344, 345.
45. *Theory of Business Enterprise*, pp. 352, 355.
46. Thorstein Veblen, *Absentee Ownership and Business Enterprise in Recent Times* (New York: B.W. Huebsch, 1923), pp. 319, 320, 322, 323.
47. Thorstein Veblen, *Essays in Our Changing Order*, ed. Leon Ardzrooni (New York: Viking Press, 1945), pp. 200ff., 217, 209, 218.
48. Veblen, *Theory of Business Enterprise*, p. 374; *Engineers and The Price System, passim*, esp. p. 169.

Chinese cannery hands aboard the ship *Balclutha*. (Courtesy of the San Francisco Maritime Museum.)

SEVEN

THREE
NATURALIST WRITERS

OVELS ARE THE CLASSIC first resource of intellectual historians, and with reason, for a novel can be a sensitive record of contemporary civilization. Creative writers, when they have acute antennae and a strong professional concern with the current climate of opinion, by clothing abstractions with life, can act as cultural middlemen in purveying to their readers the ideas that alter the configurations of intellectual life. Great writers, of course, are far more than middlemen; they are creators, not purveyors merely, of new ideas. But even hack writers absorb and transmit a particular milieu and its characteristic thought patterns.

It was inevitable that the new science of the later nineteenth century should find its way into fiction. The ideas that clustered under the rubric of Darwinism were arresting, novel, charged with dramatic potential. They were not remote and difficult to apprehend thematically, as, perhaps, were later revolutionary scientific developments like Einsteinian relativity, but directly and immediately relevant to the human condition. They were also potential weapons of revolt against prevailing literary standards.

Certainly the literary climate of opinion, as reported in the writings of contemporary critics like Frank Norris, Walt Whitman, and the philosopher Santayana, stagnated during the 1870s and 1880s. Fiction labored under the burden of the genteel tradition, with its curious bifurcation of the American mind into a practical, aggressive male mentality and a genteel, moral, feminine one. There existed two worlds: the world of affairs, peopled by men of enterprise little given to intellectualism or fussy moral scrupulousness, and the world of higher culture, presided over by ladies, for whom one must write, Frank Norris protested, in such a way as not to "call a blush to the cheek of the young." "On one side was religion; on the other, business. On one side was the divine in human beings; on the other, everything animal. On one side was art, on the other, life. On one side were women, clergymen, and university professors, all guardians of art and the ideal; on the other side were men in general immersed in their practical affairs."[1]

Such an artificial division could not endure indefinitely and had, in fact, already been breached by Walt Whitman. No doubt a revolt of some sort in the interests of realism would have occurred had there never been a Darwin, Spencer, or Tyndall: it is not clear that the realist trend to greater verisimilitude, commonplace details, ordinary rather than "dramatic" events, and characters of lower social class, owed anything to the new science. But it happened that the materials of Darwinism, together with other developments in biology and the emergent science of psychology, at the crucial moment offered themselves as tools with which to break the grip of the genteel tradition and to forge something more powerful and more complex.

Naturalism in American literature has been described as realism plus determinism, but it is difficult to define an entire movement in a phrase. Naturalism was a congeries of assumptions and attitudes, a stockpile of phrases and themes, rather than a unified movement. There were several levels of naturalism, ranging from the simple use of animal metaphors to the acceptance of a full-fledged philosophy of determinism. The influence of science made itself felt throughout—in the shift of focus away from the supernatural to the purely natural; in the use of clinical physical details, of scientific terminology, of themes straight from Darwin; in the deterministic philosophy based on the latest researches in neurological functioning.

Only at a time of enormous intellectual innovation could so many novels saturated with the same general themes have come into being. We find in the works of these writers the shock of discovery, the sense of some new and profound knowledge about ourselves that cries out for fictional form. The manner of expression varies from one writer to another, of course, as does the success with which they handle their new material. But a sympathy of interpretation is evident among them. From the twelve or fifteen novelists often termed naturalist, I have chosen three—Jack London, Frank Norris, and Theodore Dreiser—to illustrate some of the varieties and vagaries of American naturalism.

The Education of Jack London

If Jack London refused to create a literature of gentility, it was at least partly because he himself, unlike most previous novelists, was not genteel. Born poor and illegitimate, he early ran up against the Darwinian facts of life in a fantastic young manhood as oyster pirate, sailor, tramp, "work beast," and Klondiker. Having been, as he tells us, at the very bottom of the "social pit," he resolved to get an education so that he might support himself by brain rather than brawn.

Coming upon Herbert Spencer at the Oakland public library, London underwent a conversion experience that he later described in the semi-autobiographical novel *Martin Eden*: "He got into bed and opened 'First Principles.' Morning found him still reading. It was impossible for him to sleep. Nor did he write that day. He lay on the bed till his body grew tired, when he tried the hard floor, reading on his back, the book held in the air above him, or changing from side to side." In Spencer London found the clue to the universe: "There was no caprice, no chaos. All was law." Furthermore, all was unity: "What, in a way, most profoundly impressed Martin, was the correlation of knowledge—of all knowledge. All things were related to all other things from the farthermost star in the wastes of space to the myriads of atoms in the grain of sand under one's foot."[2]

With Spencer under his belt, London turned to the mastery of other writers in a veritable orgy of self-education. He emerged from his studies with a very solid grasp of the scientific literature of his time. He was so familiar with Darwin, for example, that he could quote whole passages of his work from memory. He retained a lifelong reverence for Spencer. In philosophy, however, he found

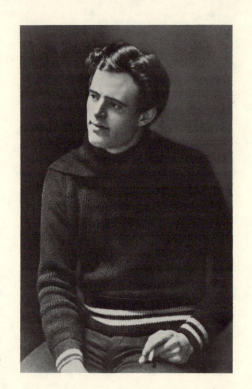

Jack London, 1876–1916.
(Courtesy of The Bettman
Archive, Inc.)

he had most in common with Ernst Haeckel, the German biologist who went beyond the skepticism and agnosticism of the English Darwinians to an uncompromising materialism. "I have always inclined toward Haeckel's position," he wrote to a friend. "In fact, 'incline' is too weak a word. I am a hopeless naturalist. I see the soul as nothing else than the sum of the activities of the organism plus personal habits, memories, experiences of the organism. *I believe that when I am dead, I am dead. I believe that with my death I am just as much obliterated as the last mosquito you or I smashed.*"[3]

London was the most insistently and directly Darwinian of the three naturalist writers under consideration. His was the universe of "Nature red in tooth and claw" carried over into fiction: "Kill or be killed, eat or be eaten, was the law," learns Buck, the dog hero of London's most popular book, *The Call of the Wild*.[4] Somewhere, perhaps, all things might work inevitably toward the good, but certainly not in the worlds London created. "I believe that life is a mess," says Wolf Larsen in a well-known passage in *The Sea Wolf*. "It is like yeast, a ferment, a thing that moves and may move for a minute, an hour, a year, or a hundred years, but that in the end will cease to move. The big eat the little that they may continue to move, the strong eat the weak that they may retain their strength. The lucky eat the most and move the longest, that is all."[5] It is because of passages like this that Maxwell Geismar writes that London's work was "the most complete and logical statement of the potential horrors of evolutionary thought."[6]

Nature and Man
in London's Fictional Universe

Since man's relation to these elemental laws could best be seen at the margins of existence, London often chose to set his stories in wild and alien terrain. He was especially fond of Alaskan scenes, having himself prospected for gold in Alaska. In the wilds, London felt, men discovered themselves as they really were, without the softnesses and artificialities of civilization: "In the young Northland, frosty and grim and menacing, men stripped off the sloth of the south and gave battle greatly. And they stripped off likewise much of the veneer of civilisation—all of its follies, most of its foibles, and perhaps a few of its virtues."[7] This rejection of the effeteness of civilization and city life as opposed to the rugged realism of the frontier is a persistent motif of several of the naturalists, reflecting perhaps the birth pains of the new urban and industrial America, and finding its counterpart in Frederick Jackson Turner's frontier thesis in American history. Turner argued that the uniqueness of American civilization was rooted in the presence of a western frontier during the formative years of the American nation. The interest in wilderness frontiers also reflects the prominent place accorded the environment in naturalist theory and practice, a prominence quite in keeping with its Darwinian roots. London once wrote, "I have always been impressed with the awful plasticity of life and I feel that I can never lay enough stress upon the marvellous power and influence of environment."[8]

So it is that the rude Northland in *A Daughter of the Snows* strips away the superficialities of civilization and separates out the weaklings and the heroes, just as the brutal environment of the schooner *Ghost* in *The Sea Wolf* engenders brutality among the crew and weeds out those, like Johnson, who cannot or will not become as elemental as their surroundings.

The power and influence of the environment could only work on what it was given, however, and London did not forget the other partner in the Darwinian process—heredity. London was, of course, an evolutionist, and therefore, he says, "a broad optimist, hence my love for the human (in the slime though he be) comes from knowing him as he is and seeing the divine possibilities ahead of him. . . ."[9] Nevertheless he preferred—and this was characteristic of one strain of naturalism—to dwell more on devolution than on evolution. Apparently the Darwinian discovery of man's close kinship with the beasts all but overwhelmed these writers, riveting their attention on the dark and unexplored mysteries beneath the surface skin of humanity. The fascination took several forms; in London's case, a preoccupation with atavism, or reversion of an individual to a more primitive type. The hero of *A Daughter of the Snows*, newly confronting the Alaskan frontier, undergoes such a reversion:

> He had not become hardened in the mould baked by his several forebears and into which he had been pressed by his mother's hands. Some atavism had been at work in the making of him, and he had reverted to that ancestor who sturdily uplifted. But so far this portion of his heritage had lain dormant. He had simply remained adjusted to a stable environment. There had been no call upon the adaptability which was his. But whensoever the call came, being so constituted, it was manifest that he should adapt, should adjust himself to the unwonted pressure of new conditions.[10]

Atavism, so beneficial in this situation, could also be a handicap in the struggle for existence, as it was for Wolf Larsen, the Sea Wolf, "the perfect type of the primitive man, born a thousand years or generations too late and an anachronism in this culminating century of civilization."[11] One has the feeling, however, that London felt more affection for his atavistic hero than for the civilization to which the Sea Wolf was so unsuited. London was convinced that violence came naturally to man, and that it was unduly repressed by the constraints of modern culture. "It must be great to give the brute the rein now and again," says Frona Welse in *A Daughter of the Snows*, "and healthy, too. Great for us who have wandered from the natural and softened to sickly ripeness."[12] Frank Norris was forever brooding over the beast within and its potentialities for evil, but London regarded his atavistic creations with admiration and nostalgia. They were the authentic ones, civilized men the deviants.

The Cult of Racial Supremacy

One of the less pleasant strains of London's Darwinism, one that he shared with Frank Norris, was a blunt racism. London felt rather obsessively proud of his own Anglo-Saxon origins and consequent "blond-beastliness." This may well have been a result of his actual uncertainty about his paternity, but whether compensatory or not, the belief was firm. "I do not believe in the universal brotherhood of man," he wrote to his good friend Cloudesley Johns. "I believe my race is the salt of the earth."[13] Nature had ordained that the race with the highest altruism would endure, and that signified the Anglo-Saxon race. But an early paean to the Anglo-Saxons suggests that he was less impressed with their altruism than with their aggressiveness and manly strength.

> We are a race of doers and fighters, of globe-encirclers and zone conquerors. . . . Will the Indian, the Negro, or the Mongol ever conquer the Teuton? Surely not! . . . All that the other races are not, the Anglo-Saxon, or Teuton if you please, is. All that the other races have not, the Teuton has. What race is to rise up and overwhelm us?[14]

London can hardly be censured very severely for acceding to a racial mythology so prevalent in his time, but it does sound a particularly anachronistic note to the modern ear. It serves, too, to remind us how closely woven was the mingling of truth with falsehood in the first flush of Darwinism, so that a writer like London can put forth what seem now like simple truisms (the importance of environment to character, the kinship of men and animals) side by side with the arrant nonsense of racialism.

A persistent and basic theme of naturalist writing was the notion of determinism. It furnished, indeed, the philosophical underpinning, so far as one could be said to exist, of the naturalist enterprise. Since the question of determinism versus free will raises serious problems not only of philosophy but of the novelist's art, it is central to any discussion of naturalism. London, we know, was a strict philosophical determinist, convinced that science had disproved freedom of the will. One of his letters records his belief that "man is not a free agent, and free will is a fallacy exploded by science long ago . . . . Whatever we do, we do because it is easier to than not to. No man ever lived who didn't do the easiest thing (for him)."[15] Hemmed in by the twin forces of environment and heredity, men moved on their appointed paths, children of nature and fate.

It is one thing to believe in such a philosophy. It is another and exceedingly difficult thing to construct a satisfying novel in which choice and vision are by definition ruled out. With a stroke of genius London hit on the device of using a dog as the hero of *The Call of the Wild*. Buck, by virtue of being nonhuman, can engage our sympathies while at the same time standing outside the domain of responsibility and free decision. For this reason *The Call of the Wild* has been termed a perfect parable of naturalism: the action is completely determined by material forces, yet it commands assent.

When London tried to fit human characters into a deterministic universe, the problems were magnified, not alone because of the difficulty of constructing a plausible plot, but because London's emotional predispositions warred with his determinism. All his life London held to a mystique of power, a cult of the superman, which became explicitly Nietzschean after London discovered that writer around 1905. All men, London thought, were moved by a will to power, but supermen more strongly than other men. Supermen, the "blond-beastly" Aryans among whom London enrolled himself, were natural leaders, not bound by the laws of the lower orders. "Conventions are worthless for such as we," Jacob Welse declares. "They are for the swine who without them would wallow deeper. The weak must obey or be crushed, not so with the strong."[16] London's strongest figures are all motivated by this intense Nietzschean will to power. Such perfervid individualism, however, hardly sits well with a philosophy of determinism. (It sits even less well with a politics of socialism, which London also espoused. London my have been the only Nietzschean socialist of our time; the tension between his individualism and his socialism ultimately flaws his most ambitious novel, *Martin Eden*.)

The Dilemma of Determinism

Theoretically, it is possible that the actions of an individual possessed of tremendous internal drive may be determined by forces beyond his control—possible, but not especially plausible. Readers of *The Sea Wolf* in fact do not see the superman hero Wolf Larsen as a puppet of fate, and this despite Larsen's own repeated assertions about the meaninglessness of life. What they see is a man, or superman, bending others to the whims of his own imperious will. The impression is indisputably one of man *choosing* his course of action, brutal and unlovely though that course may be. If Larsen is really acting in helpless conformity to exterior forces, London has failed to persuade us of that fact. A determinism that does not direct the course of the plot in any demonstrable way stands in danger of being forgotten.

A final item in London's naturalist credo, an immediate corollary of the doctrine of human helplessness, is a denial of man's responsibility for his behavior. "We are what we are," pronounced London," and we cannot help ourselves. No man is to be blamed, and no man praised."[17] But, again, it was easier for London to make the pronouncement than to honor it. The heroine in *A Daughter of the Snows* soundly castigates the villain, St. Vincent, for his cowardice. It is a judgment London's readers are clearly meant to share. And Martin Eden draws up a rather convincing indictment of the hypocrisy and shallowness of some members of the bourgeois gentility. London, in fact, never made a serious attempt to approach the compassionately objective reportage of a Theodore Dreiser; in all his works the heroes and villains come clearly labeled. In theory, London should have been willing to people his stories with heroes of any morality, or none. In practice, his heroes and heroines conformed pretty closely to the mores of early twentieth-century America. Only with Buck in *The Call of the Wild* did London feel free to portray an amoral hero, and Buck, of course, was scarcely liable to the imperatives of human ethical codes. Forcefully transplanted from his home in California to the "hostile Northland environment," Buck learns at once that morality is

> a vain thing and a handicap in the ruthless struggle for existence. It was all well enough in the Southland, under the law of love and fellowship, to respect private property and personal feelings, but in the Northland, under the law of club and fang, whoso took such things into account was a fool, and in so far as he observed them he would fail to prosper.[18]

Note that even here, however, Buck only turns to an amoral code to avoid being killed in his new environment. In his young doghood in California he had always been a perfect gentleman. One can scarcely avoid concluding that London's vaunted rebellion against the prevailing social ethos of his times was, like the trust-busting of his contemporary Theodore Roosevelt, more a matter of rhetoric than of performance.

Frank Norris:
The Naturalist as Romantic

Though they shared a common attachment to the area around San Francisco Bay, it is hard to imagine two authors more separated from one another by birth and upbringing than Jack London and Frank Norris. Later on, they were to discover in each other qualities of conviction and style that were the basis for mutual admiration, but the one had arrived at these convictions while growing up in poverty, the other out of the security of wealth.

Norris, born in Chicago to parents of wealth, spent four years at Berkeley and another year at Harvard (though he never received a degree), and also studied painting in Paris. His initiation into the rites of the new science does not appear to have been the intellectual crisis it was for both London and Dreiser, perhaps because these two, as self-educated men, had to make the passage alone, while Norris passed under the guidance of Joseph Le Conte at Berkeley. Le Conte, a widely known geologist and zoologist, had effected one of the most celebrated reconciliations of evolution and religion, on the basis of a rather drastic division between the lower, bestial nature of man and his higher, spiritual nature. Norris was later to be overridingly concerned with this dual nature of man and his potential reversion to bestiality.

It has been said that Theodore Dreiser's naturalism came to him from life itself.[19] Jack London, too, wrote his life story into his works. But Norris, unschooled in the grim culture of poverty, had to learn his naturalism from books, and somehow it never sounded quite as real. In fact, Norris's naturalism was peculiarly his own, and incorporated many elements traditionally associated with romanticism—high drama, extraordinary events, and the violent play of emotion. Romanticism, Norris believed, searched out, as realism did not, the inner nature of things, "the unplumbed depths of the human heart, and the mystery of sex, and the problems of life, and the black, unsearched penetralia of the soul of man." Norris insisted that naturalistic novels, as opposed to novels of realism, must involve characters in situations of awe and terror far removed from ordinary life. Unlike London or Dreiser, Norris was a student of literary theory and acknowledged a literary master, the great French naturalist Émile Zola. His debt to Zola extended not only to general themes and concepts but to particular episodes and apparently even, in some cases, to details. Yet he was by no means a slavish imitator of Zola, and does not seem to have taken very seriously either Zola's aspiration to construct "experimental" novels, that is, novels in which life could be dissected with the clinical rigor of a scientific experiment, or his explicit and elaborate philosophy of determinism.

For all that, Norris's novels exhibit certain phases of naturalism very well. Norris gives no evidence of having had any serious interest in scientific ideas as such. The avidity with which he absorbed Le Conte's lectures on evolution, for example, seems to have derived less from an intellectual appreciation of Darwinism than from satisfaction with the way in which Le Conte explained as elements of man's lower nature the sensual urges that the youthful Norris was experiencing with some dismay. Certainly, like so many of his fellow students who created flourishing "Evolution Clubs" during his years at Berkeley, Norris was caught up in the general mania for the idea of evolution. Evolution appealed to him not scientifically but romantically, as an epic affair both great and awe-inspiring. To one irresistibly attracted by bigness, a universal process like evolution—whether or not he understood the scientific theory behind it—could serve as a symbol of titanic natural force. Hence, we find Norris invoking the evolutionary process, in the shape of the cycle of growth of the California wheat crop, to control the structure of his most ambitious novel, *The Octopus*. (Actually, *The Octopus* was the first of a proposed trilogy on the growth, distribution, and consumption of wheat; the second volume was *The Pit*; the final volume was never written.) Preoccupation with evolutionary ideas in one form or another was of course scarcely remarkable for a novelist in those evolution-saturated days, but putting evolution at the very core of the novel's structure was less common.

Man the Civilized Beast

In Norris's earlier works the dominant scientific and naturalistic motif is that of the beast within. Doubtless a psychiatrist could detect all sorts of personal reasons for Norris's intense, indeed very nearly obsessive, concern with human bestiality (*Vandover and the Brute*, the story of a man's decline through debauchery, has been adjudged by competent authorities to be partially autobiographical.) At the same time, it must be said that Norris was here recording a more than private reaction, shared by all those who interpreted Darwin to mean that the animal ancestry of man left him a brute under the skin, a brute who at any moment of weakness might explode. Jack London's treatment of atavism was one version of this theme, Norris's treatment of degeneracy another.

Vandover and the Brute[20] provides the fullest airing of the bestial motif. It tells of a young man of wealth and breeding who falls into habits of drunkenness and sexual immorality and degenerates into a mental and physical wreck. The accompaniment and symbol of Vandover's decline is a mental illness called lycanthropy, in which the victim imagines himself a wolf and prowls about on all fours—doubtless the most graphic presentation of this particular Darwinian strand. Repeatedly during the novel's progression we are made aware of the hidden presence within poor Vandover of a lower self, growing in strength as it feeds upon "all that was highest and best in him," until eventually it assumes complete mastery. The telling is vivid and convincing. But a little reflection provokes a basic question. Whence comes Vandover's dreadful affliction? Classic naturalist theory would insist that Vandover's fate is fixed by his heredity, or by the circumstances of life. There are indeed suggestions to this effect. The lycanthropy itself is apparently intended to be a manifestation of syphilis, and insofar as Vandover's mental illness is responsible for his subsequent fall from grace he certainly cannot help himself. But Norris makes it perfectly clear that Vandover has indeed "fallen from grace": no pressure of heredity or environment determined his initial lapses from straight living, but rather a weak will. Norris makes a point of emphasizing how easygoing Vandover is, how quickly adaptable to any situation, how lacking in strength of character. Vandover, in short, is responsible for his own fate. Once unleashed, his lower nature gradually takes over to the point where Vandover can no longer resist. But his tragedy is not inevitable. He need not have succumbed.

The presence of concepts of sin and responsibility and contingency obviously make a fatal breach in the ethic of determinism. Norris was not a consistent determinist. The dramatic force of the story is blurred by the confusion between an ethic of free will and responsibility and a philosophy of impersonal determinism. Free will is suggested by the unmistakable note of auctorial condemnation: "It was the punishment that he had brought upon himself, some fearful nervous disease, the result of his long indulgence in vice". At other times, Norris clearly implies that Vandover is fated to be destroyed whatever he might do: "Even that vast mysterious power, to which he had cried *could* not help him now, . . . could not stay the inexorable law of nature, could not reverse that terrible engine with its myriad spinning wheels that was riding him down relentlessly, grinding him into the dust."[21] Vandover's destruction, just insofar as it seems plausible, bears witness to the terrible temptations besetting young men with more money than morals in the big city. It does not bear witness to "that terrible engine with its myriad spinning wheels," the godly machine of the author's intrusive reflections.

McTeague, more consistently determinist (though both stories were written at about the same time), develops the theme of man's subsurface beastliness in a rather different and in some ways more plausible fashion. McTeague, a huge and stupid dentist with an office on Polk Street in San Francisco, marries a pretty young woman by the name of Trina, and the two, suffering various reverses of fortune, sink gradually into depravity—he through drunkenness and physical cruelty, she through miserliness and greed. At last, enraged by her avarice, he murders her and escapes to the desert. The book ends with McTeague handcuffed to the dead body of his enemy Marcus Shouler, alone and without water in the heart of Death Valley.

In *McTeague*, Norris hews far more to the line of determinism, and here the determinism is far more explicit than that of *Vandover and the Brute*. Chance reigns, Norris asserts, and not choice. The fatal marriage of McTeague and Trina was not of their making: "From the first they had not sought each other. Chance had brought them face to face, and mysterious instincts as ungovernable as the winds of heaven were at work knitting their lives together."[22] Men are not responsible for the impulses generated by the inner beast, since they cannot control them. McTeague first becomes conscious of his animality when he feels an overpowering urge to kiss Trina, whom he does not yet know, as she lies anaesthetized in the dental chair before him. "Suddenly the animal in the man stirred and woke; the evil instincts that in him were so close to the surface leaped to life, shouting and clamoring." McTeague does not fully understand what is going on within him, but we are made to know at once that he is not at fault: "What was this perverse, vicious thing that lived within him, knitted to his flesh? Below the fine fabric of all that was good in him ran the foul stream of hereditary evil, like a sewer. The vices and sins of his father and of his father's father, to the third and fourth and five hundredth generation, tainted him. Why should it be? He did not desire it. Was he to blame?"[23]

Norris's horrified comment on this breach of etiquette suggests—and other evidence supports the suggestion—that Norris had not altogether emancipated himself from the genteel tradition. But granting for a moment that impulsive physical desire is evil, we can see that McTeague's sensual urges are the product of an unfortunate inheritance and that they are brought into play by a chance conjunction of circumstances. The universe Norris has created in *McTeague* is logically and ethically of a piece. The characters are dominated by the combined forces of heredity and environment, and until the final episode of McTeague's pursuit by Marcus Shouler in the desert, where, in effect, all the evildoers are punished for their sins, there are no lapses into moralism. For this reason *McTeague* is, except for its conclusion, a more credible piece of work than *Vandover*.

At the same time there is a danger in *McTeague* that the reader will keep himself at an emotional distance from the denizens of Polk Street, seemingly so lacking in resources of wisdom and inner strength. The use of characters from the lower levels of society was an explicit element in the naturalist canon, for, as Donald Pizer has written, naturalism embodied the belief "that even the least significant human being can feel and strive powerfully and can suffer the extraordinary consequences of his emotions." Surely this is a legitimate point of view. Indeed, McTeague does represent, in part, the theme of man "trapped in the universal net of sex," unable to shake off the burden of his animal past.[24] But Norris barely resists the temptation to patronize his characters; one senses a thinly veiled amusement at their pretensions to the good life that works against the reader's sympathy and compassion. A fully persuasive presentation of Norris's philosophy would seem to require characters with whom we share more fellow feeling so that we could participate vicariously in the working out of inscrutable Fate. Dreiser created many characters of this type. Norris, in *McTeague*, did not.

The Octopus: Economic
Determinism and Evolutionary Optimism

In *The Octopus*, however, Norris did create sympathetic characters. In place of the decline and fall of individuals, Norris was here after bigger game—the collapse of an entire social group. *The Octopus* tells of the great struggle between a number of wheat ranchers in the San Joaquin Valley of California and their enemy, the Pacific and Southwestern Railroad, the "octopus" of the title. Ultimately the ranchers are crushed: six of them die in a battle with a Federal posse, and the rest are financially ruined. Lesser figures, too, suffer in the holocaust, until only the poet Presley, and the mystical shepherd Vanamee, are left unscathed. The railroad's triumph is complete.

The Octopus is naturalistic in its emphasis on the economic forces which shape the lives of all those within its pages, naturalistic, too, in its cosmic philosophy. Norris shared that delight in throwing up to man his own insignificance that characterized one strain of naturalist thought.

> Men were nothings, mere animalculae, mere ephemerides that fluttered and fell and were forgotten between dawn and dusk. . . . Men were naught, death was naught, life was naught; FORCE only existed—FORCE that brought men into the world, FORCE that crowded them out of it to make way for the succeeding generation, FORCE that made the wheat grow, FORCE that garnered it from the soil to give place to the succeeding crop.[25]

Perhaps, but the animalculae and ephemerides are likely to go on thinking that they have a hand in the sowing and the reaping and that they count for something after all. Norris, who sought to chronicle the great cosmic force, found himself dealing with the same hopes, despairs, fears, joys, and human tragedies that fill the works of less cosmically conscious authors. Indeed, Norris's superb repertorial skill, his ability to convey the appearance, the texture, the very smell of reality, work powerfully to make the reader forget that the epic tragedy of *The Octopus* is only an incident in "these heated tiny squabbles, this feverish, small bustle of mankind, this minute swarming of the human insect . . . "[26] In the opinion of one critic, Norris failed to achieve a convincing synthesis of philosophy and art. He tried to integrate the free will and moral sense we experience as actors with the determinism of naturalist theory, but the two refused to mesh. *The Octopus*, according to this view, does not convey man's helplessness in the toils of fate; rather, it projects "a Homeric conflict between free agents and a fatal but malign institution."[27] It is not that the forces which Norris depicts—the wheat, the railroad—are inherently uncontrollable; it is only that Norris has not created figures of sufficient stature to control them.[28]

Another apparent paradox that has long puzzled students of *The Octopus* is the contradiction between the tragic burden of the story and the final casting of accounts. In the concluding paragraphs, after we have watched the ranchers killed or ruined in the San Joaquin Valley and then witnessed the death by starvation of the widow of a ranchhand in San Francisco, we are asked to accept a "larger" view:

> Falseness dies, injustice and oppression in the end of everything fade and vanish away. Greed, cruelty, selfishness, and inhumanity are short-lived; the individual suffers, but the race goes on . . . . The large view always and through all shams, all wickedness, discovers the Truth that will, in the end, prevail, and all things surely, inevitably, resistlessly work together for good.[29]

Such a cheerful teleology jars with the mood of the story and is an aesthetic flaw, but it is not inconsistent with the theme. For the entire story is meant to illustrate the proposition—and a good Darwinian proposition it is—that the individual and his sufferings are unimportant in comparison with the cosmic forces of nature which work always for the larger good. The trouble with *The Octopus* an an illustration of this point of view is that it never makes credible the reality of an ultimate good, while it does overwhelmingly demonstrate the reality of proximate evil.

How do we know that "Truth will, in the end, prevail"? We don't. Such an assertion is a confession of faith, and, indeed, Warren French has shown that underlying all of Norris's work is an abiding transcendental faith in the essential rightness and benevolence of nature. Furthermore, one of the striking features of *The Octopus* is its translation of the supernatural into the natural. Norris actually offers in this novel a religious system, with nature in the place of God. His natural laws are naturalized Christian beliefs. Nature, in the role of God, is omnipotent, though man has free will; it rewards and punishes and is beneficent to those who conform themselves to its norms.[30] (Though it cannot be said that nature is a very maternal surrogate for God. Norris, like Stephen Crane and Jack London, loved to dwell on the "colossal indifference" of nature, an indifference hardly distinguishable from cruelty: "Nature was, then, a gigantic engine, a vast cyclopean power, huge, terrible, a leviathan with a heart of steel, knowing no compunction, no forgiveness, no tolerance . . . ")[31] Doubtless the most striking instance of nature as an actor occurs near the end of the book, when the wheat itself smothers the evil S. Behrman, agent of the railroad, in the hold of a freighter.

The Octopus is an example of the transmutation of values from one frame of reference to another, when the earlier frame of reference, but not the values, begins to appear outmoded. It is a bible of secular theology, a Darwinian testament. Norris, ever the moralist, could even go the New Testament one better by proclaiming the ultimate triumph of good. Such a faith cannot be disproved, of course, but more and more it becomes implausible, and unlike the faith in final salvation that sustained sufferers under the Christian dispensation, it is hard to see how the lesson of the individual's unimportance in a benevolent cosmos is going to console the suffering wheat ranchers even a little.

Theodore Dreiser, Compassionate Darwinian

With Theodore Dreiser we turn to a more authentic naturalism. After a childhood and adolescence less swashbuckling than Jack London's but fully as impoverished, Dreiser managed to land a job as a newspaper reporter on the Chicago *Globe*. Two years later in Pittsburgh, at the age of 23, Dreiser underwent the naturalist rites of passage, absorbing Huxley, Spencer, Darwin, and Tyndall, and experiencing a conversion not, like London's, exhilarating, but painful. Dreiser, who had rebelled against a harshly Catholic upbringing but had not abandoned his belief in God and a moral order, reported that the dual assault of Huxley and Spencer "quite blew me, intellectually, to bits."

The same pages of *First Principles* that revealed to London a universe of law, opened up to Dreiser a vision of the precariousness of man's existence: "all I deemed substantial—man's place in nature, his importance in the universe, this too, too solid earth, man's very identity save as an infinitesimal speck of energy or a 'suspended equation' drawn or blown here and there by larger forces in which he moved quite unconsciously as an atom—all questioned and dissolved into other and less understandable things . . . " It was an overwhelming revelation. "I was completely thrown down in my conceptions or non-conceptions of life." There was then no spiritual hereafter, and no significance to life in the present. All a man's "ideals, struggles, deprivations, sorrows and joys" were so many "chemic compulsions." Man, in short, was "a mechanism, undevised and uncreated, and a badly and carelessly driven one at that." Dreiser claims to have been completely depressed by this view of reality, all his "gravest fears" about the "brutality of life" confirmed. "I felt low and hopeless at times as a beggar of the streets."[32]

So he may have felt for the moment. But he was only 23, and could not remain low and hopeless indefinitely. After weathering the initial shock, Dreiser seems to have found the mechanist philosophy of life tolerable. There was really nothing in it so very new to him. Newspaper reporting was a veritable school of naturalism, and Dreiser had already found that the reporters with whom he worked shared, almost to a man, a tough-minded estimate of humanity as driven by self-seeking compulsions to which terms like "morality" simply did not apply. Alfred Kazin goes so far as to suggest that Dreiser's reading of Darwin and Spencer and the rest was less a discovery than a confirmation, legitimizing his own previous reflections. According to Kazin, Dreiser learned all about the survival of the fittest simply by growing up. He was one of those naturalists "who know [naturalism's] drab environment from personal experience, to whom writing is always a form of autobiographical discourse," as compared with those (cf. Frank Norris) "who employ it as a literary idea . . . . Naturalism was Dreiser's instinctive response to life."[33]

It is true that Dreiser's naturalism is almost never didactic; it is simply there, suffusing the entire atmosphere of his stories. He himself warned against taking theory too seriously. To a student who had requested his theory of writing, he responded, "It is just as well to remember that all critical and aesthetic theories arose after the fact." Novels sprang not from theory but from emotion; they expressed "feeling for life."[34] Because it has so little to do with theory, Dreiser's naturalism has been defined by some Dreiser critics very broadly. F. O. Matthiessen, for example, speaks of it thus: "His mind became more and more absorbed in understanding the broad processes of nature, and in making his fiction correspond with them."[35]

But it would be quite wrong to infer from all this that Dreiser was an untaught primitive, a genius who did no more than put down on paper the naturalism he lived. In fact, Dreiser was seriously engaged with ideas as ideas. He did, after all, care enough to read the great English naturalists, and he did come to some conclusions about the nature of man and man's place in nature—if only to conclude that we could draw no conclusions. To the end of his life, Dreiser remained acutely interested in the research of scientists, especially life scientists, as it bore on a mechanist philosophy. "The more we know *exactly*, about the chemic and biologic and social complexities by which we find ourselves generated, regulated, and ended, the better," he once wrote.[36] When, around 1910 or 1912, Dreiser came across the work of the biologist Jacques Loeb, he decided that Loeb's well-known book, *The Mechanistic Philosophy of Life*, had put the case for mechanism more forcefully than anything else he had read. As late as 1935 Dreiser was writing to Calvin Bridges of the California Institute of Technology to inquire if Loeb had ever been contradicted; and in a second letter of the same year he wrote, "The more I examine the various scientific attempts at an interpretation of life the more I respect and admire Loeb."[37] The pursuit of science even took Dreiser into the laboratories themselves. He made long summer visits to the marine biological laboratories at Woods Hole, Massachusetts in 1928 and to Cold Spring Harbor, Long Island in 1937, where he watched experiments and talked to researchers, gazing in fascination through their microscopes.

Lobsters, Squids, and People

The most obvious, if superficial, indication that Dreiser writes as a post-Darwinian is his fondness for animal imagery. Jack London had created a dog-hero, and insofar as his readers could identify their emotions with Buck's, they could conclude that men and dogs were not very different after all. Dreiser went a step further in making the bond explicit, introducing a group of very solid citizens of Chicago, members of the Union Club, as figures "with eyes and jaws which varied from those of the tiger, lynx, and bear to those of the fox, the tolerant mastiff, and the surly bulldog."[38] *The Financier* has a number of animal symbols, the most vivid probably being the description of Cowperwood as "a wolf prowling . . . in the night . . . looking down into the humble folds of simple men."[39]

Dreiser's people live in a Darwinian universe, symbolized by the famous battle in *The Financier* between the lobster and the squid in a tank in the Chicago marketplace. Frank Cowperwood observes the struggle, and takes away from it the lesson that will guide his future career: "Things lived on each other." Lobsters lived on squid, men lived on lobsters, and strong men lived on weak. Dreiser reinforces the moral of the episode later in the tale: "Life was a dark, insoluble mystery, but whatever it was, strength and weakness were its two constituents. Strength would win—weakness lose."[40] Dreiser himself, it seems clear from his admiration for his Darwinian hero Cowperwood, held to some such philosophy at the time he was writing the Cowperwood trilogy. But as he grew older he pointedly disavowed the Darwinian law. "For certainly," he wrote, "the thousands-of-years growth of organized society augurs desire on the part of Nature to avoid the extreme and bloody individualism of the jungle . . . ."[41] By this time Dreiser was a convinced socialist.

Dreiser's greatest achievement on behalf of naturalism is his successful combination of a philosophy that seems to deny any intrinsic meaning to life with a compassion that endows each individual life with profound meaning. "How curious are the vagaries of fortune," might well be the motto of his first novel, *Sister Carrie*.[42] The randomness of existence, the absence of any clear pattern or design, is a theme Dreiser accepted in the real as well as the fictional universe. Reminiscing about his brother in 1922, Dreiser recalled that "whenever I saw him I felt sad, because, like so many millions of others in this grinding world, he had never had a real chance. Life is so casual, and luck comes to many who sleep and flies from those who try."[43] Dreiser could make out no ultimate sense in the way of the world. "Life is to me too much a welter and play of inscrutable forces to permit, in my case at least, any significant comment," he wrote. "As I see him the utterly infinitesimal individual weaves among the mysteries a floss-like and wholly meaningless course—if course it be. In short I catch no meaning from all I have seen . . . "[44] Dreiser favored the term "chemism" and believed that man's behavior could be explained as a reaction of "glands, chemisms, hormones, and compulsions" to the environment. Man did not have free will. "All of us are more or less pawns," says Lester Kane in *Jennie Gerhardt*.[45] And yet, out of the meaninglessness and the helplessness, poignant stories issued from Dreiser's pen, replete with engrossing vicissitudes, intensely human characters. For, in truth, Dreiser's philosophical speculations are not terribly important to the unfolding of his tales. We ought perhaps to find it difficult to sympathize with pawns, but their humanity transcends philosophy.

Toward the end of his life Dreiser became more and more impressed by the mystery of life, and began to feel the need to press his inquiry into the essence of being beyond the limits of scientific evidence. His trip to Woods Hole in 1928 was undertaken partly to try to corroborate his own growing sense of a universal directive force. (The scientists, not surprisingly, could offer little hard evidence along these lines.) At Cold Spring Harbor he had a mystic experience evoked by the unity in design shared by the tiny organism under the microscope and the yellow flowers blossoming outside the laboratory. Perhaps the creative force that he had been accustomed to think of as blind might be intelligent, even benevolent. But Dreiser was not ready to abandon determinism intellectually, and continued to affirm belief in the controlling forces of physiology and environment. Taxed with inconsistency in being at once socialist and determinist, he simply replied that he could not be otherwise. It seems likely that he kept his intellectual life and his emotional life apart to some extent, as so many of us do, accepting determinism as a theory but not something to live by. For certainly a tension existed between his belief in the sufficiency of biological explanations and his awed contemplation of the "mystery of life," just as between his search for transcendental meaning in life—for some universal creative force—and his firm adherence to a philosophy of mechanism.

Dreiser's Determinism in Practice

The fictional world Dreiser elaborated conforms perhaps as closely as fiction can conform to the rules of determinism. In Clyde Griffiths, central character of *An American Tragedy*, Dreiser created the prototype of the naturalistic character—the man hemmed in by circumstance, the helpless product of forces outside his control. Griffiths is at the mercy of an environment which has made him and which proceeds to unmake him. He is Dreiser's weakest character, that is, he is the least autonomous, the most fully accounted for by hereditary and environmental factors. We never feel that Clyde Griffiths is truly acting, but rather that he is acted upon. Again and again Dreiser shows him incapable of making a genuine, reasoned decision; he continually refuses the plea of his pregnant sweetheart Roberta to marry, but is unable to come up with an alternative solution and drifts for days without an answer. His final resolve to murder Roberta is reached only in consequence of her threat to return to her hometown and to reveal their relationship: Clyde's will "recede[d] in precipitate flight, leaving only panic and temporary unreason in its wake." The climax to indecisiveness comes in the murder scene at Big Bittern Lake, when Clyde, in "a sudden palsy of will," is unable to carry out his fatal resolve. Roberta drowns, but the drowning is accidental, for Clyde has once more failed to adhere to a planned course of action.

Other Dreiser characters do act. Frank Cowperwood acts, strongly and vigorously, and so, in her own way, does Carrie Meeber. What, then, becomes of Dreiser's determinism? It has been suggested that it breaks down at this point; Eliseo Vivas has written that "in spite of his futilitarian philosophy, his characters never genuinely lacked guiding purpose."[46] Charles Walcutt has attempted to rescue Dreiser's determinism by showing how these "guiding purposes," apparently free, are nonetheless rendered impotent by external pressures.[47] That is a useful insight, but one cannot help wondering how much a deterministic philosophy, so defined, can really enter into the fiber of the narrative. Would it not be perfectly possible for a believer in free will and ethical responsibility to construct a story like *Sister Carrie* or the Cowperwood saga? To put it another way, would *The Titan*, say, be altered in any material way were we to assume human freedom rather than environmental determinism? Indeed, the rise and fall of Frank Cowperwood has elements of moral drama—of transgression and retribution—just as it stands. As for Dreiser's belief in the capriciousness of chance, it is assuredly not just the determinist who believes that chance is a real factor in the human equation (cf.

Theodore Dreiser,
1871–1945. (Courtesy of
Culver Pictures, Inc.)

William James), or that choice is conditioned by multiple pressures from within and without. Perhaps it is safe to say that determinism makes its presence strongly felt only where the characters are so simple and elemental (as in *An American Tragedy* or *McTeague*) that they patently do not have genuine power of choice. Any appearance of free will or forceful behavior, however illusory the author assures us it may be, destroys the logical compulsion of determinism—though we may of course still accept it on faith. To that extent, determinism in the naturalistic novel is peripheral.

Another aspect of Dreiser's naturalism, one that follows from his personal philosophy, is his view of morality. When *Sister Carrie* was first published in 1889 Dreiser became involved in a cause célèbre with his publisher, Doubleday, because of the unconventional nature of the book's ethics. Carrie Meeber, while never a prostitute, was certainly a kept woman, and she was kept by more than one man. Such figures had appeared in fiction before, but hitherto the "fallen woman" had met her just deserts, or repented and reformed. What was astonishing and shocking in *Sister Carrie* was Carrie's failure to do either; rather, her wayward behavior seemed to carry her from strength to strength. Dreiser not only refused to pass judgment on her behavior but rewarded it. In a meaningless world, he seemed to be saying, conventional ethics are as out of date as the medieval veneration of saintly relics. Human impulses are natural and good, but old-fashioned codes of ethics stultify and demean.

Dreiser was writing in the cause of compassionate objectivity. But there was a polemical edge to his writing as well. If mistresses could be superior human beings, if financial entrepreneurs could and did prosper by means of chicanery and fraud, what real meaning or validity was there in the pious horror of traditional moralists? Surely it was ill-suited to the realities of the world as it actually is. Dreiser defiantly put more genuine goodness into the character of Jennie Gerhardt, mistress to two prominent men, than into any of his other characters. At the same time he could not be horrified at the behavior of the amoral financier Frank Cowperwood. For the most part, he admired him. Cowperwood was only following the main chance, which was the way people really behaved. Conventional morality was hypocrisy and fraud, so Dreiser concluded; it concealed behind a fog of cant what actually goes on. As he wrote in an essay, "Life seems to prove but one thing to me, and that is that the various statements concerning right, truth, justice, mercy are palaver merely, an earnest and necessitous attempt, perhaps, at balance and equation where all things are so very much unbalanced, paradoxical and contradictory—the small-change names for a thing or things of which we have not yet caught the meaning."[48]

Dreiser's contempt for prevailing morals resembles Jack London's. London, too, found contemporary ethical codes empty and hypocritical—but he said so only in private, or through the mouth of an anti-hero like Wolf Larsen. For public consumption, his heroines were ever chaste, his heroes honest and true. Those of his characters who could not measure up fell by the wayside. London explained that he had to conform to the tastes of his readership, and no doubt his conventionality saved him from the kind of controversies in which Dreiser was periodically embroiled. (Of course, Dreiser's private life was also considerably more unorthodox than London's.) But London thereby forfeited the opportunity to educate the public to what he considered a more genuinely moral stance. Dreiser seriously undertook this task, in essays as well as in fiction. He gained a goodly measure of notoriety for doing so, but he did live to see a drastic alteration in the American attitude toward sex.

The Legacy of Naturalism

Naturalism owed a heavy debt to Victorian science. Science had disclosed whole new worlds to the fascinated gaze of the naturalists, and had altered the very shape and meaning of the old. It had radically transformed the ancient concept of the Great Chain of Being by setting men firmly down among the animals. The naturalists were eager students, and the lessons they learned were those of their times—lessons of heredity and circumstance, of force external and internal, of fragility and necessity and the complex chemistry of human behavior. For all that, it is no disparagement of the scientific component of naturalism to suggest that something like naturalism would have arisen with or without the biological revolution. A man like Theodore Dreiser could have written in no other way; he wrote what he lived and knew. He was indebted to science, certainly, for the language and imagery of Darwinism and, later, Freudianism. He was indebted to science, too, for the formulas that seemed to explain why men behaved the way they did, and for confirmation of his own intuitive sense of the drift and meaninglessness of life. But Dreiser and Stephen Crane and, to some extent, Frank Norris were responding above all to the dynamism of the new urban and industrial culture that they saw in the making around them, a new culture whose multitudes—not Anglo-Saxon, not genteel, not affluent for the most part—had yet to gain admission to the pages of genteel literature. This new culture was the phenomenon the best naturalists burned to describe, and they called on science to help them achieve their aim. They recognized what earlier writers had been slow to admit, that we cannot expect life to provide us with moral homilies; that, indeed, there is often enough little relation between goodness and earthly reward. In theory, naturalists would have liked to abolish distinctions like good and evil, in recognition of the forces that shape man's ends. To this end they were wary of judgment and, in

Dreiser's case, generous with compassion. Yet they often wrote as if goodness and evil were realities that could be experienced and defined. Of Jennie Gerhardt, his favorite character, Dreiser wrote, "From her earliest youth goodness and mercy had molded her every impulse." Jennie is made to ask, "Did anything matter except goodness—goodness of heart? What else was there that was real?"[49]

I have dealt at some length with the question of determinism in naturalist literature because it is a genuine issue and because it has been of central concern in the past. Was naturalism just realism plus determinism? The results of this examination show that a simple equation of naturalism with determinism is overly simple. In the first place, an author's personal affirmation of determinism is no guarantee that he will be able to present that philosophy effectively in his novels. Forceful action destroys the semblance of determinism, which appears tenable only so long as the characters are nonhuman (as in *The Call of the Wild*), or subhuman (as in *McTeague*), or totally lacking in autonomy (*An American Tragedy*). William James once observed that a world of determinism differs in no essential way to the observer from a world of freedom: two people may hold opposing views on the constitution of the universe but the world presents the same face to both. So it would seem that the presence or absence of a deterministic philosophy cannot satisfactorily define naturalism.

All the more is this true because not all naturalist writers were unequivocally determinist. Donald Pizer, analyzing Frank Norris, has gone so far as to speak of the "absence of a philosophical center" in American naturalism, and it is clear that there was considerable variety in the way these writers approached philosophical concerns. Determinism, in any case, will only be dramatically effective when counterpointed against freedom. If there were not the possibility, however slight, of some small chink in the block universe of determinism; or, failing that, if there were not at least a lingering sense of regret that free will is an illusion, the novel of determinism would lose its poignancy and its bittersweet savor. Tension and ambiguity thus become the stock in trade of naturalist writers, who balance the sternness of their conceptions about the human condition with a tender concern for the significance of individual lives. "The tension here," observes Pizer, "is that between the naturalist's desire to represent in fiction the new, discomforting truths which he has found in the ideas and life of his late nineteenth-century world, and also his desire to find some meaning in experience which reasserts the validity of the human enterprise."[50]

For all these reasons American naturalism cannot, in the end, be most usefully judged by philosophical norms. When it succeeded, it did so because it was faithful not to a formula but to the experience of life. In appraising this faithfulness, we find a number of reasons why Dreiser continues to seem modern by contrast to Norris and London. Dreiser was willing to let his stories go it alone, for one thing, free of moralism. He was immensely more sophisticated about the use of literary techniques like symbolism, even though his style could be inferior at times to that of the other two writers. Dreiser was an urban man, above all, and he, together with Stephen Crane, first successfully translated the naturalist vision into the new environment of the city. London disliked the city, preferring to set his tales in the wilderness, where the artifices of civilization had no place. Norris sometimes used the city as a backdrop for his stories, but most frequently, like London, with strong undertones of distrust for urban civilization and all its works. Classic Darwinian theory applied most obviously to man in the wilderness, where he must pit himself against the forces of nature merely to survive. But such direct applications of Darwinism were increasingly less relevant to late nineteenth-century culture, and, in the end, largely devoid of human interest. For what was peculiarly human about man, as Lester Frank Ward and John Dewey unceasingly pointed out, was his power to create an artificial environment.

Dreiser understood that society needed to be conceived as an extension of nature, that a close analysis of the forces of social life would show that civilization, whatever its complexities, was no stranger to the law of tooth and claw. In an urban world Darwinism must be translated into the push and pull of social pressures, "the physico-chemical stimuli of the urban scene: the lights and noise."[51] By the time he wrote *An American Tragedy* Dreiser did, of course, have the advantage of familiarity with the ideas of Loeb and Freud and other scientists, who could show him more precisely how man was a creature of drives and forces beyond his ken; but even *Sister Carrie*, written at the turn of the century, demonstrates the superior insight of Dreiser into the forces shaping American life. The frontier had closed by 1890; the new frontier was the city. So *The Call of the Wild* remained a fable, though a nearly perfect one of its kind, an "atavism," as London might have said, while *Sister Carrie* offered a glimpse of things to come.

NOTES

1. Malcolm Cowley, "Naturalism in American Literature in Stow Persons, ed., *Evolutionary Thought in America*, p. 301.
2. Jack London, *Martin Eden,* pp. 107, 108.
3. Letter of June, 1914 to Ralph Kasper in King Hendricks and Irving Shepard, eds., *Letters from Jack London* (New York: Odyssey Press, 1965), p. 145.
4. Jack London, *The Call of the Wild* (New York: The Macmillan Co., 1903), p. 167.
5. Jack London, *The Sea Wolf* (New York: The Macmillan Co., 1904), p. 50.
6. Maxwell Geismar, *Rebels and Ancestors, The American Novel 1890– 1915* (Boston: Houghton Mifflin Co., 1953), p. 196.
7. Jack London, *A Daughter of the Snows* (Philadelphia: J. B. Lippincott, 1902), p. 202.
8. Quoted in Charmian London, *The Book of Jack London* (2 vols., London, 1921), 2: 69.
9. Ibid., p. 69.
10. London, *A Daughter of the Snows*, p. 76.
11. London, *The Sea Wolf*, p. 75.
12. London, *A Daughter of the Snows*, p. 135.
13. Letter of Dec. 12, 1899 in *Letters from Jack London*, p. 74.
14. London, *A Daughter of the Snows*, p. 83.
15. Letter of Jan. 6, 1902 in *Letters from Jack London*, p. 128.
16. London, *A Daughter of the Snows*, p. 184.
17. *Letters from Jack London*, p. 128.
18. London, *The Call of the Wild*, pp. 59–60.
19. Alfred Kazin, "Theodore Dreiser: His Education and Ours," in Alfred Kazin, ed., *The Stature of Theodore Dreiser* (Bloomington, Ind.: Indiana University Press, 1955), p. 158.
20. Frank Norris, *Vandover and the Brute* (Garden City, N.Y.: Doubleday, Page & Co., 1914).
21. Norris, *Vandover and the Brute,* pp. 244–245.
22. Frank Norris, *McTeague* (New York: Doubleday, Page & Co. 1900), p. 89.
23. Ibid., pp. 30, 32.

24. Donald Pizer, *Realism and Naturalism in Nineteenth Century American Literature* (Carbondale, Ill.: Southern Illinois University Press, 1966), pp. 13–14, 18.

25. Frank Norris, *The Octopus* (New York: Doubleday, Page & Co., 1901), p. 634.

26. Ibid., p. 448.

27. Charles Child Walcutt, *American Literary Naturalism, A Divided Stream* (Minneapolis: University of Minnesota Press, 1956), p. 145.

28. Warren French, *Frank Norris* (New York, 1962), p. 96.

29. Norris, *The Octopus*, pp. 651–652.

30. Donald Pizer, *The Novels of Frank Norris* (Bloomington, Ind.: Indiana University Press, 1966), p. 22.

31. Norris, *The Octopus*, p. 577.

32. Theodore Dreiser, *A Book About Myself* (New York: Boni & Liveright, 1922), pp. 458–459.

33. Kazin, "Theodore Dreiser," in *The Stature of Theodore Dreiser,* pp. 155, 158.

34. Theodore Dreiser, *Letters of Theodore Dreiser*, ed. Robert H. Elias, 3 vols. (Philadelphia: 1959), 3: 795.

35. F. O. Matthiessen, *Theodore Dreiser*, American Men of Letters Series (New York: Wm. Sloane Associates, 1951), p. 170.

36. Quoted in Matthiessen, *Theodore Dreiser*, p. 236.

37. Letter of April, 1935 in *Letters*, 2: 742.

38. Theodore Dreiser, *The Titan* (New York: John Lane Co., 1914), p. 10.

39. Theodore Dreiser, *The Financier* (New York: Boni & Liveright, 1927), p. 495.

40. Ibid., pp. 3–5, 272.

41. In an article in the *New Masses* quoted in William Swanberg, *Dreiser* (New York: Charles Scribner's Sons, 1965), p. 391.

42. Walcutt, *American Literary Naturalism*, p. 189.

43. Theodore Dreiser, *A Book About Myself* (New York: Boni & Liveright, 1922), p. 253.

44. In an article in the *Bookman* quoted in Robert Elias, *Theodore Dreiser: Apostle of Nature* (New York: Alfred A. Knopf, Inc., 1949), p. 239.

45. Theodore Dreiser, *Jennie Gerhardt* (New York: Harper & Bros., 1911), p. 342.

46. Eliseo Vivas, "Dreiser, An Inconsistent Mechanist," in Kazin, *The Stature of Theodore Dreiser*, p. 244.

47. Walcutt, *American Literary Naturalism*, p. 197.

48. Theodore Dreiser, *Hey Rub-a-Dub-Dub: A Book of the Mystery and Wonder and Terror of Life* (New York: Boni & Liveright, 1920), p. 17.

49. Dreiser, *Jennie Gerhardt*, pp. 15–16.

50. Pizer, *Realism and Naturalism,* p. 13.

51. Ellen Moers, *Two Dreisers* (New York: Viking Press, 1969), p. 255.

New York. Ink, pencil, and watercolor drawing (30⁵/₈″ × 21³/₄″) by Abraham Walkowitz, 1917. (Collection of the Whitney Museum of American Art. Gift of the artist in memory of Juliana Force.)

EIGHT

THE DEMISE
OF CERTITUDE

O FAR AS THE OUTER world is intelligible to us, the immediate portion in which we live our lives is simply a machine, so orderly and compact, so simple in construction, that we may reckon its past and gauge something of its future with almost as much certitude as that of a dynamo or a waterwheel. In its motions there is no uncertainty, no mystery . . . . This is the first fact which modern science has to offer to the philosophic mind."[1]

The machinelike certainty of nature, here celebrated by the scientific popularizer Carl Snyder early in the twentieth century, would be quite possibly the last fact that science in our own time would offer to the philosophic mind. A revolution in the way we think about physical nature has intervened to make Snyder's paean to the simplicity of the cosmos seem as remote and archaic from us as Paley and the Bridgewater Treatises. Today Robert Hofstadter, a Nobel-prize winning physicist, can write instead, "Man will never find the end of the trail."[2] Yet it was perfectly reasonable to write a passage such as Snyder's in 1904. To be sure, here and there scientists had begun to question the buoyant Victorian faith in the certitudes of science. In thermodynamics it had already become apparent that when dealing with very small entities strict determinism had to give way, for all practical purposes, to statistical analysis. Worse, some of the more reflective scientists—Pearson and Mach, Ostwald and Poincaré and Duhem—had themselves begun to look askance at claims of scientific omniscience. But the overall mood of most men of science remained one of supreme confidence.

Why should it not? Since Newton, it had been customary to view the world through the lenses of classical physics. Triumph after triumph in the unraveling of nature's complexities had followed in the wake of this view. The great work of Darwin could itself be taken as a tremendous vindication of the classical vision of a causally determined universe. For through Darwin, biology rid itself of the residue of mysticism that had been driven out of the study of inorganic nature a century and more before. Natural selection demonstrated that the cosmic mechanism worked among the animals fully as inexorably as among the planets, sifting and preserving, altering and rejecting, pursuing its hidden purpose in accordance with definite laws.

The New Physics

The classical vision of physics was comprehensive, it was elegant, it was surpassingly neat. It was also wrong. Three developments, taking place within the period from 1870 to 1930 sufficed to ring down the curtain on the age of Newton—the electromagnetic theory of radiation, the theory of relativity, and the quantum theory. Taken together they refuted or corrected virtually all the core conceptions of Newtonian mechanics—most startlingly the absoluteness of space, time, and mass and the principle of action at a distance.

The first of these breakthroughs in our understanding of the physical world occurred with the finding by Clerk Maxwell that light could not be mechanical but must be electromagnetic in nature and the subsequent downfall of the theory of ether. Starting out with the accepted mechanical premises, Maxwell wound up with a series of equations which simply could not be rendered in the familiar mechanical terms. Very few physicists at the time accepted the clear implication of Maxwell's equations: that the new field concepts might be irreducible, and their presumed mechanical foundation a myth. Traditionally, light had been considered as mechanical waves in an elastic solid, the ether, and it was exceedingly difficult for Maxwell's colleagues to jettison the notion of ether upon which they had lavished much ingenuity. Maxwell himself did not believe his theory to be in conflict with traditional physics; indeed, he fully shared the conviction that light waves traveled through a material ether. But there was nothing in his account of electromagnetism to support the idea, and a good deal tending to make it dubious. Though it required some forty years for the full import of Maxwell's work to be felt, his theory was really the opening wedge in undermining the concept of a thoroughgoing mechanism.

Einstein posed the second and graver threat to the billiard ball universe in 1905, when he published his special theory of relativity. Reflecting on the famous Michelson-Morley experiment of 1887, which had failed to reveal any trace of a material ether through which the earth might be moving, Einstein came to the radical conclusion that space, time, and mass could not be absolutes, as they had been considered to be in Newtonian physics. Instead, all these entities must be seen as relative to the observer, and varying in accordance with his position. Thus a bullet moving past a stationary observer had a different mass from the same bullet at rest, and the length of a table carried in a truck past the person measuring it was shorter than the length of the same table when standing still. Newtonian physics, Einstein asserted, gave correct results for motion at relatively slow speeds, but it broke down at speeds approaching the velocity of light. The familiar three-dimensional Euclidean universe of boxlike space and evenly flowing time must give way to a universe quite beyond the bounds of Euclidean geometry, one in which space and time joined together, in some almost unimaginable way, into a four-dimensional space-time. The basic concepts of Newton's system could hardly have been more directly challenged.

An even more fundamental rejection of the assumptions of classical physics took place with the development of quantum physics, culminating in Heisenberg's uncertainty principle in 1927. For even relativity theory, though it had certainly cast doubt on the validity of Newton's definitions and assumptions, did not necessarily question the conviction that the processes of the universe could in theory, if not in practice, be fully determined. Such a complete determinism meant providing causal explanations for literally everything under the sun, and this in turn required tracking down the position and velocity of every least element. Already thermodynamics, and the general development of the statistical outlook, seemed to imply the impossibility of ever carrying out this program in reality. But one could still hold that our inability to deal simultaneously with large numbers only revealed human limitations, the frailty of men as measuring instruments, not any inherent indeterminacy in the things themselves.

It was just this opinion that became dubious in the light of quantum physics. The new physics pointed to the impossibility in principle as well as in practice of determining at the same time both the position and the velocity of individual electrons. In order to measure the position of an electron a beam of light must be directed at it, but this beam knocks the electron out of its original position, disturbing its velocity in the process. It is possible to determine either the position or the velocity, within some limits, but the more accurately scientists determine the position, the less accurate becomes their measurement of velocity, and vice versa; so that the product of uncertainty of position times uncertainty of velocity can never be reduced below the quantum constant h. Indeed, it may be misleading to speak of electrons as having definite position and velocity at all, since they behave under different circumstances both as particles and as waves. Physicists now speak of electrons as waves permanently occupying a whole ellipse, not as discrete entities travelling around it. More than that they simply cannot express verbally, and they must resort to the language of mathematics, at a level far beyond the grasp of the layman. The electron, which in Bohr's atomic model seemed to be perfectly understandable—a satellite, just like the earth, orbiting about a massy nucleus—has receded to the very outermost limits of intelligibility, and there does not appear to be any immediate prospect of salvaging it for the comprehension of the average man.

Of course, the retreat of the electron, suggestive as it is of how much we still have to learn about the ultimate composition of things, is not the important point. What is important is that uncertainty and ambiguity may be built in to our attempts to fathom that composition. Beyond a certain point definite knowledge gives way to a calculus of probabilities and nothing we can do can conjure it back.[3]

So major a reorientation of thought naturally produced a sense of displacement in many minds. It was perhaps less unsettling to laymen—whose intellectual horizons had already been so rudely ruffled by Darwinism that they could scarcely be further disturbed—than it was to scientists, many of whom had committed themselves to a belief in the determinism of nature. The physicist suddenly found himself, wrote Bridgman, "in a world from which the bottom has dropped out." He had to "give up his most cherished convictions and faith . . . . The world is not intrinsically reasonable or understandable; it acquires these properties in ever-increasing degree as we ascend from the realm of the very little to the realm of everyday things."[4] Not everyone, indeed, could accept these results. Einstein himself spent the better part of his later years in a search, now considered by some of those competent to judge to have been futile, for the clue to a reconciliation of the new findings with the old classical interpretation. But the mainstream of scientific thought gradually began adjusting to a new and more complex philosophy of nature than that cherished by the Victorians, one which could live in peace with the apparent fact that uncertainty is a constant in our deepening knowledge of the world. There may well be definite limitations to what we can hope to know of reality; La Place's spirit has been laid to rest.

Following closely upon the heels of the Darwinian revolution, the revolution in physics cut across the influence of Darwinism in a rather fundamental way. It marked the end of the period of intensive reaction to Darwinian theory on the part of other fields of thought, and reasserted the claims of physical theory on a philosophy that could see no other science but biology. At the same time, by failing to confirm the notion of the perfect determinism of nature it made possible the reconsideration of certain conceptions of chance or freedom, of the complexity of nature, that Darwinism had made unfashionable. That being so, it makes sense to review here the distinctive contributions of Darwinism and especially to try to evaluate which ones did, and which ones did not, have sufficient staying power to endure the overthrow of mechanism.

Darwinism
Reconsidered: The Method

We ought, in the first place, to make a preliminary distinction between the method and the content of Darwin's theory. When Charles Darwin published the *Origin* he had no notion that his method was in any way unusual, as indeed it was not, being the ordinary scientific combination of observation, experiment, hypothesis-making and hypothesis-testing. He differed from his scientific contemporaries largely in the brilliance of his scientific imagination, and in the incredible degree of patience and persistence with which he pursued his facts, marshaling them into the overwhelming array of which the *Origin* was to have been just an abstract. His concern was not for method but for message—the message of natural selection as the cause of evolution. And this was the way Darwinism was received by the public: it was certainly the ideas Darwin propagated, not the medium of their propagation, that kindled the great controversies.

Yet it is possible to consider the eventual triumph of Darwinism a triumph more of method than of doctrine. John Dewey, for one, considered it to be so, and few people have spoken on Darwin with greater insight than Dewey. According to Dewey, the great importance of the *Origin of Species* was in "laying hands upon the sacred ark of absolute permanency," by virtue of which it "introduced a mode of thinking that in the end was bound to transform the logic of knowledge, and hence the treatment of morals, politics, and religion."[5] In a similar vein, Sidney Ratner, one of Darwin's more militant admirers, writes that "the most significant effect of Darwin's discovery was, not the triumph of certain specific scientific theories, but a revolutionary change in the very process by which men arrived at their convictions."[6]

Darwinism did, of course, lead to a heavy emphasis on genetic analysis, as a way of getting around the deductive, static, nonhistorical approach then dominant in many areas of scholarship. And this in itself was a tremendously fruitful innovation that revolutionized procedures in the nascent social sciences. According to James Mark Baldwin, "the rise of the evolution theory in biology supplied the direct motive to a genetic psychology. . . . The contribution consisted in extending to the mind the methods of positive and comparative research, and the formulation of a principle, that of natural selection, which established genetic continuity and on the basis of which research could be directed and controlled."[7] So also with the other social sciences, all of which, soon or late, were ignited by the Darwinian tinder.

But the revolution Ratner refers to went far beyond the particular process of genetic inquiry to include a more general and hugely significant shift in the basis of certitude on which men anchor their convictions—the shift from some kind of unverifiable or ethical base to one grounded in science and concrete data. One can observe this transition in the life of John Dewey, prophet of post-Darwinian philosophic reconstruction. Dewey as a young man revolted violently against the dualisms of his New England tradition, which pitted body against mind, and matter against spirit. He found philosophic surcease in the doctrines of Hegelian idealism, with their vision of reality as unity and process. He appreciated Hegel's emphasis on the creative mind, and on the interdependence of that mind with its social milieu. When, gradually, Dewey became aware of the implications of Darwinism for his psychology and philosophy, he was able to pursue them with enthusiasm and insight because so many of the Darwinian categories—process, history, organism, environment—were also Hegelian. But Darwin provided what Hegel never could—materials for an empirical analysis of reality in terms of minds and their transactions with their surroundings. So, painlessly, Dewey emerged from the chrysalis of Hegelian idealism into maturity as a Darwinian empiricist.

We may conclude that Darwin did inaugurate a permanent change in our views on the propriety and scope of scientific method. At the threshold of the Darwinian era, for example, it was still considered out of the question in many quarters to study the mind by any method other than that of introspection, guided by the pieties of orthodox morality. Ethics was a wholly deductive enterprise based on a set of presumably self-evident axioms. Contrast such a situation with that of our own day, when the human mind and consciousness has become the focal point of a whole battery of sciences ranging from neurophysiology to clinical psychology, and a flourishing new discipline, ethology, is wholly given over to studying the behavior of animals for the clues their behavior can supply to an understanding of our own. The modern habit of expecting an authoritative reply from science on almost any subject where hard data can be found dates from Darwin. Scientific method, we have come to believe, cannot be walled off into a few "safe" areas; wherever empirical evidence exists, there the method of science belongs. Insofar as the significance of the Darwinian revolution resides in the impetus it gave to the spread of scientific method, the battle has been won. No future thought revolution is likely to endanger the primacy of scientific method in western culture.

Darwinism Reconsidered: The Doctrine

With respect to Darwinian doctrine, the issue is more complex. The theory of natural selection is and will continue to be the core and vital center of biology, most evidently, perhaps, in the field of genetics. Since Darwin first enunciated this principle, it has undergone some correcting and refining that makes its phraseology less belligerent than formerly. The "struggle for survival" has been replaced by the less colorful but more accurate notion of differential reproduction: the fittest organisms prove their fitness by producing more offspring than their rivals. The process need not involve any bloody competition at all. But in its essentials selection theory remains as it was one hundred years ago, and the essentials are beyond controversy. For many years it was possible to doubt the validity of Darwin's theory, but skepticism is not a tenable position today.

Not surprisingly, the net value of evolution theory for areas outside biology is less easy to judge. For one thing, it is not always clear when Darwinian evolution provoked new ideas or when it merely reinforced those already in existence. There is considerable evidence, for example, that the nineteenth century was already beginning to think historically long before Darwin. This was true of both the human and the nonhuman record. The historian Herder, and after him Hegel and Comte and Marx, to name only a few, had by 1850 firmly established the notion of a cosmic history moving through time toward some predetermined goal; so that the social sciences inspired by these men, and especially sociology, were already marked by the idea of temporal progression and development. Still, it is fair to say that the idea of evolution greatly accelerated this "discovery of time" among the sciences of man by assimilating man to nature and thereby making human development part of a universal process of change.[8]

Assessing the effects of Darwinism on the social sciences is made much more difficult by the need to distinguish between evolution generally and natural selection theory in particular. This distinction, which makes no sense in natural science, where evolution *is* natural selection, becomes necessary outside the natural sciences, where evolution and natural selection are separable. For while it is clear that man as an animal has evolved in much the same way as the other animals, it is not at all certain—indeed, it appears highly dubious—that there exists an identity between organic evolution and social development. "In the main," as Morris Ginsberg has written, " . . . it remains that years of controversy have led to the general rejection of the theory that social evolution depends on natural selection, and to the acceptance of the view that the principal factors of social change are social rather than genetic, depending on changes in organization, knowledge and belief, rather than on changes in the inherited structure, under the influence of selection."[9]

Early uncritical attempts to assimilate social theory to biology resulted in the proliferation of crude Social Darwinisms, which all too often substituted rhetoric for reflection, and in so doing sheltered some unpalatable social philosophies of the "might makes right" variety. This development cannot with justice be blamed on the theory of natural selection itself, it is true, for the basic concepts of that theory were open to more than a single interpretation. Indeed, one of the great accomplishments of genetic theory was to demonstrate the radical shift in the course of evolution brought on by the advent of a social, rather than a purely physical, environment. The social environment perforce generates its own standards of behavior, so the new scholarship insisted. The individualistic, egoistic Darwinian universe simply can not be taken unreservedly as a working model of human life.

This more adequate and sophisticated interpretation of Darwinism took time to develop. Only after a concerted attack on the part of reformers, logicians, psychologists, and some biologists did the jungle version of Darwinism give way to one that recognized in intellect both the supreme product of natural selection and the creator of new, distinctively human environments. The initial impact of natural selection ideas on social theory was rather to efface intellect almost entirely, and it must therefore be judged, on balance, as probably detrimental to the development of social thought.

If we turn from the influence of natural selection to the influence of evolution, taken more generally, on social theory, we find ourselves on less controversial ground. The idea of evolution did great service in calling attention to the bond between ideas and environments, and in clarifying judgments on contemporary institutions by a study of the matrices out of which they had arisen. It is true that in certain instances evolutionary enthusiasm outran good sense. In sociology and anthropology, for example, a form of cultural evolutionism based on a rather distorted reading of Darwin arose and flourished at the turn of the century. The theory assumed a sequence of stages through which every culture was presumed to pass, thereby suggesting that the evolutionary process had a definite path and goal. This kind of evolutionism, perhaps best illustrated in the work of the anthropologist Lewis Henry Morgan, was patently false to several cardinal principles of Darwinism—notably random variation and the absence of teleology. It turned out, in addition, to be false to the facts. So the whole idea of evolution in the social sciences fell into disrepute for many years. Still, its adoption into the study of men and society was for the most part very beneficial. Before Darwin, time and change were only beginning to enter into explanations of whole areas of behavior. The Darwinian emphasis on origins and on variations working over innumerable generations, and the radical denial of the eternal fixity of species, introduced the Victorian era to time, and to the need to examine particular situations. It de-mythologized, as it enriched, contemporary understanding of manners and morals.

Ethics and Religion after Darwin

It was, above all, in the two most sensitive areas of public culture, ethics and religion, that evolution by natural selection disturbed the Victorian horizon. Here, truly, the philosophical implications of Darwinism bore down most heavily, and the harbingers of reconciliation, as of rejection, labored most vigorously. In these areas, evolutionary notions of any kind were bound to be distressing, for they could only lead to the conclusion that values and religions are

time conditioned, and that no moral codes and no religious formu-
lations, however noble, are valid absolutely and forever. Such a
conclusion was breathtaking enough. The subsidiary notion of
natural selection, in itself, could scarcely shock the Victorian mind
more. God, after all, could have chosen natural selection as his way
of working in the world, as various liberal theologians (and even
some conservatives) did not fail to point out. Likewise, in ethical
theory it was possible to interpret natural selection in ways that
took account of the social nature of men, thereby blunting the
"dog-eat-dog" versions of Darwinian ethics. But, unfortunately,
natural selection could not be taken by itself, devoid of metaphysical implications. It was frequently taken (as indeed Darwin intended it to be) as the example par excellence of the mechanistic
structure of a world purely natural in origin and operation. For this
reason—because it was symbolic of godless mechanism—natural
selection had to be firmly refuted by many theistic philosophers
and theologians who managed to muster enthusiasm, or at least
tolerance, for some variety of evolution.

In ethics, evolution suggested the emergence of human morality
from animal instinct as an adaptive response to the environment.
Naturally, it was unsettling to learn that man was so much more
akin to his hairy brethren in matters of morality than he had ever
imagined himself to be. Not that recognizing the animal origins of
ethical behavior necessarily involved denying traditional moral
values. Many, probably most, of the early evolutionary moralists
continued to pay allegiance to the prevailing Victorian mores.
What did change was the *standard* of morality, not the values themselves. Thus, in the crudely hedonistic ethics of Herbert Spencer
the standard of morality became simply life itself, and the good,
that which promotes survival.

Now, it was not difficult to point out the shallowness of Spencerian ethics by demonstrating that survival, plain and simple, could
never be a sufficient criterion of the moral life. Neither was it
difficult to show that tracing complex moral codes back to their
primitive origins could not serve as a satisfactory judgment on the
worth of those codes, for this was to confuse a *useful* and perhaps
necessary mode of explanation with a *sufficient* one. These initial
responses to the impetus of evolution were clearly inadequate. But
refuting Spencer did not refute Darwin, and Darwinism applied to
morals pointed toward a revision of the standards of morality.

Once the standard of morality had been undermined, it was only a question of time until the beliefs themselves were challenged. By tracing the varying conceptions of the moral life which men had held at different times and places, evolutionary ethics tended to promote some form of cultural relativism, and to replace moral absolutism with situation ethics. This challenge to traditional values could not be easily refuted, as the earliest intrusions of evolution into ethics had been. The question of relativism versus absolutism, the validity of situation ethics—these are live issues in our own time. Insofar as evolution promoted cultural and moral relativism, then, it did challenge the verities of its time, and doubtless promoted the erosion of established principles. But whether one considers this good or bad, one cannot in fact claim the growth of relativism as a distinctive product of the evolutionary outlook. For historical and anthropological studies would have established the great diversity of cultures even without the impetus of evolution. What evolution did was to link contemporary Western civilization to these other peoples and remote cultures in one vast developmental process, so that men could no longer assume that the ethics of nineteenth-century Victorian England and America expressed an inherent and fundamentally timeless righteousness.

As with ethics, so with religion. Quite apart from Darwinism, the higher criticism, the "search for the historical Jesus," the corrosive attacks of Renan and Strauss and Schleiermacher and the rest upon traditional religion, had their effect—and it was telling—on the beliefs of many. We have evidence that the Darwinian revolution led some particularly thoughtful people away from the faith of their fathers, but one suspects the seeds of disbelief had been previously planted. Darwin did not himself lapse from religious belief because of Darwinism; disbelief came upon him gradually over a period of many years, and rather from aesthetic and emotional than from intellectual distaste. He could not believe in a God who permitted as much suffering as seemed to exist in the animate world, or who condemned to eternal punishment unbelievers like his father and brother.

Logically, it is hard to make a strong case for the incompatibility of Darwinism with traditional religion. The case that one can make rests not with the idea of evolution, but with natural selection seen as a mechanism in a mechanistic universe. There is no question that Darwin's discernment of a wholly natural explanation for fitness and adaptation exploded forever the natural theology of Paley. God could not be proved through his creation. But the fact is that natural selection conflicts with religious belief only when it is assumed that the laws of nature have no origin outside nature itself. And this is an assumption that, like God, lies beyond the empirical evidence. It was not wise of Christian thinkers to place such a heavy burden of proof on nature, but, still, if God cannot be proved in his creation, neither can he be disproved. Darwin has often been called the Newton of biology; his work, it is suggested, was really an extension into the animate world of the mechanized pattern of the Newtonian universe. If this is so, then truly there was no more reason to abandon the deity after Darwin than after Newton.

Of course, logic is not everything. Mood counts for much. The latter part of the nineteenth century was not a particularly glorious period for European or American Christianity. To an institution whose power to bear witness to the message of Christ was already severely impaired by spiritual and intellectual torpor, the shock of Darwinian evolution was greater than it might otherwise have been. Many people were prone to attribute to Darwin what really came about through a complex of factors. Darwinism did not undermine religion. It could and did provide evidence furthering the case of the philosophical alternative to religion, which was naturalism. As long as Christianity and naturalism both insisted on trying to offer concrete proof of the unprovable, every increment to our comprehension of the thoroughly natural working of the universe automatically decreased by so much the plausibility of the existence of God. Thus Darwinism, strengthening the claim of naturalism, weakened that of religion. But it did not, as indeed it could not, disprove it.

Darwinism
in American Thought—A Summary

If we try to estimate the significance of the Darwinian revolution and its aftermath for American intellectual life, it is hard to avoid the impression that Americans were able to have their cake and eat it too. America, in the years after the Civil War, was so clearly ripe for innovative thought. Philosophers occupied themselves with flattening out reality to the banalities of Scottish common sense when they were not enveloping it in Hegelian mysticism. Religion had all but capitulated to the idol of the marketplace. Literature remained captive to the genteel tradition. Everywhere in the life of the mind, sentiment made do for rigor, and good form for realism, while rigor and realism, devoid of sentiment, transformed the industrial environment.

In fact, two revolutions—the one of mind, the other of society—were taking place concurrently. We have looked at some of the changes that followed in the wake of Darwinism very much as if they occurred in a vacuum. Of course they did not. It is interesting to consider to what extent the two transformations were related, and whether some sort of crisis in American thought was not in the making without the added impetus from biology. For example, as I have previously suggested, religion did not owe its difficulties in the first place to Darwin. Natural selection was not the cause of the defection of such eminent English Victorians as Leslie Stephen, John Stuart Mill, George Eliot, James Anthony Froude, or Darwin himself. Clearly some sort of intellectual and emotional unrest was abroad in the Atlantic community, quite probably the concomitant of the transformation of society from rural to urban, and from agricultural to industrial life.

Would American thought have undergone reconstruction even without the help of Darwin? No one can say, obviously, but we might surmise that some sort of new departure would have taken place. Darwinism, superficially so sensational, actually focused the inchoate stirrings of an even more basic shift in thought patterns—away from supernaturalism, ultimate reality, and final causes. John Dewey emphasized this theme again and again throughout his writings: the turning away from teleology and finality that the *Origin* initiated, and the consequent reorientation of philosophy around more mundane concerns. But, in fact, the *Origin* did not so much initiate as accelerate a long-term trend that can be traced back at least as far as the Renaissance, a trend toward secularism and humanism in the broadest sense. There can be little doubt that the rough direction of this trend had been well established long before Darwin.

Furthermore, cultures do respond, if tardily, to fundamental changes in social structure. It is very likely that the urbanization of America, with all the difficult and intensely practical problems that process created, would have evoked present-mindedness in a sensitive spirit like Dewey's even without the Darwinian stimulus to a redirection of thought. Darwinism was frequently accused of degrading the image of humanity and replacing uplift with ugliness. But the ugliness that Jane Addams and Jack London and all those other discoverers of the urban poor found in the squalid reality of the city streets owed nothing to Darwinism. The reign of the robber barons did not depend on tutelage in the principles of selection and survival.

All of the above seems true, but more would be pure speculation. The fact is that the times were ripe for a reorientation of intellect, and Darwinism offered itself as symbol and mechanism of such a reorientation. If one can imagine a modern mentality coming into existence without the help of Darwin, it is nevertheless impossible to imagine that its contours would be identical with the mentality that actually exists. Undeniably, the Darwinian episode served as a vehicle for propelling whole areas of thought forward toward the twentieth century.

We can see now that the proponents of Darwinism, as all proponents are wont to do, claimed for their doctrine too much, not certainly in its own proper sphere of biology, where the development of genetics only led natural selection theory on from strength to strength, but as an intellectual way of life. The supremacy of naturalism and the death of supernaturalism, the sufficiency of genetic explanation, the primacy of chance over design—these ideas could not be proven by the triumph of natural selection theory, although selection theory could be a powerful support in arguing their case. Indeed, the first and last of these issues could not be proven at all, certainly not in any strictly scientific way, for they went beyond empirical evidence. Nevertheless, some of the more dogmatic Darwinians (not always or necessarily the scientists themselves) claimed for Darwinian science a certitude that had hitherto been claimed only for theology. It was generally assumed by these proponents of "German Darwinism" (as Chauncey Wright termed the speculative use of Darwin's theory) that the final conquest of nature was only a matter of time, that the general shape of the universe had already been outlined and only the details remained to be drawn in. A monistic metaphysics erected on this basis preached the sufficiency of matter and energy for a complete description of reality.

The spinning out of a new metaphysics from the conclusions of scientists like Darwin was, on the face of it, a rather curious phenomenon, for one of the forceful lessons of the whole Darwinian episode was surely the danger of dogmatism. Even as certain elements in the scientific community were growing complacent over the apparent simplicity and clarity of nature, new forces—in the shape of indeterminacy and relativity—were arising to challenge all complacency. Like the theologians who had once and for all established the age of the earth as 6000 years, like the biologists who staked their reputations on the separate creation of species, like the followers of Paley rejoicing in the evidence of God as shown in the structure of the eye—like all these, the dogmatic interpreters of science found themselves offering obsolete wares. For the new physics felt much less secure about laying down the final framework of how things really are. Physicists probed the atom and found not order and certainty but a principle of uncertainty. This made many of them reluctant to profess in human affairs a determinism for which they could find no warrant in nature. (Equally, of course, there was no warrant for asserting freedom of the will based on indeterminacy in the electron. Extrapolation of philosophical inference from the world of subatomic particles to our own macrocosmic world is probably a risky enterprise at best.)[10]

The typical scientist today is a good deal more restrained in making his research bear the weight of philosophical speculation than was his great-grandfather. Science has for the most part ceased to serve as a platform for polemics, or at least for polemics of a metaphysical nature, and where new problems are generated by scientific advance—as they have been, for example, in the ethics of organ transplantation and genetic manipulation—it is common to insist that science will not, of itself, offer solutions. The abstention of scientists (as scientists) from metaphysical speculation results partly from a feeling shared by many scientists that metaphysics is nonexistent or meaningless. But probably even more, it results from a belief that whether metaphysics (or religion or ethics) is nonexistent and meaningless, or real and intelligible, is simply not a question for science at all. Metaphysics is not physics, and the metaphysical enterprise cannot profitably be undertaken by scientists (in their professional capacity, though as disciplined thinkers scientists can and do undertake it). The boundary between science and philosophy is certainly not sealed—a great deal of philosophical ink, for example, was expended in the nineteenth century on discussions of space and time, only to have these topics revolutionized by Einstein. Wherever any sort of empirical information exists, science comes into play. But where we have no hard data, no way of proving or disproving ideas once and for all with solid facts, then science cannot function. We are free at that point to decide that no area can exist beyond the domains of science, or to maintain a healthy skepticism, or, finally, to believe in the existence of meta-scientific reality, but the choice will be based on grounds that are not themselves within the province of science.

Such a conclusion is not novel. It was cogently argued nearly a century ago by Chauncey Wright in his doctrine of the neutrality of science. Indeed, if there could be an intellectual hero in a book such as this, it might very well be Wright, a man only beginning to emerge from a century of obscurity. Immersed as he was in the immediate issue of Darwinism—and no one went more surely to the core of its meaning than he—Wright was nonetheless able to fit the intellectual turmoil of his time into a more enduring framework, one that survives into our own time. Had he not died prematurely, and had he been in a position to make himself more widely heard, the nation might have been spared some of the acute philosophical indigestion brought on by Darwinism, and the advent of a mutually agreeable relationship between science and the "other culture" markedly hastened. As it was, Darwin and Darwinism became a national preoccupation among the thoughtful for some fifty years. If much of the energy expended on the effort to comprehend Darwinism led to nothing of permanent value, it nonetheless contributed to reshaping the mainstream of American intellectual life in a way so fundamental that we still, with Thorstein Veblen, speak of pre- and post-Darwinian as a watershed in the life of the mind.

We find ourselves today farther removed in spirit from the generation of 1870 or 1875, with rare exceptions, than that generation was from the Pilgrim fathers. Two major wars have intervened between us, and a cataclysmic depression, and the atomic bomb. But the beginnings of our modern mentality are rooted in that earlier time when the ape and the angel were rallying points, and certitude lost an epic battle to ambiguity.

NOTES

1. Snyder, *The World Machine*, p. 465.
2. Loren Eiseley, *The Night Country* (New York: Charles Scribner's Sons, 1971), p. 214.
3. Modern physical theory, insofar as it is accessible to the layman, can be gleaned from a number of accounts, among them Henry Margenau, *The Nature of Physical Reality* (New York: McGraw-Hill Book Co., 1950); Louis de Broglie, *The Revolution in Physics* (New York: Noonday Press, 1953); and George Gamow, *The Atom and Its Nucleus* (Englewood Cliffs, N.J.: Prentice-Hall, 1961).
4. P. W. Bridgman, "The New Vision of Science," *Harper's*, 158 (1928–29): 450.
5. Dewey, *The Influence of Darwin*, pp. 1–2.
6. Sidney Ratner, "Evolution and the Rise of the Scientific Spirit in America," *Philosophy of Science*, 3 (1936): 105.
7. James Mark Baldwin, *Darwin and the Humanities,* pp. 79–80.
8. A compact summary of the emergence of the historical mode of thought in the nineteenth century, with due attention to Darwin, is Stephen Toulmin and June Goodfield, *The Discovery of Time* (New York: Harper & Row, 1965).
9. Morris Ginsberg, "Social Evolution" in *Darwinism and the Study of Society*, ed. Michael Banton (London: Tavistock Publications, 1961), p. 105.
10. For one philosopher's skepticism about inferring human freedom from the indeterminacy of subatomic particles—a skepticism which, however, denies equally that the causal principle negates "free will"—see L. Susan Stebbing, *Philosophy and the Physicists* (London: Methuen & Co., Ltd., 1937).

SUGGESTIONS FOR
FURTHER READING

The following reading list is composed almost entirely of secondary sources. Interested readers will without question want to consult the classic original works of the figures treated in the text, works such as William James, *Pragmatism*, Thorstein Veblen, *The Theory of the Leisure Class*, Henry Adams, *The Education of Henry Adams*, and Theodore Dreiser, *An American Tragedy*. These works are readily available, however, and are therefore not included in this brief list.

On the general topic of the American mind in the post-Civil War period and its reaction to evolutionary ideas, several older studies are still very much worth consulting: Ralph Henry Gabriel, *The Course of American Democratic Thought* (New York: Ronald Press Co., 1940); Merle Curti, *The Growth of American Thought* (New York and London: Harper & Bros., 1943); and Henry Steele Commager, *The American Mind* (New Haven: Yale University Press, 1950). Stow Persons has reassessed the flow of American intellectual life in a sophisticated study, *American Minds: A History of Ideas* (New York: Henry Holt & Co., 1958), with a provocative section on "the naturalistic mind." The classic and not-to-be-outdated work on American receptivity to Darwinism and Spencerianism is Richard Hofstadter, *Social Darwinism in American Thought* (Boston: Beacon Press, 1955). Paul Boller includes a great deal of lively information in his *American Thought in Transition: The Impact of Evolutionary Naturalism, 1865–1900* (Chicago: Rand McNally & Co., 1969). Boller also has an excellent bibliography. Morton White, *Social Thought in America* (New York: Viking Press, 1949) treats Veblen and Dewey, among others, as revolutionaries

221

against formalism in thought. Collections of contemporary material, both with excellent introductory essays, are Perry Miller, ed., *American Thought, Civil War to World War I* (New York: Holt, Rinehart and Winston, 1954) and R. J. Wilson, ed., *Darwinism and the American Intellectual* (Homewood, Ill.: Dorsey Press, 1967). Finally, Philip Appleman has put together a massive compilation of both nineteenth- and twentieth-century material on all aspects of Darwinism, both scientific and more broadly cultural, entitled simply *Darwin* (New York: Norton, 1970).

Chapter 1.   Useful books on Darwin and the making of the Darwinian revolution include Loren Eiseley, *Darwin's Century: Evolution and the Men Who Discovered It* (Garden City, New York: Doubleday Anchor Books, 1958); William Irvine, *Apes, Angels, and Victorians* (New York: McGraw-Hill Book Co. 1955); and Gertrude Himmelfarb, *Darwin and the Darwinian Revolution* (Garden City, N.Y.: Doubleday Anchor Books, 1962), though Himmelfarb's interpretations are dubious. For the reception of Darwinism in America, an early article by Bert J. Loewenberg is standard: "Darwinism Comes to America, 1859--1900," *Miss. Valley Historical Review*, 28 (December, 1941). The two most important American protagonists in the scientific dispute over Darwinism are ably treated in A. Hunter Dupree, *Asa Gray, 1810--1888* (Cambridge, Mass.: Harvard University Press, 1959) and Edward Lurie, *Louis Agassiz, A Life in Science* (Chicago: University of Chicago Press, 1960).

Chapter 2.   Perspective on American religious life in the post-Civil War period can be gained from Sydney Ahlstrom, *A Religious History of the American People* (New Haven: Yale University Press, 1972) and James Ward Smith and A. Leland Jamison, eds., *Religion in American Life* (4 vols., Princeton: Princeton University Press, 1961) which includes an excellent full bibliography. Stow Persons has a chapter on theological reconstruction after Darwin in his edited volume of essays, *Evolutionary Thought in America* (New Haven: Yale University Press, 1950). A good biography of one of the most ardent and voluble religious evolutionists is Ira V. Brown, *Lyman Abbott, Christian Evolutionist* (Cambridge, Mass.: Harvard University Press, 1953).

Chapter 3.   A persuasive and readable interpretation of Chauncey Wright, Charles Peirce, William James, and John Dewey, among others, addressed to the conflict in American thought between "science" and "sentiment," or head and heart, is Morton White, *Science and Sentiment in America: Philosophical Thought from Jonathan Edwards to John Dewey* (London and New York: Oxford University Press, 1972). Philip P. Wiener, *Evolution and the Founders of Pragmatism* (New

York: Harper & Row, 1965) is central to the topic of this chapter. Useful biographies or studies of individual figures include Milton Berman, *John Fiske, The Evolution of a Popularizer* (Cambridge, Mass.: Harvard University Press, 1961); H. Burnell Pannill, *The Religious Faith of John Fiske* (Chapel Hill, N.C.: Duke University Press, 1957); Edward H. Madden, *Chauncey Wright and the Foundations of Pragmatism* (Seattle: University of Washington Press, 1963); Ralph Barton Perry's fascinating *The Thought and Character of William James* (2 vols., Boston: Little, Brown & Co., 1935); and T. A. Goudge, *The Thought of C. S. Peirce* (Toronto: Univ. of Toronto Press, 1950).

Chapter 4. For the reaction of Northern intellectuals to the Civil War, and its influence on subsequent social thought, see George Fredrickson, *The Inner Civil War* (New York: Harper & Row, 1968). Richard Hofstadter's *Social Darwinism* remains the starting point for explorations of that topic. A newer view of the relationship of businessmen to ideologies of Social Darwinism can be found in Irvin G. Wyllie, "Social Darwinism and the Businessman," *Proceedings of the American Philosophical Society,* 103 (October, 1959): 629–635; Edward C. Kirkland, *Dream and Thought in the Business Community* (Ithaca, N.Y.: Cornell University Press, 1956); and Richard M. Huber, *The American Idea of Success* (New York: McGraw-Hill, 1971). An excellent biography of a prominent business figure, which revises our view of his slavish devotion to the ideas of Herbert Spencer, is Joseph Frazier Wall, *Andrew Carnegie* (New York: Oxford University Press, 1970). Thomas F. Gossett, *Race: the History of an Idea in America* (Dallas: Southern Methodist University Press, 1963) is standard. See also, for a richly detailed discussion of late nineteenth-century race theory, John S. Haller, Jr., *Outcasts from Evolution: Scientific Attitudes of Racial Inferiority* (Urbana, Ill.: University of Illinois Press, 1971). John Higham, *Strangers in the Land: Patterns of American Nativism, 1860–1925* (New York: Atheneum Publishers, 1970) treats racism as one strand of a developing American nativism. R. Jackson Wilson, *In Quest of Community* (New York: John Wiley & Sons, 1968) and David Noble, *The Paradox of Progressive Thought* (Minneapolis: University of Minnesota Press, 1958) examine the attitudes of some prominent post-Darwinian social theorists.

Chapter 5. Ernest Samuels' biography of Henry Adams in three volumes, *The Young Henry Adams, Henry Adams, the Middle Years,* and *Henry Adams, the Major Phase* (Cambridge, Mass.: Harvard University Press, 1948, 1958, 1964) sets the stage for detailed Adams studies like William C. Jordy, *Henry Adams: Scientific Historian* (New Haven: Yale

University Press, 1952); J. C. Levenson, *The Mind and Art of Henry Adams* (Stanford: Stanford University Press, 1957); and Henry Hirsch Wasser, *The Scientific Thought of Henry Adams* (Thessaloniki, 1956).

Chapter 6. The basic source on Veblen is the massive *Thorstein Veblen and His America* by Joseph Dorfman (New York: Viking Press, 1934). Veblen is perceptively discussed elsewhere in Daniel Aaron, *Men of Good Hope* (New York: Oxford University Press, 1951), in Morton G. White, *Social Thought in America* (New York, 1949), in Stow Persons, *American Minds* (New York, 1958), and in Max Lerner's editorial introduction to *The Portable Veblen* (New York: Viking Press, 1964).

Chapter 7. A lively tour of fin-de-siècle literature is Larzer Ziff, *The American 1890's* (New York: Viking Press, 1966). Charles Child Walcutt, *American Literary Naturalism, A Divided Stream* (Minneapolis: University of Minnesota Press, 1956) is helpful. More recent criticism is represented in Donald Pizer, *The Novels of Frank Norris* (Bloomington, Ind.: Indiana University Press, 1966) and *Realism and Naturalism in Nineteenth Century American Literature* (Carbondale, Ill.: Southern Illinois University Press, 1966). Alfred Kazin is a reliable guide in *On Native Grounds* (New York: Reynal & Hitchcock, 1942). Kazin has also edited *The Stature of Theodore Dreiser* (Bloomington, Ind.; Indiana University Press, 1955). Two useful biographies are Warren French, *Frank Norris* (New York: Twayne Publishers, 1962) and Robert Elias, *Theodore Dreiser, Apostle of Nature* (New York: Alfred A. Knopf, Inc., 1948).

INDEX